Understanding the Language Classroom

Understanding the Language Classroom

Edited by

Simon Gieve
University of Leicester, UK

and

Inés K. Miller
Pontifical Catholic University of Rio de Janeiro, Brazil

with a Foreword by Kathleen M. Bailey

We dedicate this book to Dick Allwright, Lancaster University 1978–2003, our intellectual mentor, inspiring colleague and dear friend, who has motivated a generation of language teachers and researchers, and taught us the meaning of thinking.

Contents

List of Figures

Foreword

Kathleen M. Bailey

The title of this book, *Understanding the Language Classroom*, is well chosen. The authors and editors have all been influenced by Dick Allwright's thinking, and Dick has spent his entire professional life trying to understand (and help others to understand) life in language classrooms. His work has profoundly influenced a broad sphere of investigation called 'language classroom research'.

What is 'language classroom research'? A good place to start is van Lier's (1988: 47) definition of a *language classroom*: 'The L2 [second-language] classroom can be defined as the gathering, for a given period of time, of two or more persons (one of whom generally assumes the role of instructor) for the purposes of language learning.' An earlier definition came from Long's paper entitled 'Inside the Black Box'. There he said, 'the investigation of classroom language learning may be defined as research on second language learning and teaching, all or part of whose data are derived from the observation or measurement of the classroom performance of teachers and students' (Long, 1980: 3). The mysterious 'black box' in Long's title suggests how little we understood language classroom processes in the late 1970s, and how many challenges we would face.

Dick Allwright has been gently shaking the 'black box' and peeking into it for years. In addition to conducting his own explorations, he has been instrumental in getting language teaching professionals to discuss their own classroom-based investigations. In particular, he helped to organize several of the colloquia on this topic at TESOL conventions throughout the 1980s. In 1983, the *TESOL Quarterly* published several articles from the colloquium at the 1982 convention (Allwright, 1983; Gaies, 1983; Long, 1983; Seliger, 1983). In his own *TESOL Quarterly* paper, Allwright (1983: 191) broadened our definition, when he wrote:

> Classroom-centered research is just that – research *centered* on the classroom, as distinct from, for example, research that concentrates on the *inputs to* the classroom (the syllabus, the teaching materials) or on the *outputs from* the classroom (learner achievement scores). It does not ignore in any way or try to devalue the importance of such

inputs and outputs. It simply tries to investigate what happens inside the classroom when learners and teachers come together. At its most narrow, classroom-centered research is in fact research that treats the language classroom not just as the *setting for* investigation but, more importantly, as the *object of* investigation. Classroom processes become the central focus. (Allwright, 1983: emphases in the original)

Thus, 'language classroom research' became 'a cover term . . . for a whole range of research studies on classroom language learning and teaching. The obvious unifying factor is that the emphasis is solidly on trying to understand what goes on in the classroom setting' (Allwright, 1983: 192).

This emphasis on trying to understand has not changed, though the profession itself has grown. As the literature has developed, different authors have viewed our emerging field of inquiry in various ways. For example, Chaudron (1988) discussed four traditions in classroom research: the psychometric tradition, interaction analysis, discourse analysis and the ethnographic tradition. In 1990, Brumfit and Mitchell identified three main types of research: pure research, policy-oriented research and action research (1990a: 8–9). Ellis (1990: 10–15) also described three main categories of empirical research in language classrooms: (1) classroom process research, (2) the study of classroom interaction and L2 acquisition and (3) the study of formal instruction and L2 acquisition. In 1994, Cumming edited a report about seven different methods or research orientations: analyses of learners' language, verbal reports on learning strategies, text analysis, classroom interaction analysis, ethnography, participatory action research and critical pedagogical approaches to research. Bailey (1998) compared experimental research, naturalistic inquiry and action research as three approaches to classroom language learning and teaching. Kumaravadivelu (1999) discussed three approaches: classroom interaction analysis, classroom discourse analysis and critical classroom discourse analysis. In short, we have witnessed tremendous methodological diversification since the early days of the once-dominant experimental method.

Collections of classroom research articles have been published (see, for example, Bailey and Nunan, 1996; Brumfit and Mitchell, 1990b; Das, 1987; Schachter and Gass, 1996; Seliger and Long, 1983), and qualitative procedures for data collection and analysis are now better understood and more widely used than they were just twenty years ago (Chaudron, 1986; Davis and Lazaraton, 1995). Teachers' knowledge (Allwright, 1997; Allwright and Lenzuen, 1997; Freeman, 1996) and teachers' beliefs and decision-making (Woods, 1996) have been highlighted as essential, researchable areas of professional understanding and as appropriate foci for investigation.

Since the 1970s, the role of the teacher in classroom research has also expanded greatly (Nunan, 1997a, 1997b). The field has moved from an experimentally motivated view of teachers primarily as subjects or as implementers of treatments, to a broader view of teachers as partners in the research enterprise, and teachers as producers of research. Pica (1997) described the evolving relationship of research and teaching as moving from coexistence to collaboration and complementarity. Indeed, the term 'teacher research' has been used increasingly in recent years to refer to any systematic investigations conducted by teachers, regardless of the methodological approach employed. Numerous books intended for a wide reading audience have addressed classroom data collection and analysis issues (see, for example, Allwright and Bailey, 1991; Burns, 1998; Chaudron, 1988; Freeman, 1998; Nunan, 1989; Wallace, 1998). It is interesting to note that many of these works use the word 'understanding' in their titles (Freeman, 1998; Johnson, 1998, 1999; Nunan, 1989; van Lier, 1994). Since the 1990s, Allwright himself (2005) has emphasized the importance of the work for understanding being done by practitioners themselves – the teachers *and* the learners, thus arguing for the notion of practitioner research as a way forward for the profession.

In 1980, I visited Dick Allwright when he was teaching at the University of New Mexico. In a presentation about classroom research that weekend, Steve Gaies said, 'The classroom is the crucible' (1980). This phrase captured the science, the art and the mystery of instructed language learning and language teaching as we saw it at the time. In the twenty-five years since then applied linguistics has developed in a number of disparate directions. On the one hand, researchers have penetrated further into the 'black box' as cognitivist accounts have made progress, and the Chomskian paradigm has become a major force in second language acquisition studies. In some instances, this direction has become increasingly technical and remote from the everyday understandings and everyday concerns of teachers and learners. On the other hand, we have also become concerned with what lies *outside* the crucible: a different school of research, strongly influenced by critical theory or post-structuralist accounts of subjectivity, has expanded our understanding of the role of the social context of learning, and led to a greater appreciation of the role of identity in language learning (Canagarajah, 1999; Norton, 2000). In addition, more attention has been paid to cultural factors (for example, Cortazzi and Jin, 1999;

Holliday, 1994), which affect the behaviours and beliefs that learners and teachers bring with them into the classroom. In the past twenty-five years also our understanding of the *content* of language instruction (what the language-to-be-learned consists of) has developed in such areas as pragmatics and discourse. Increasing recognition has been given to new varieties of English, and all of these developments have led to increasing demands on teachers' knowledge base. As part of the wider world the smaller world of language learning and teaching has become more connected, more speeded up, more vulnerable to demands for change. Allwright's own response to these developments in his 'directions' (Allwright, 2006) is to continue to insist on the primacy of the meeting point between teachers and learners in their own classrooms, emphasizing their central role in working for their own understandings of classroom life, accommodating the local to the global and the old to the new. The chapters in this volume contribute to this perspective.

In this brief Foreword I have tried to capture some of the historical developments in language classroom research. The various chapters in this book exemplify both Allwright's vision and the changing nature of the field. The challenges have not abated, however. As Rounds and Schachter point out, 'classroom based research entails a very large number of human and institutional factors that can affect research design and outcomes in many unforeseen and unforeseeable ways. It is not for the timid' (1996: 108).

The contributors to this volume have all added to our understanding of language classroom life. I hope this book will encourage others to do the same, even though the effort is indeed 'not for the timid'.

KATHLEEN M. BAILEY
Monterey, California

References

Allwright, D. 1983. Classroom-centered research on language teaching and learning: a brief historical overview. *TESOL Quarterly* 17, 2: 191–204.

Allwright, D. 1997. Quality and sustainability in teacher-research. *TESOL Quarterly* 31, 2: 368–70.

Allwright, D. 2005. From teaching points to learning opportunities and beyond. *TESOL Quarterly* 39, 1: 9–31.

Allwright, D. 2006. Six promising directions in Applied Linguistics. In: *Understanding the language classroom*, eds S. Gieve and I.K. Miller. London: Palgrave Macmillan, Chapter 1 in this volume.

Allwright, D. and K.M. Bailey 1991. *Focus on the classroom: an introduction to classroom research for language teachers*. Cambridge: Cambridge University Press.

Allwright, D. and R. Lenzuen 1997. Exploratory practice: work at the Cultura Inglesa, Rio de Janeiro, Brazil. *Language Teaching Research* 1, 1:73–9.

Bailey, K.M. 1998. Approaches to empirical research in instructional language settings. In: *Learning foreign and second languages: perspectives in research and scholarship*, ed. H. Byrnes, 75–104. New York: Modern Language Association of America.

Bailey, K.M. and D. Nunan, eds 1996. *Voices from the language classroom: qualitative research on language education.* New York: Cambridge University Press.

Brumfit, C. and R. Mitchell 1990a. The language classroom as a focus for research. In: *Research in the language classroom: ELT Documents 133*, eds C. Brumfit and R. Mitchell, 3–15. London: Modern English Publications and British Council.

Brumfit, C. and R. Mitchell, eds 1990b. *Research in the language classroom: ELT Documents 133.* London: Modern English Publications and British Council.

Burns, A. 1998. *Collaborative action research for English language teachers.* Cambridge: Cambridge University Press.

Canagarajah, A.S. 1999. *Resisting linguistic imperialism.* Oxford: Oxford University Press.

Chaudron, C. 1986. The interaction of quantitative and qualitative approaches to research: a view of the second language classroom. *TESOL Quarterly 20*, 4:709–17.

Chaudron, C. 1988. *Second language classrooms: research on teaching and learning.* Cambridge: Cambridge University Press.

Cortazzi, M. and L. Jin 1999. Cultural mirrors: materials and methods in the EFL classroom. In: *Culture in second language teaching and learning*, ed. E. Hinkel, 196–219. Cambridge: Cambridge University Press.

Cumming, A., ed. 1994. Alternatives in TESOL research: descriptive, interpretive and ideological orientations. *TESOL Quarterly 28*, 4:673–703.

Das, B.K., ed. 1987. *Patterns of classroom interaction in Southeast Asia* (Anthology Series 17). Singapore: SEAMEO Regional Language Centre.

Davis, K.A. and A. Lazaraton, eds 1995. *Qualitative research in ESOL.* A special issue of *TESOL Quarterly 29*, 3.

Ellis, R. 1990. *Instructed second language acquisition: learning in the classroom.* Oxford: Basil Blackwell.

Freeman, D. 1996. Redefining the relationship between research and what teachers know. In: *Voices from the language classroom: qualitative research on language education*, eds K.M. Bailey and D. Nunan, 88–115. New York: Cambridge University Press.

Freeman, D. 1998. *Doing teacher research: from inquiry to understanding.* Boston: Heinle & Heinle.

Gaies, S.J. 1980. *Classroom-centered research: some consumer guidelines.* Paper presented at the TESOL Summer Meeting, Albuquerque, NM.

Gaies, S.J. 1983. The investigation of language classroom processes. *TESOL Quarterly 17*, 2:205–17.

Holliday, A. 1994. *Appropriate methodology and social context.* Cambridge: Cambridge University Press.

Johnson, K.E. 1998. *Teachers understanding teaching.* Boston: Heinle & Heinle.

Johnson, K.E. 1999. *Understanding language teaching: reasoning in action.* Boston: Heinle & Heinle.

Kumaravadivelu, B. 1999. Critical classroom discourse analysis. *TESOL Quarterly* 33, 3:453–84.

Long, M.H. 1980. Inside the 'black box': methodological issues in research on language teaching and learning. *Language Learning* 30, 1:1–42. Reprinted in *Classroom oriented research in second language acquisition*, eds H.W. Seliger and M.H. Long, 1983: 3–35. Rowley, MA: Newbury House.

Long, M.H. 1983. Does second language instruction make a difference? *TESOL Quarterly* 17, 3:359–82.

Norton, B. 2000. *Identity and language learning: gender, ethnicity and educational change.* Harlow: Pearson Education.

Nunan, D. 1989. *Understanding language classrooms: a guide for teacher-initiated action.* New York: Prentice Hall.

Nunan, D. 1997a. Developing standards for teacher-research in TESOL. *TESOL Quarterly* 31, 2:365–7.

Nunan, D. 1997b. Research, the teacher and classrooms of tomorrow. In: *Language classrooms of tomorrow: issues and responses*, ed. G.M. Jacobs, 183–94. Singapore: SEAMEO Regional Language Center.

Pica, T. 1997. Second language teaching and research relationships: a North American view. *Language Teaching Research* 1, 1:48–72.

Rounds, P.L. and J. Schachter 1996. The balancing act: theoretical, acquisitional and pedagogical issues in second language research. In: *Second language classroom research: issues and opportunities*, eds J. Schachter and S. Gass, 99–116. Mahwah, NJ: Lawrence Erlbaum Associates.

Schachter, J. and S. Gass, eds 1996. *Second language classroom research: issues and opportunities.* Mahwah, NJ: Lawrence Erlbaum Associates.

Seliger, H.W. 1983. Classroom-centered research in language teaching: two articles on the state of the art. *TESOL Quarterly* 17, 2:189–90.

Seliger, H.W. and M.H. Long, eds 1983. *Classroom oriented research in second language acquisition.* Rowley, MA: Newbury House.

van Lier, L. 1988. *The classroom and the language learner: ethnography and second language classroom research.* London: Longman.

van Lier, L. 1994. Forks and hope: pursuing understanding in different ways. *Applied Linguistics* 15, 3: 328–46.

Wallace, M.J. 1998. *Action research for language teachers.* Cambridge: Cambridge University Press.

Woods, D. 1996. *Teacher cognition in language teaching: beliefs, decision-making and classroom practice.* Cambridge: Cambridge University Press.

Acknowledgements

First, we are very grateful to Dick Allwright for having agreed to share his manuscript *Six promising directions in Applied Linguistics* with his colleagues as a way of contributing to our editorial project, which is dedicated to him.

We also wish to thank all our contributors, who promptly welcomed the idea of focusing on language classroom life in a collegial effort to think around an 'Allwrightian' perspective on our field. Other authors who had expressed an interest in engaging in dialogue with Dick's thinking at earlier stages could not join us for various personal or professional reasons, and we are sorry not have been able to include their contributions. Special thanks to all and especially to those who supported us all along in the midst of their (and our) busy academic lives!

Our thanks should also go to our students and colleagues, in both Leicester and in Rio de Janeiro, who have followed and nurtured the development of the ideas and our editorial ups and downs in the past three years. Simon is especially grateful to colleagues at the School of Education, University of Leicester, whose agreement to share workloads at a time of heavy institutional demand, which enabled the completion of the editing, shows a spirit of true collegiality.

Thanks are also due to the reviewers at Palgrave Macmillan for finding in our proposal a volume that could become worthwhile reading for those related in different ways to (language) classroom life. Specifically, we thank Jill Lake for her patience and support at every stage of the process.

We also need to express our gratitude (although it may never be sufficient!) to our families for the hours spent on 'the book', which came only a few years after 'the thesis'. Simon, then, thanks his wife, Sonia, and his daughters, Celeste and Giulietta, while Inés thanks especially her husband, Leão, for his enormous help, and her parents, Sida and Mario, who would have been very proud of this achievement.

Last but not least, as co-editors, we also thank each other for the opportunities for mutual understanding, professional development and encouragement that helped us reach this point. We have fulfilled our shared desire to honour Dick, somewhat belatedly, on his institutional retirement but, most importantly, to celebrate the fact that he is as productive and insightful as ever in his thinking about language classroom life.

Leicester   SIMON GIEVE
Rio de Janeiro   INÉS K. MILLER

Notes on the Contributors

Dick Allwright originally trained to teach primary French in the UK, but instead taught English to adults in Sweden for two years before going to Edinburgh University to study applied linguistics. From there, he went to Essex University to teach applied linguistics in 1969, where he pioneered language classroom research, moving to Lancaster University in 1978. At Lancaster, his interest in classroom research shifted towards research as a contribution to teacher, and learner, development, via the notion of 'Exploratory Practice', a form of practitioner research involving teachers and learners working together, during language lessons, to explore and develop their understandings of their classroom lives. Retired since 2003, he is still actively pursuing his interest in teacher, and especially learner, development.

Kathleen M. Bailey is Professor of Applied Linguistics at the Monterey Institute of International Studies in California, USA. Her research interests include the teaching of speaking, teacher development, language assessment and classroom research. In 1998–9 she was the president of the international TESOL association.

Roger Barnard is Senior Lecturer at the Department of General and Applied Linguistics of the University of Waikato, New Zealand. Before taking up this appointment in 1995, he worked for many years with language teachers in England, Italy, the Netherlands, Yemen and Oman. He publishes frequently on issues relating to the classroom socialisation of (young) learners for whom English is an additional language, and was co-editor of *Bilingual children's language and literacy development* (2003).

Michael P. Breen was for over thirty years until his recent retirement, involved in language education and language teacher development. He worked directly with Dick Allwright at Lancaster before becoming Professor of Language Education at Edith Cowan University, Western Australia and holding a similar position at the University of Stirling. His major research work has been on literacy education and language teachers' thinking and classroom experience. He has also published on curriculum innovation and second language classroom research.

Maria Antonieta Alba Celani is Professor Emerita at the Pontifical Catholic University of São Paulo (PUC-SP), Brazil. She teaches in the Post-Graduate Programme in Applied Linguistics and is involved in research in the area of English teacher education.

Hywel Coleman is Honorary Senior Research Fellow in the School of Education, University of Leeds, UK. He has been involved in education in Indonesia for over thirty years; he is currently Team Leader for School Based Management in the Decentralised Basic Education Project in Indonesia. Recently he has also contributed to education development projects in Iraq, Saudi Arabia, Sri Lanka, Tajikistan, Uzbekistan and elsewhere.

John F. Fanselow divides his time between Tokyo and New York doing workshops and consulting. He is Professor Emeritus of Columbia University, Teachers College, New York where he studied and taught from 1964 to 1997. He has been active in TESOL and New York TESOL, serving as president of both.

Donald Freeman is Director of Teacher Education and Associate Professor of Education at the School of Education, University of Michigan, and Senior Faculty Fellow at the School for International Training. His work focuses on the connections among teacher learning, student learning, and school change.

Simon Gieve is Lecturer in Applied Linguistics at the University of Leicester, UK. He started his life as a language educator in Thailand, and subsequently taught for many years in Japan and later in Britain. His interests are in classroom language learning, teacher education, critical discourse analysis, and the social relationship between first and second language speakers.

Adrian Holliday is Professor of Applied Linguistics at Canterbury Christ Church University, UK, where he directs doctoral research in the critical sociology of TESOL. His recent publications have been in the areas of intercultural communication, qualitative research methodology, and cultural chauvinism in TESOL.

Roz Ivanič is Professor of Linguistics in Education at the Department of Linguistics and English Language, and Associate Director of the Literacy Research Centre at Lancaster University, UK. Her current research interests include literacies across the curriculum in Further Education, the learning and teaching of writing, integrating research with practice, pedagogy in adult literacy provision and how it relates to learners' lives and purposes for learning. She is currently Director of the ESRC-funded Literacies for Learning in Further Education research and is working on the NRDC project comparing embedded and non-embedded teaching of literacy, language and numeracy for learners on vocational pro- grammes. Her publications include *Writing and identity: the discoursal construction of identity in academic writing* (1998), and *The politics of writing* (1997).

Inés K. Miller is Assistant Professor at the Pontifical Catholic University of Rio de Janeiro (PUC-Rio), Brazil. She is involved in English language teaching as well as teacher education and development at undergraduate and post-graduate levels. Her research interests focus on the discourse of professional reflection generated by teachers, teacher educators and consultants. As a core member of the Lancaster University-based Exploratory Practice Centre (EPCentre) and the Exploratory Practice Group in Rio (EPGroup-Rio), she has also been actively engaged in the development and dissemination of Exploratory Practice.

Elaine E. Tarone is the Director of the Center for Advanced Research on Language Acquisition (CARLA), and Distinguished Teaching Professor and Chair of the English as a Second Language Program in the Institute of Linguistics, ESL and Slavic Languages and Literatures at the University of Minnesota, USA. Her research publications focus on the impact of social context on learner language and second language acquisition, interlanguage variation, learners' interactions in immersion classrooms, communication strategies, language play and, most recently, the impact of literacy on oral language processing.

Ming-i Lydia Tseng is Assistant Professor in the Department of Applied Linguistics and Language Studies, Chung Yuan Christian University, Taiwan. Her Ph.D. research at the Department of Linguistics and English Language, Lancaster University, UK was concerned with under- standing more about EFL students' learning of academic writing in English, in particular, the role of classroom interaction in the develop- ment of academic literacy. Her general interest is in the area of language education: the teaching and learning of literacy in the context in which English is used as a second or foreign language, the integration of research with classroom teaching and learning (especially 'Exploratory Practice'), and curriculum design.

Tony Wright is Professor of Language Education in the Centre for International Education at University College Plymouth St Mark & St John. He leads postgraduate courses for teacher educators in Plymouth and abroad and conducts consultancies in all aspects of English language education worldwide. His professional interests, as well as in teacher education and professional development, are researching classroom life, language awareness and online and distance education. His previous publications include *Classroom management in language education* (2005) and *Roles of teachers and learners* (1987).

Devon Woods is Associate Professor at Carleton University, Canada, teaching courses in second language acquisition and second language classroom research. His research interests are in decision-making processes in language teaching and learning, instructional strategies, the social construction of language learning, teacher cognition, teacher beliefs-assumptions-knowledge, learner cognition, learner beliefs-assumptions-knowledge, strategies in language learning and ethics in applied language research. He is the author of *Teacher cognition in language teaching: beliefs, decision-making and classroom practice* (1996).

Introduction

Simon Gieve and Inés K. Miller

The idea for this book arose out of a short paper that Dick Allwright originally wrote in 2001 for the benefit of his Masters course students in Hong Kong. We asked him if he would care to make it available in an expanded form as a 'starter paper' to which invited contributors would be invited to respond, and he agreed to do so. This paper appears as Chapter 1 of this volume. It offers a very particular view of applied linguistics (seen as the study of language teaching and learning); it is not interested in cognitivist approaches which attempt to shine a light into the 'black box' and specify links between input and uptake or the development of language skills. In Allwright's view, the relative productivity of various methodological solutions to teaching and learning language are of little interest, and competency-based approaches to teacher education are not seen as useful. Allwright's perspective on promising directions for applied linguistics derives from his original insight, formulated in his (1984a) and (1984b) papers, that learners don't simply learn what teachers teach, but that learning arises out of the *learning opportunities* that emerge through interaction in the classroom. Learners have as much of a role in this process as teachers. In this perspective, it is fruitless to search for and refine the 'best method', a view echoed by Prabhu in his (1990) paper, although this has not deterred other investigators from their current search for the 'perfect task'. Allwright's turn away, as an academic, from trying to specify the ideal conditions for language learning, and ideal behaviours for language teachers, is not just for reasons connected to research methodology, although certainly it is not possible, as a researcher, to control all the variables that might make a difference to learning outcomes without encountering serious ethical constraints. It is because of his growing perception of the *inherent complexity* of language classrooms, and their

1

situatedness. Once these features have been given primacy it makes little sense even for teachers in their own classrooms to investigate what happens in them with a view to 'fixing' them – to tackling 'problems' as if they were always amenable to direct teacher interventions. This was the position that Allwright and Bailey had taken in their (1991) volume *Focus on the language classroom*, but even before they had finished they realized that even teacher research on their own classrooms was not going to lead to problems being solved, let alone research by academics, applied to language classrooms across the world in disparate contexts, with disparate traditions and conditions, sizes, resources and purposes.

Since then, Allwright himself has achieved a great deal in pioneering an approach to practitioner-based *understanding* of their own classrooms, as an essential condition of, and preliminary to, any attempt at change – when the only change that then seems sensible may be a change in understanding itself rather than behaviour. This has resulted in his proposal for 'Exploratory Practice' (see the Exploratory Practice Centre website address in the Reference list, p. 10). This is not a book about Allwright's own contribution in this respect, however, but a book about how Allwright's perspective represents and finds echoes in the thinking of others. You do not need to have followed Allwright's own direction to be part of the general movement in applied linguistics that arose from a shared perception that a 'scientific' approach to language teaching, such as that which resulted in audio-lingualism for example, was not (ever) going to produce the expected results. This at a time when, as Breen (Chapter 10) and Freeman (Chapter 12) point out, policy-makers, politicians and the marketization of education, have been making more and more demands on teachers to 'come up with the goods', which has inevitably led to pressure for accountability, efficiency and productivity. In these conditions the increasing 'technologisation' of education has seemed the obvious solution: the specification of external syllabi, the honing of methodologies and their justification by second language acquisition theory and research, the training of learners to be better learners, the embrace of new technology. But it is not in these directions that Allwright sees the most promising directions for applied linguistics.

In Chapter 1, then, 'Six promising directions in Applied Linguistics', Dick Allwright provides the starting point for the contributions that follow. He offers a brief interpretation of six interwoven directions in the study of language teaching and learning since the 1950s, guided by his own sense of what appears to be 'promising' in these directions – what he would choose to encourage. Each proposal grows out of the one that precedes it. Direction 1 is that *From prescription to description to under-standing* between the 1950s and 1990s, which is linked to a growing awareness of the 'inherent complexity' of the teaching–learning situation (direction 2, *From simplicity to complexity*), rather than a simple matter of finding and implementing a 'best method'. Direction 3 is a move *From commonality to idiosyncrasy*: the awareness that if classrooms are complex, then there cannot be general solutions to general problems, but 'local' solutions are required. Direction 4 is *From precision to scattergun*, from the idea that the 'best' teaching precisely focuses on what gets learning done to the idea that we cannot hope to achieve that, and that all we can do is to generate a wide range of productive learning oppor-tunities. Direction 5 is *From teaching and learning as 'work' to teaching and learning as 'life'*; here Allwright makes the suggestion that 'efficiency' cannot be the ultimate aim in the provision of rich learning opportunities, but that they best arise if the quality of classroom life enables them to occur. He then suggests that the quality of classroom life itself is in fact the 'primary consideration'. Direction 6 is *From academics to practitioners as the knowledge-makers in the field*, as it becomes plain that professional 'understanding' is an alternative goal to 'problem-solving'. This leads him to his own proposal for Exploratory Practice as an alternative research paradigm for the field. Being aware of the elusiveness of the concept of 'progress' in applied linguistics he is hopeful, but does not wish to be optimistic, that the six 'promising directions' he currently identifies will last as guiding values for the profession in the future.

It is to this proposal that our eleven other contributors have responded, each in their own way. It is not a coincidence, of course, that they all seem to find in Allwright's thinking a resonance with their own attempts to understand classroom life, and an identification with the promise of his 'directions'. It is not that we, as editors, removed discordant notes from the contributions, but that we adopted the policy of approaching potential contributors whom we thought would add flesh to Allwright's skeletal argument. They have all, in one way or another, been closely associated with Dick Allwright over the years, worked with him, or been taught by him, or been influenced by his thinking. The contributions fall into two main areas of interest: what goes on inside language classrooms (Chapters 2–8), and language teacher education and development (Chapters 9–12). The main themes in the contributions, the common ideas that have found most resonance in our contributors' attempts at understanding language classroom life, are *the inherent complexity and idiosyncrasy of classroom life* (Holliday, Wright, Woods, Coleman, Tseng and Ivanič, Tarone, Fanselow and Barnard, Celani,

Freeman); *the central importance of participants' own understandings* (Gieve and Miller, Holliday, Woods, Tseng and Ivanič, Fanselow and Barnard, Breen, Celani, Freeman); *the relationship between classroom life and teachers' and students' lives* (Gieve and Miller, Wright, Woods, Tseng and Ivanič, Tarone, Breen, Celani); *negotiation between teachers and learners* (Gieve and Miller, Wright, Woods, Freeman); *the relationship between the local and the global* (Holliday, Coleman, Breen), and *the quality of classroom life* (Gieve and Miller, Wright).

In Chapter 2, Simon Gieve and Inés K. Miller ask 'What do we mean by "quality of classroom life?"', following up explicitly on Allwright's direction 5 in exploring a process approach to quality of life in the classroom (QoCRL). This is in opposition to the dominant technicist approach to quality in, and of, education, which is primarily concerned with the 'work' side of classrooms, and they try to redress the balance by valuing 'life' alongside work aspects of quality. The process approach that they propose is essentially relativizing in accepting that the quality of the classroom experience is best understood by participants in any particular classroom, and that such understanding cannot be automatically transferred to other contexts. It also means that QoCRL depends on the degree to which attention is paid to it, and the authors argue for the notion of 'classroom awareness' which arises through the process of teachers and learners together attempting joint understanding. Gieve and Miller draw on Bakhtin, using his concepts of *addressivity* and *speaker's speech plan* or *speech will* in emphasizing the situatedness of classroom discourse, in which *people talk to people* in the context of an exclusively shared history of interaction. In the third section of the chapter a range of examples of participant based classroom investigations in search of understanding of classroom life, based on Allwright's principles of Exploratory Practice, are used to illustrate how jointly working towards understanding informs QoCRL.

In Chapter 3, 'What happens between people: Who we are and what we do', Adrian Holliday bases his discussion of the messiness and complexity of professional puzzles in TESOL on what he sees as a postmodernist conception of the embeddedness of ideology in the everyday discourses of the profession. The ideologically invested concept of *native-speakerism*, an aspect of *culturism*, is seen as a central issue in TESOL, which features a cultural division marked by the distinction between 'native' and 'non-native speakers'. Organising his discussion around the first four of Allwright's directions, Holliday produces examples of how careful descriptive ethnographies of classrooms can help to unravel culturist prescriptions, and he adds insider reports drawn from email interviews with practitioners from the periphery. He focuses on the importance of idiosyncrasy and complexity in local conditions and preferences, and the inadequacy of attempts at precision, in discussing how 'non-native speakers' can resist culturist impositions within TESOL. True to his convictions, Holliday sees periphery practitioners' own struggles to understand their puzzles as more relevant to their unravelling than what he, as a Western 'expert' might have to say.

In Chapter 4, 'Managing classroom life', we see a clear realisation of the implications of the complexity of language classrooms, a focus on the *life* of the classroom, and life *in* the classroom, and a concern for the *quality* of that life. Tony Wright outlines an understanding of 'managing' that goes beyond *organising* and *controlling* to include its *coping* as well as *initiating* and *responding* senses, contrasting an 'order' view of classroom management with an 'opportunity' view. This is based on an acknowledgment of the *complexity* of classroom life, in which social and pedagogic aspects are intertwined, and in which *care* is an important feature. Wright also points out how classroom life is contextualized by institutional forces, sociocultural expectations and 'real life' outside the classroom. He discusses the contribution of five elements of classroom life in the opportunity view of classroom management: time, space, affective engagement, social participation and material and cognitive resources. This perspective on managing classroom life has implications for both classroom research (especially participant-based research) and language teacher education, but his ultimate goal for the opportunity view of classroom management is to maximize the quality of classroom life.

In Chapter 5, Devon Woods examines the question 'Who does what in the management of language learning?', quickly deciding that while this question is in principle unanswerable, it leads us to the more interesting question of '*how* is who does what decided?', which leads to an examination of both teachers' and learners' goal-directed decision-making processes in planning actions and evaluating events, and the negotiations between participants over 'whose job it is to do what'. Following a theoretical discussion of what is involved in decision-making and relationships between decisions, conceptually and in time, Woods reports on extended empirical classroom investigations of decision-making in relation to the process of *planning* by both teachers and learners. Planning extends from the level of life and career, through choice of programme, course, activity, to the utterance and word levels. The general characteristics of learner and teacher planning as well features of the negotiation of planning between teacher and learners are noted. Attention then shifts to the concepts of 'attending' and 'engagement' (which are relevant to discussions of 'focus on form', for example), their relationship to motivation, and how teacher and learners see their roles in these respects, in particular negotiation around responsibility for attending to learner errors. The constructivist nature of the language classroom is emphasized, and related to Allwright's 'directions' 1, 2, 3, 5 – *understanding, complexity, idiosyncrasy* and *teaching/learning as life*.

In Chapter 6, 'Darwin and the large class', Hywel Coleman proposes a Darwinian metaphor to help in the understanding of large classes, in contrast to approaches defined by over-simplistic technical prescriptions aimed at improving pedagogical efficiency. These have tended to be unsatisfactory in terms of offering either understanding or better results in contexts other than those in which they were generated. The author proposes that each classroom represents the best available 'local adaptation' for the environmental niche in which it occurs. Darwinism, Coleman explains, does not carry any sense of *progress*, but attempts to explain variation through gradual mutation. In this perspective, classrooms are characterized by their *relative stability and continuity*, coupled with *uniqueness* in individual occurrences (that is, both commonality and idiosyncrasy). Innovations or modifications introduced into classrooms may be benign, negative (and therefore short-lived), or bring advantages – in which case the 'mutation' may be gradually introduced as a feature of that classroom. Two case studies are reported which show how particular classroom events constituted best-fit local adaptations to local circumstances. These were not determined by considerations of efficiency of learning outcomes. Finally, Coleman presents a model in which eight variables are identified which determine the achievement of local adaptations in the lives of classrooms.

Chapter 7, 'Recognizing complexity in adult literacy research and practice', by Ming-i Lydia Tseng and Roz Ivanič, expands the volume's central concern with ELT classrooms in showing the applicability of Allwright's thinking to the domain of adult literacy learning. The authors' appreciation of *complexity* as a central concept derives from their recognition that learning is not the total sum of what has been taught in a class. The authors build a conceptual framework for adult literacy education in which the relationship between teaching and learning takes into account adult learners' *idiosyncrasy*, moves away from *precision*, and acknowledges the integration between teaching, learning and *life*. This model consists of factors that enter into teaching–learning events, features that characterize the nature of learning–teaching events, the learning opportunities that may be made available in learning–teaching events as these two sets of factors intersect, and the different types of learning ('uptake') that may result. Tseng and Ivanič also endorse Allwright's proposal of 'Exploratory Practice' as a viable way for *practitioners* to integrate their work for 'locally helpful understandings' into their learning–teaching events. Finally, the authors highlight the harmony between adult literacy *practitioner* work and the principles that orient the New Literacy Studies as well as much research and practice in adult literacy education.

In Chapter 8, 'Language lessons: a complex, local co-production of all participants', Elaine E. Tarone summarizes and reviews studies supporting Dick Allwright's view that the development of local, detailed descriptions of classroom learners, teachers and their activities is more helpful than global prescriptive statements. Data from descriptive case studies of child language learners in French, Spanish and English immersion classrooms, as well as findings from studies of the second language learning processes of young adults in college-level language classrooms, all support the view that second language classes can be viewed as speech communities, within which there are complex social relationships constituting sub-communities, with important implications for students' second language use. Students' patterns of language use with one another in desk work and in structured teacher-initiated activities are affected by their social identities and their relationships with the teacher and one another, and may influence their acquisition of the second language in complex and often unexpected ways. Since the complex and idiosyncratic sociolinguistic dynamics identified in these studies were not easily predictable either by the teacher or the researcher – or, most importantly, controlled by the immersion teachers – Tarone concludes that more such studies should be done to promote deeper researchers' and teachers' understandings of the complex nature of language classrooms.

Chapter 9, 'Take 1, Take 2, Take 3: a suggested three-stage approach to Exploratory Practice', by John F. Fanselow and Roger Barnard, proposes a particular interpretation of what might constitute 'Exploratory Practice' by teachers and learners (rather than academics) seeking to understand classrooms: the examination of records of classroom interaction from various contrasting perspectives. Allwright's directions 1 and 2 – of *understanding* (as opposed to prescription, or even description) and *complexity* – are central to their thinking and underlie their approach. The essence of their proposal is the generation of multiple perspectives. The 'three stages' of their title are *recreating interaction* (preparing classroom transcripts which seem to offer leverage on a particular issue or puzzle); *reflection on*

action (consisting of insiders' emic knowledge and alternative etic interpretations, based on theoretical perspectives, made with no knowledge
of the context itself); and *reconstruction for action* on which the three
perspectives of stage two are compared in order to generate alternative
possibilities for classroom practice from those which appeared in the
transcript. The three stages could then be repeated on the reconstructed
classroom practice as enacted. The process is described making use of
two examples of classroom transcript, and a third transcript is supplied
to encourage readers to follow the process for themselves (a set of
possible interpretations is supplied in an appendix). This is not an
approach to be followed as an everyday activity, however, but a tool to be
used sparingly by practitioners to explore and develop understanding of
particular aspects of professional activity.

In Chapter 10, 'Collegial development in ELT: the interface between
global processes and local understandings', Michael P. Breen identifies
pressures on language teachers' professional identities in late modernity,
when teachers are obliged to locate their own local action within global
processes. The purpose is to consider aspects of teacher development
that, in responding to shifts in professionalism, may be contributing to
professional *uncertainty* rather than facilitative of understanding and
adaptation. Four key aspects of the work of ELT practitioners that
are now under challenge are identified: what it is that teachers are
supposed to know; pressures for change in the ways that teachers are
expected to teach; a preoccupation with *performativity*, which affects the
degree of accountability to which teachers are being held; and insecurity
in working conditions. He asks how professional development may
help teachers to deal with these pressures. While prevailing approaches
to in-service teacher training provision are seen as inadequate, Breen
cautions against reliance on locally authentic vernacular pedagogies,
seeing strength in the possibility of *hybridity*. The potential of both
reflective practice and action research for teacher development are
examined and their basis in the rationalisation of personal experience is
questioned in the light of the complexity of classroom life and the
limitations of enquiry restricted to teachers' own immediate work. The
potential of a collaborative critical reflection approach is outlined, and
Allwright's proposal for Exploratory Practice as a means of understanding
the quality of life of the classroom, rooted in a concern for the quality
of teachers' lives, is seen as offering space for critical reflexivity. Finally,
Breen proposes seven desirable features of collegial language teacher
development that is both grounded in localized communities of practice
and engages with global issues: it should recognize teachers as integrated

individuals, as members of communities, as 'cultural workers', and as responsible for their own development, and it should promote collegiality, discoursiveness and evolutionary change.

In Chapter 11, 'Language teacher educators in search of "locally helpful understandings"', Maria Antonieta Alba Celani, extends Allwright's 'directions' to the world of teacher education, as she reflexively discusses the challenges faced by the inter-institutional team that conceptualized and managed a wide-scale in-service English teacher education programme in São Paulo, Brazil. In contrast to the normally available teacher development opportunities for English teachers, which emphasize technical efficiency heavily based on such notions as the appropriateness of techniques or the myth of the best method, Celani finds in their programme strong echoes of Allwright's tenets on teacher development. Collaborative reflection by teachers as agents, not subjects, of their continuing process of professional reconstruction are highlighted as central issues in an attempt to disassociate teacher education from simplistic problem-solving, with a view towards a stronger recognition of the need to question and understand the complex, idiosyncratic features of classroom lives in the Brazilian school system. Taking a critical stance and considering that there is no best method for teacher education, Celani also reflects on the team's 'puzzles', on their 'learning opportunities' and on the possibilities for peer teachers to act as researchers, becoming 'knowledge-makers' in the sense of 'reaching locally helpful understandings'. Finally, the author exploits new relations between the notions of 'quality of work' and 'quality of life' to reflect on life inside *and* outside classrooms in school settings *as well as* in teacher education contexts.

In the final chapter, Chapter 12, 'Teaching and learning in "the age of reform": The problem of the verb', Donald Freeman approaches an understanding of the relationship between teaching and learning in the form of an enquiry into what verb we would choose to connect the two parts of the sentence *'What teachers know and do——what students know and do'*. Freeman argues that understanding this is central to making any progress in teachers' professional development. He identifies three potential 'dead ends' in working towards such an understanding. First, the idea that what happens in classrooms is about *individuals* rather than collectivities; he makes use of Engeström's activity theory (Engeström, Miettinen and Punamäki, 1999) here in exploring the role of 'interconnectedness' in classroom life. The second 'dead end' Freeman identifies is that of *immediacy*, or the *presentist* perspective that the here-and-now is what matters most in teaching and learning, ignoring all historical processes. The third is that of attributing *causality* – the notion that the actions of an individual teacher *causes* individual learning. Freeman focuses in particular on the role of 'instruments' or 'tools' in Engeström's activity theory model (taking as an example a graphing calculator used in algebra classes), extended into the role of 'symbolic tools' for professional learning.

In this Introduction, we have outlined our thinking behind the volume and the central themes that have emerged in the texts – and anticipated how the contributors have related their thinking to Allwright's 'six directions'. At this point, it also seems important to share with our readers Allwright's awareness, at the initial stage of our project, that his document was not exhaustive in itself of all the directions he could have indicated, and that proposals for other 'directions' would be desirable/ stimulating for the field. With this in mind, we have taken the editorial decision of sharing Allwright's initial 'six directions' document with our readers. We hope that this decision will motivate others to join in the responsive process started in this book and that it will generate the proposal of other 'directions' for the field of applied linguistics and for the enhancement of our understandings of language classroom life.

References

Allwright, R.L. 1984a. Why don't learners learn what teachers teach? – The interaction hypothesis. In: *Language learning in formal and informal contexts*, eds D.M. Singleton and D.G. Little, 3–18. Dublin: IRAAL.

Allwright, R.L. 1984b. The importance of interaction in classroom language learning. *Applied Linguistics* 5, 2:156–71

Allwright, D. and K.M. Bailey 1991. *Focus on the language classroom: an introduction to classroom research for language teachers.* Cambridge: Cambridge University Press.

Bakhtin, M.M. 1986. *Speech genres and other late essays.* Trans. V.W. McGee, eds C. Emerson and M. Holquist. Austin: University of Texas Press.

Engeström, Y., R. Miettinen and R.-L. Punamäki, eds 1999. *Perspectives on activity theory.* New York: Cambridge University Press.

Exploratory Practice Centre http://www.lehras.puc-rio.br/epcentre/epcentre. htm

Prabhu, N.S. 1990. There is no best method, why? *TESOL Quarterly* 24, 2:161–17.

1

Six Promising Directions in Applied Linguistics

Dick Allwright

Introduction

What follows started out as a somewhat hastily composed handout for a Masters course I was teaching in Hong Kong. I was seeking to help the students gain a sense of the history of Applied Linguistics (seen narrowly as the study of language teaching and learning), but it is now obvious that all I was able to do was tell my own personal story, of the development of my own thinking over more than forty years of serious involvement with language teaching and learning.

I have revised that original handout to strengthen it generally, and in particular to strengthen its relationship to the general applied linguistics and educational research literature. But it remains a highly personal account (one that helps me get a sense of coherence for my own career in applied linguistics), rather than one claiming to summarize the entire field with authority (for fuller discussion of the issues, see Allwright and Hanks, in press). I hope it will nevertheless serve as a productive starting point for the other contributions to this volume, whether or not they share my sense of what is *promising*.

1. From prescription to description to understanding

Prescription

In the 1950s and through to the late 1960s the job of applied linguists was seen as one of doing the sort of research that would enable applied linguists to tell language teachers what to do for the best for their learners. From this came the famous experiments (Scherer and Wertheimer, 1964; Smith, 1970, for example) comparing an exciting new way of teaching a language (audio-lingualism) to an old, and beginning to be discredited, way of teaching (grammar-translation).

Description

The failure of such methodological comparisons experiments in the mid- and late 1960s to get definitive results (and thus serve the above prescriptive aim) prompted a switch to a descriptive approach to pedagogical research, because part of the problem of the comparisons research had been a failure to adequately describe the teaching that actually happened during the experiments (Allwright, 1972, 1988; Clark, 1969; Otto, 1969).

At the same time as the methodological comparisons experiments were being conducted, however, a descriptive approach was already being advocated in teacher training (Allwright, 1972; Jarvis, 1968; Moskowitz, 1971). Initially this too was often allied to a prescriptive aim – to describe what a teacher was doing so that the teacher could be advised to do things somewhat differently.

Gradually, however, as confidence in prescription further weakened, the focus of description in teacher training shifted to emphasize the value already noted by Moskowitz in the 1960s of description as a feedback system for teachers to look at their own teaching and decide for themselves if they wanted to change it in any way (Fanselow, 1977; Moskowitz, 1968).

Understanding

But research through the 1970s kept on revealing, for me at least, more and more layers of complexity (Allwright, 1975; Smith and Geoffrey, 1968), especially when I saw that general education researchers (for example, Mehan, 1974) were arguing persuasively that lessons were best seen as a co-production of all participants, so that you could no longer expect a teacher to be able to simply change what happened in the classroom, unilaterally, at will (Allwright, 1980).

At the same time, this revelation of increasing complexity began slowly to suggest to classroom researchers like myself that the description of what could be seen through direct observation was clearly not going to be adequate to the task of understanding (Allwright, 1987, 1988).

And in teacher training people gradually began to realize that initial training was in some ways less important than in-service work, and that experienced teachers could be helped more by equipping them to better understand their situation than by simply trying 'to teach old dogs new tricks' (for an excellent example of this development see Breen et al., 1989).

In my own work I began, in the late 1980s and through the 1990s, slowly to equate this with the idea that the proper concern of both research and teacher development work was to focus on *understanding* rather than *problem-solving*, and on understanding as something potentially of value in its own right, not simply as a road to technical 'improvements in teaching efficiency' (Allwright and Bailey, 1991: Epilogue).

2. From simplicity to complexity

Another way of looking at the shift from prescription to description and then to understanding is to think of it more generally as a move from a simplistic way of looking at the world of applied linguistics (for example, thinking, universalistically and causally, that there *ought* to be just one best method for language teaching, for all languages, for all learners, for all teachers, and for all time), towards a recognition of the essential and irreducible complexity of the phenomenon of classroom language learning and teaching.

3. From commonality to idiosyncracy

Part of this recognition of complexity meant that it was no longer worth looking for general solutions to general problems, because all 'problems' are reducible, ultimately, and in practice, to 'local' ones, and so require 'local' solutions, solutions that respect the uniqueness of all human situations, and of all humans (Allwright, 2003). For example, Perpignan (2001), working with seven learners on the development of their academic writing, did find some commonalities, but found their idiosyncracies to be much more important.

It is quite clear that there are plenty of people still looking for essential commonalities, as if this were the best (perhaps the only) way for them to make a useful contribution to the field, but the more I look, the more I find idiosyncracy to be the more important phenomenon, not commonality.

4. From precision to scattergun

If you accept the notion of the essential idiosyncracy of humanity, then logically there are two possible responses that can be made. Either you can try to match, on a one-to-one basis, the individual differences of the people around you, which in language teaching could mean trying to tailor your teaching to each learner separately ('individualisation' in the north American tradition, see Altman and James, 1980), or you can acknowledge that this is asking far too much and decide instead to adopt a 'scattergun' approach, whereby you offer a multitude of learning opportunities for learners, and expect them to select according to their own particular needs ('autonomy' in the European tradition, see Holec, 1988). *A less militaristic metaphor would be to contrast the individual planting of seeds in specially dug holes to the traditional technique of sowing seeds by 'broadcasting', throwing them all around you, in the expectation that some will fall on 'stony ground' but that at least some others will fall on fertile ground, by chance alone.*

Curiously, this 'broadcasting' approach found an early champion in Krashen (1982), who in the late 1970s and early 1980s began advocating that the provision of 'comprehensible input' was best guaranteed by avoiding a linguistic syllabus altogether, and substituting for it teacher talk that merely tried to communicate effectively on any topic of interest to the learners. See also Prabhu's 'Communicational' Language Teaching project (1987).

Another development of interest with regard to the issue of precision is 'task-based language teaching' (see Ellis, 2000; Long, 1985; Nunan, 1989). Sometimes it appears that task designers are trying to get more and more precise in their design, to guarantee that particular things will be learned from carrying out particular tasks, and sometimes it appears that the best task design will not seek to determine what shall be learned, but only to guarantee the provision of a wide-range of learning opportunities, *among which all the participants will be able to find something of use.*

Behind all such thinking is the idea that the best teaching will be the teaching that gets nearest to a one-to-one relationship between what gets taught and what gets learned. My preferred alternative is to suggest that the 'best' teaching (if the notion has any value at all) will be that which generates the most, and the most productive, learning opportunities.

5. From teaching and learning as 'work' to teaching and learning as 'life'

If we do make the shift outlined above towards the provision of learning opportunities then we may appear still to be buying into the notion that 'efficiency' is the ultimate aim. An alternative take on this is to say that the productivity of learning opportunities may depend less on the quality of the work that goes into them than to the quality of the classroom life in which they arise. But this still accepts that the ultimate aim is short-term productivity – teaching efficiency.

A further, more radical, alternative is to suggest that the quality of classroom life is itself the most important matter, both for the long-term mental health of humanity (and the mental health of the language teacher!), and for the sake of encouraging people to be lifelong learners, rather than people resentful of having to spend years of their lives as 'captive' learners, and therefore put off further learning for life. I find this shift has very intriguing parallels in management studies (see Blackler and Kennedy, 2001).

6. From academics to practitioners as the knowledge-makers in the field

Work on teacher education (for teachers in general as well as for language teachers in particular) has been moving for some time in the direction of looking to the *practitioners* as the people who will conduct the most productive research in the field. This started with the renewed interest in the paradigm of Action Research, whereby teachers were invited to identify practical classroom problems, and then try out possible solutions (the 'action' part), and to continue to make changes until they solved the original problem (see Kemmis and McTaggart, 1988). For this purpose it was considered unnecessary for them to follow standard academic research practice and thus try to run a 'control' group alongside the class they were experimenting with. But in other respects they were encouraged to follow standard academic practices of data collection and analysis, in order to reach professionally valid conclusions about what worked for them and what did not (see Nunan, 1989: 12–14).

I think it is now becoming increasingly clear (within the social sciences more generally, and within management studies also) that a more radical approach to finding a professionally viable research approach is needed, as the emphasis is increasingly placed on the supreme importance of *understanding*, as being logically prior to, and potentially a substitute for, *problem-solving*. My own proposal for a professionally viable alternative research paradigm is '*Exploratory Practice*'. But accepting Exploratory Practice would also mean re-thinking the idea of teachers as knowledge-makers (Allwright, 2003). First, Exploratory Practice would see practitioners as people trying to reach locally helpful *understandings*, not *new knowledge*. And, secondly, Exploratory Practice would specifically include learners as seekers after understanding. Exploratory Practice is thus conceived as a way of getting teaching and learning done, not as a way of getting research done. But it is a way of getting teaching and learning done so that the teachers and the learners simultaneously develop *their own understanding of what they are doing* as learners and teachers. And they can perhaps best do this, as suggested in the previous section, by focusing on trying to understand the factors that affect the quality of *life* in the language classroom, rather by focusing directly on trying to achieve a high quality of *work*.

So what?

Using the term 'promising directions' in my title suggested optimism, a sense that we know where we have been, that we know where we are going and that we are reasonably confident of making progress towards well-chosen goals. But the concept of 'progress' is a very elusive one in our field (Allwright, 2000). Each of us needs a sense (or at least the illusion) of personal intellectual progress, but at the same time we also perhaps need a strong sense that the past was not exclusively populated with fools, and that our own efforts at understanding will no doubt one day look at least as foolish as anything that has preceded us looks foolish to us now.

So, in response to 'So what?' we can hope only that our current, apparently 'promising', ideas are going to prove worth pursuing at least for a while longer. More than that would be too much to ask.

References

Allwright, R.L. 1972. Prescription and description in the training of language teachers. In: *Applied linguistics: problems and solutions*, eds J. Qvistgaard, H. Schwarz and H. Spang-Hanssen, 155–66. Volume III of the Proceedings of the Third AILA Congress, Copenhagen. Heidelberg: Julius Groos Verlag,

Allwright, R.L. 1975. Problems in the study of the language teacher's treatment of learner error. In: *New directions in second language learning, teaching, and bilingual education*, eds H.C. Dulay and M.K. Burt, 96–109. Washington, DC: TESOL.

Allwright, R.L. 1980. Turns, topics, and tasks: patterns of participation in language learning and teaching. In: *Discourse analysis in second language research*, ed. D. Larsen-Freeman, 165–87. Rowley, Mass.: Newbury House,

Allwright, R.L. and J. Hanks (forthcoming). *The Developing Language Learner: An Introduction to Exploratory Practice*. Basingstoke: Palgrave Macmillan.

Allwright, D. 1987. Classroom observation: problems and possibilities. In: *Patterns of classroom interaction in Southeast Asia*, ed. B.K. Das, 88–102. Singapore: SEAMEO Regional Language Centre.

Allwright, D. 1988. *Observation in the language classroom*. London: Longman.

Allwright, D. 2000. The notion of progress in research on language teaching and learning. Unpublished monograph, available from the author at the Department of Linguistics, Lancaster University, UK.

Allwright, D. 2003. Exploratory Practice: re-thinking practitioner research in language teaching. *Language Teaching Research* 7, 2:113–41.

Allwright, D. and K.M. Bailey 1991. *Focus on the language classroom: an introduction for language teachers.* Cambridge: Cambridge University Press.

Altman, H.B. and C.V. James 1980. *Foreign language teaching: meeting individual needs.* Oxford: Pergamon Press.

Blackler, F. and A. Kennedy 2001. The design of a development programme for experienced top managers from the public sector. Draft paper from a Management Sciences Research Seminar, Lancaster, March.

Breen, M.P., C. Candlin, L. Dam and G. Gabrielsen 1989. The evolution of a teacher training programme. In: *The second language curriculum,* ed. K. Johnson, 111–35. Cambridge: Cambridge University Press.

Clark, J.L.D. 1969. The Pennsylvania Project and the 'audio-lingual vs traditional' question. *Modern Language Journal* 53: 388–96.

Ellis, R. 2000. Task-based research and language pedagogy. *Language Teaching Research* 4, 3: 193–220.

Fanselow, J.F. 1977. Beyond *Rashomon:* conceptualising and describing the teaching act. *TESOL Quarterly* 11, 1: 17–39.

Holec, H., ed. 1988. *Autonomy and self-directed learning: present fields of application.* Strasburg: Council of Europe.

Jarvis, G.A. 1968. A behavioral observation system for classroom foreign language skill acquisition. *Modern Language Journal* 52: 335–41.

Kemmis, S. and R. McTaggart, eds 1988. *The action research planner.* 3rd edition, Geelong, Australia: Deakin University Press.

Krashen, S.D. 1982. *Principles and practice in second language acquisition.* Oxford: Pergamon Press.

Long, M.H. 1985. A role for instruction in second language acquisition: task-based language training. In: *Modelling and assessing second language acquisition,* eds K. Hyltenstam and M. Pienemann, 77–100. Clevedon: Multilingual Matters.

Mehan, H. 1974. Accomplishing classroom lessons. In: *Language use and school performance,* eds A.V.Cicourel, K.H. Jennings, S.H.M. Jennings, K.C.W. Leiter, R. McKay, H. Mehan and D. Roth, 76–142. New York: Academic Press,

Moskowitz, G. 1968. The effects of training foreign language teachers in interaction analysis. *Foreign Language Annals* 1, 3: 218–35.

Moskowitz, G. 1971. Interaction Analysis – a new modern language for supervisors. *Foreign Language Annals* 5, 2: 211–21.

Nunan, D. 1989. *Designing tasks for the communicative classroom.* Cambridge, Cambridge University Press.

Otto, F. 1969. The teacher in the Pennsylvania Project. *Modern Language Journal* 53: 411–20.

Perpignan, H. 2001. Teacher-written feedback to language learners: promoting a dialogue for understanding. Unpublished PhD thesis, Lancaster University.

Prabhu, N.S. 1987. *Second language pedagogy.* Oxford: Oxford University Press.

Scherer, G.A.C. and M. Wertheimer 1964. *A psycholinguistic experiment in foreign language teaching.* New York: McGraw-Hill.

Smith, L. and W. Geoffrey 1968. *The complexities of an urban classroom.* New York: Holt, Rinehart & Winston.

Smith, P.D. 1970. *A comparison of the cognitive and audiolingual approaches to foreign language instruction: The Pennsylvania Project.* Philadelphia: Center for Curriculum Development.

2
What Do We Mean by 'Quality of Classroom Life'?

Simon Gieve and Inés K. Miller

> [T]he quality of classroom life is itself the most important matter.
>
> Allwright (2006, Chapter 1 in this volume)

Introduction

In this chapter, we explore the complexity and subtlety of the notion of 'quality of life' in the classroom as we find that it underlies some tensions that we perceive in the fields of applied linguistics and, more specifically, in the area of (foreign) language education. One such perennial tension seems to exist between those who believe in and promote technicist and problem-solution orientations in education and those who strive for authentically humanistic and process-oriented views of classroom life. Our interest resonates with the latest developments in Allwright's thinking as delineated especially in his *Six promising directions for applied linguistics* (Allwright, 2006, Chapter 1 in this volume). We, together with Allwright and the other contributors to this book, wish to problematize the generalized perception that educational quality can be accessed via description leading to prescription and, in simplistic ways that highlight commonalities and precision with an emphasis on externally determined productivity as the ultimate aim.

In facing the challenge of addressing some dimensions of the elusive notion of 'quality' and relating them to our position on published research on 'quality' in the fields of education and (foreign) language (teacher) education we propose a practitioner-based view of 'quality of classroom life' (QoCRL). In the third section of this chapter, we report on an illustrative sample of practitioner-based work for classroom understanding that has emerged in volunteer teacher and learner development situations set within the Exploratory Practice paradigm and within the post-graduate academic context of PUC-Rio, Brazil. We interpret 'practitioner thinking' of this kind as a form of grass-root resistance to, and of potential transformation of, the dominating technicist paradigm. Born out of the tension between the product and problem-solution orientations favoured within educational institutions and the local everyday classroom realities, we find teachers and learners as practitioner researchers creating and exploiting opportunities to reflect on what puzzles *them* about their teaching–learning processes. We have found that the Rio teachers engaged in the EP programme prioritize issues related to their *lives* – *in*side as well as *out*side classrooms – over such work-oriented issues as content proficiency, technical efficiency or productivity. In various ways, these practitioners are resolving their classroom dilemmas by prioritising quality of classroom life over the overwhelming institutional emphasis given to quality of classroom work. They resist the colonization of the life-world by technologies of education by redefining notions such as motivation, anxiety, discipline, learners' and teachers' beliefs, or patterns of classroom interaction, in *life* rather than *work* terms.

Why our concern with the quality of classroom life?

We address the notion of QoCRL in order to highlight some central issues that have also been recurrent in Allwright's thinking; namely, that our personal and our professional lives are interwoven, that understanding and learning are so intrinsically constitutive of life that they cannot be measured in terms of efficiency and that the 'quality' of an experience can best be felt, or known, by its experiencer.

As teachers and learners, we weave together our schoolwork lives with our personal lives. We agree with Wenger, when he observes that 'communities of practice are an integral part of our daily lives' (1998: 7) and that 'in learning an occupation we weave together our work with our private lives' (1998: 41). As members of our communities of practice, we have multiple and complex identities; teachers are not *only* teachers and students are not *only* students (work lives), who respond to each other as if the sum total of their interaction is rooted in their respective roles as teachers and learners. They are also *people who speak to each other* (personal lives). There is an inherent integration between our personal and institutional lives in the classroom, which is paradoxically ignored in most educational contexts. We believe that addressing this tension is one way of redressing the balance between 'life' and 'work' in the classroom.

Along these lines, Allwright has emphasized, since the 1990s, that 'our first priority is to address the issue of the *quality of life* in whatever setting is under consideration' and has also proposed that this ought to be the case 'even if the *quality of work* is initially seen to be the central issue' (Allwright, 2002: 1). By focusing on 'classroom life' issues we are not advocating, of course, a dichotomising separation between 'classroom life' and 'classroom work'. Quite the contrary, our thinking reveals a 'life' orientation *as well as* a 'work' orientation. We are trying to highlight the strong integration we see between 'life' and 'work' – 'work' being a part of 'life' and 'life' being a part of 'work', or, possibly, 'work' being a form of 'life' and 'life' a form of 'work'. And we are doing so because we are observing that the 'work' part has been hitherto predominant, while the 'life' part has been forgotten or suppressed.

We find this 'non-efficiency' orientation towards *understanding* in Allwright and Bailey (1991: 196), when they explain their intention to' 'help teachers *understand* better their own, and their learners', classroom lives', not as a short cut to "more effective learning"'. We also align ourselves with Allwright (2006), when he makes the even more radical point that

> the quality of classroom life is itself the most important matter, both for the long-term mental health of humanity (and the mental health of the language teacher!), and for the sake of encouraging people to be lifelong learners, rather than people resentful of having to spend years of their lives as 'captive' learners, and therefore put off further learning for life.

More recently, in his proposal for broadening innovation beyond the notion of 'success', Allwright (2004a: 7) suggests that 'the notion of "quality" does not in itself necessarily invoke a world of measurable "qualities" (like the notion of quality of life in different cities, for example). Instead it can evoke the notion of an interest in the "nature" of life in the classroom.'

Such an interest in 'what is going on' (Goffman, 1974) in the classroom leads us to address the complexity and idiosyncrasy involved in what it means to understand QoCRL and question whose understandings of 'quality' counts. In this process, some puzzlement arises. Understanding the QoCRL involves multifaceted interpretive processes based on frameworks of expectations of what constitutes a *good* or a *poor* quality of classroom experience. Since these frameworks are necessarily socio-historically situated and interpersonally constructed in complex and idiosyncratic ways, understandings not only tend to vary among classroom participants but are also bound to be different from the perspective of an external observer of the classroom situation. The tension between the emic understandings of participants and the etic view of external observers helps us perceive the complexity involved in assessing classroom life according to how well what is going on serves the purposes of the moment, which can be about product (progress in language learning, for instance) *as well as* about process (quality of the human interaction).

What needs to be seriously avoided is for external interpretations of local observations to be translated into local or global recommendations for improving learning processes or for enhancing results. This position allies our thinking to that of Allwright's sixth direction (Allwright, 2006) advocacy of practitioner research, and of Exploratory Practice as a form of practitioner research that offers opportunities for teachers and learners to work for their local understandings of their classroom lives. By integrating teachers, learners and pedagogic practice within a collegially developed investigative attitude, Exploratory Practice strengthens the agency potential of classroom insiders as those necessarily pivotal in any search for serious understanding of what goes on in classrooms. We claim that 'quality of classroom life' can be best understood by insiders and, possibly, that these understandings can be most useful to *them* as experiencers of their classroom lives. This does not suggest, of course, that insider understandings cannot illuminate or inspire outsiders. Or that, regarding the emic–etic dilemma, we cannot consider the possibility of an outsider participating as catalyst in insiders' work for understandings. In the role of consultant, colleague or, simply, friend, a respectful outsider inspired by a collegial belief in mutual professional development can participate in the process of understanding a local situation (Miller, 2003a; Miller and Moraes Bezerra, 2005).

As outlined in this section, we shall be working towards a *process* view of QoCRL (White, 1998: 135), but one that emphasizes the contributions of both teachers and learners, not the post-Fordist notion of the professionalized teacher as put forward by Tuffs (1995). This necessarily involves adopting a relativist, phenomenological approach to understanding quality, which we distinguish from a universalistic approach. Figure 2.1 summarizes some aspects of this complex distinction. But being aware of this complexity and avoiding the danger of simplistic dichotomizations, we consider various characterizing aspects of each tendency as dimensions of a *continuum* between relativising and universalizing tendencies.

Relativizing Tendency	Universalizing Tendency
← —————————————— →	
Varies between participants at any one time	Can be 'averaged out' at any one time
Fitness for moment-to-moment personal needs	Fitness for generalized values
Socially, culturally, historically and contextually situated	Objective criteria can be transferred across classrooms, schools, times
Participants and observers may disagree	Observers' and participants' evaluations are averaged out
Equal focus on process and product	Tendency to favour product criteria
Best understood, and therefore subject to control by insiders	Outsiders can propose global management (best practice) solutions
Individual concerns, locally relevant	Institutional concerns, compromised by QoCR work, globally relevant
Puzzle orientation	Problem orientation
Research to enhance understanding of quality of classroom life is best done by insiders	Research to enhance understanding of quality of classroom life can be done by academics
Understanding comes through participation	Understanding can be taught

Figure 2.1   Aspects of relativizing and universalizing approaches to the 'quality of classroom life'

We see an essential tension in thinking about QoCRL between internal and external criteria, between participants' subjective responses and classroom outsiders' objective evaluations and between insiders' and outsiders' agency in the investigative processes of understanding QoCRL. Naturally the two are not independent: classroom participants, both teachers and learners, will have a reflexive eye on external criteria ('Am I doing what others expect me to do in the way of learning, here? Am I teaching in a way that will satisfy others?'), and external understandings of the quality of classroom life will also take into account participants' subjective experience ('One way that I know about the quality of classroom life here is what the participants feel about their experience').

Adopting a process approach to QoCRL essentially means that quality depends on the degree to which attention is paid to it. This attention needs to be continuously maintained. We believe that QoCRL *is* what teachers and learners understand, and/or try to understand, about their joint experience in classrooms, and that these understandings are of greater intrinsic importance to them than how productive or efficient classroom outcomes are by external standards. We see these local understandings being striven for not in order to improve learning processes or enhance results but because the process appears to constitute an inherent way of *being* in the classroom.

We shall return to this theme in due course and in the third section, where we review some studies which demonstrate what can happen when attention is paid to understanding QoCRL within a practitioner research framework. The message of this work in relation to the insider–outsider paradox is the perception that these practitioner understandings were locally co-constructed (between 'internal' teachers and their learners and/or 'external' teacher–researchers) within an investigative perspective and not produced for global mass-consumption. This movement appears to be echoing Palmer's (1998: 66) belief that 'when we think together, we reclaim the life force in the world, in our students, in ourselves'.

Approaches to the idea of the quality of classroom life

In exploring the notion of QoCRL we will be drawing in this section on philosophical thinking about quality in education, on empirical research on measures of quality of school life and on understandings specifically within the field of language education. But first, we turn our own attention to more abstract understandings of the idea of 'quality' itself.

What is 'quality' in QoCRL?

There is no doubt that 'quality' is a complex notion. Pirsig ([1974] 1989) in *Zen and the art of motorcycle maintenance* writes:

Quality...you know what it is, yet you don't know what it is. But that's self-contradictory. But some things *are* better than others, that is, they have more quality. But when you try to say what the quality is, apart from the things that have it, it all goes *poof!* There's nothing to talk about. But if you can't say what Quality is, how do you know what it is, or how do you know that it even exists? If no one knows what it is, then for all practical purposes it doesn't exist at all. But for all practical purposes it really *does* exist...Obviously some things are better than others...but what's the betterness?...So round and round you go, spinning mental wheels and nowhere finding anyplace to get traction. What the hell is Quality? What *is* it? ([1974] 1989: [187], emphases in the original)

The *Oxford English Dictionary* defines quality in terms of the *nature* or *attribute* of an entity as well as its *degree of excellence or superiority*. In thinking about QoCRL we hold on to the polyphony of the word 'quality' as referring to both *goodness* and *what kind of stuff it is*. It may be, however, that this distinction is a false one, and that when people refer to the quality of something the idea of the *nature* of it is always related to *how well* it does its supposed job, or how much it is valued. Quality is thus not inherent in nature. We cannot have a *good-quality* mountain or tree *per se*, although they could be 'good' relative to the aesthetic sensibilities of an observer looking at them, or their intention and ability to climb them, and we can have good-quality rock or wood, only because it suits certain purposes we have for it.

Thus in assessing the *quality* of a classroom we add to its *nature* an idea of fitness to purpose (see Coleman, 2006, Chapter 6 in this volume), which derives from criteria tied to expectations not only of what the purpose of the classroom is, but also what we want out of our own lives, and how those two match. These criteria have cultural roots and depend on shared cultural values (whatever may constitute that culture), and also a social dimension related to our understanding of how classroom participants (which may be ourselves or others) fit into their social world. The *nature* of classroom life is about what it is like to be in that classroom, but at the same time as 'feeling being there' participants will have their own ideas about what might make it *better* to be there. These ideas can be clarified only if work towards understanding the situation is undertaken before work towards improvement gets started. They can also be contradictory, both between participants and internal to participants' own criteria, and again there can be no *gain* in quality unless work is done to explore and, probably resolve, those contradictions, according to local understandings, needs and constraints. The idea that quality can be determined externally, and that ways of improving quality can be prescribed, relies of course on the idea that there is no difference between local situations, and crucially that the participants' own understandings do not vary across each local situation.

Educational research on QoCRL

A good deal of educational research has been devoted to defining quality in education, driven by the need for public accountability and a concern with standards in education as well as value-for-money (Winch, 1996). Objective indicators of school quality measure pupil attainments, drop-out rates, facilities, expenditures per pupil, staff ratios and the like. The Organisation for Economic Co-operation and Development (OECD, 1994) definition of *teaching quality* includes: knowledge of the subject matter; pedagogical skill with a repertoire of teaching strategies; the ability for reflection and to be self-critical; 'empathy and commitment to the acknowledgement of the dignity of others' in pursuit of affective as well as cognitive outcomes; and managerial competence (cited in Ramsay and Oliver, 1995). In practice, however, a 'good teacher' is often defined on the basis of students' examination performances, as in Ramsay and Oliver's own (1995) study of primary school teachers in New Zealand, or from an *a priori* values-led definition of what good teachers do, as in Hargreaves (1988), where teaching quality is defined in terms of avoiding reliance on 'narrow transmission teaching', or from check-lists of teacher competencies.

Another strand of educational research has looked at the connection between teachers' personal and professional lives. Poppleton and Riseborough (1990), for example, have looked at the concept of work centrality, and teachers' degree of commitment to work and how much it dominates their lives at different times. Goodson (1991) argues that we cannot *improve* practice by focusing *on* practice alone, and that the teachers' voice (a personal voice rooted in their own lives) has to be brought into the quality equation. Huberman (1988, 1989, 1993) and Ball and Goodson (1989) also discuss teachers' career trajectories, stress, commitment and burn-out. There is considerable research literature on teacher job satisfaction, morale, motivation, stress and burn-out (see, for example, Csikszentmihalyi, 1997; Dunham and Varma, 1998; Evans, 1998; Lumsden, 1998; Pennington, 1995) which is effectively summarized in Chang (2004). There is no doubt that how teachers feel about their work must significantly affect their own QoCRL (Celani, 2006, Chapter 11 in this volume). There is also a certain amount of work within applied linguistics on how *learners'* articulate the connections between their personal lives and their classroom lives – for example Norton's (2001) discussion of 'imagined communities', and Benson and Nunan's (2004) edited collection of 'learners' stories'.

Research on the quality of school life collected in Epstein (1981) took the students' perspective, using their reactions to the school and their teachers and their commitment to classwork as measures of the quality of school life (QSL), seen as 'school climate'. Moos and David (1981), for example, constructed a 'Classroom Environment Scale' to access junior and senior high school pupils' response to 'environmental press' – the social context of the classroom – in terms of 'ways of doing things' and human relations (the 'environment of feeling'). There were three groups of measures of 'classroom climate': (1) Relationship (student involvement, interest and participation in class activities, affiliation amongst students – how much they help each other, teacher support – how much help, interest, trust or friendship teachers show towards students); (2) Goal Orientation (task orientation – the importance of completing activities; amount of emphasis on competition between students); (3) System Maintenance and Change (emphasis on orderliness in class; rule clarity; strictness of teacher control and punishment; innovation by students and teacher in planned activities). A more recent study by Karatzias, Power and Swanson (2001) had similar objectives, and they devised a Quality of School Life scale with fourteen domains.

Gerson, a sociologist, describes an 'individualist' conception of quality of life as 'the degree to which an individual succeeds in accomplishing his desires despite the constraints put upon him by a hostile or indifferent nature, God or social order' (Gerson, 1976: 794). In this sense of quality of life (QoL), individual learners experience a better quality of classroom life when their individual learning needs are met, whether those are defined intrinsically or extrinsically (whether individual desires to understand or to communicate are met, or whether they are enabled to pass required examinations, perhaps). The other common approach to QoL described by Gerson is what is called the 'transcendental' conception, which defines individual QoL as 'the degree to which a person carries out his place in the larger social order' (1976: 795). The focus here is on the 'character of the larger order; to the extent that the larger community was properly constituted and maintained, then QoL was largely achieved'. Here the interests of the community-at-large take precedence, and individual loyalty and solidarity furthering the stability of the community is stressed. Personal achievements obtained alongside the interests of the community are largely irrelevant. In the classroom, this might be manifest as orderly classroom management and routines, specified learning objectives held in common (as defined by an external syllabus, perhaps), an overall class success rate in general examinations and the complete dedication of time to these common objectives. A 'good' classroom in this conception would be one which has smoothly running routines, completes the external syllabus or textbook and does not suffer from 'interruptions' in the sense of individual learning needs being given more than occasional precedence over the group syllabus. We might wish to correlate these two approaches to quality of life with learner-centred and teacher-fronted or 'lock-step' classrooms, and note that they are two routes to the same end. The problem with the individualist approach, says Gerson, is that of order. How indeed is every learner in a classroom to pursue their individual agenda in competition with their peers? In practice, individuals rarely pursue their own interests to the detriment of social order in the classroom; when that does happen it is considered a 'failed' classroom. The problem with transcendentalist conceptions of QoL, on the other hand, is to distinguish between individual actions which contribute to the larger social order and those which do not. Gerson concludes that neither individualist nor transcendental conceptions of QoL can adequately define individual quality of life nor specify a form of social organization which will ensure the highest quality of life for the community as whole or for individuals (1976: 796). His solution is to avoid dichotomizing 'individual' and 'society' and focus attention on patterns of negotiations among people which result in patterns of commitment made by individuals between settings, and by settings to individuals. According to Gerson, these patterns of commitment can be measured as the joint allocation of *money, time, skill* and *sentiment*. Thus a *good* QoL is marked by the compatibility of individual commitments of resources with those flowing in the system. This compatibility is achieved by joint participation in negotiation around the organization of commitments.

The quality of classroom interaction

Of the factors that may influence the QoCRL, we shall focus on those which are under the most direct control of participants. We shall leave aside, for the purpose of this chapter, curriculum variables such as time-tabling, examination requirements, external syllabi and externally chosen materials. We shall also leave aside the physical environment – the size of classrooms, their construction and the equipment found in them, class size and composition, which are obviously also relevant (see Coleman, 2006, Chapter 6 in this volume) and the allocation of a particular teacher to a particular class. It is not that these variables are not relevant, but that they are normally so far out of the control of classroom participants as to be taken as givens. It is up to others to manage, hopefully in the knowledge of the effect they have on QoCRL – a knowledge that is best communicated to them by classroom participants themselves. What is important about these 'externals' so far as we are concerned is how classroom participants understand them, and how well they understand them – as constraints, as affordances (what they can offer that allows things to get done), or as sites of resistance – and, having understood that, to know how they feel about them and how they allow externals to affect what they themselves do. We shall concentrate then on *what happens between classroom participants* as the main site in which teachers and learners can work on understanding QoCRL. Understanding is prioritized; whether or not that leads to changes in behaviour, attitude and belief, or not, will depend on participants' understandings.

Classrooms are shared social spaces and as such cannot function without communication between participants, but they are also institutional spaces, with a power dynamic which derives from the nature of the pedagogical relationship as well as the institutional setting. It is under these conditions that teachers 'manage' classrooms (Wright, 2006, Chapter 4 in this volume) and learners and teachers make their decisions about teaching and learning (Woods, 2006, Chapter 5 in this volume), which is about how they participate in the shared social space. The quality of interaction, in the senses of both nature and goodness (Tarone, 2006, Chapter 8; Barnard and Fanselow, 2006, Chapter 9 in this volume), is determined by and also determines how participants understand the QoCRL.

There are a range of approaches to discourse analysis, including exchange structure (Sinclair and Coulthard, 1975), conversation analysis (Seedhouse, 2004), pedagogic genres (Bernstein, 1996; Christie, 1993; Gieve, 1999), critical discourse analysis (Fairclough, 1995; Rogers, 2004) and Cazden's (1988) and Mercer's (1995) approaches to classroom discourse, aimed at describing classroom interaction. More recently, attention has been focused on multiple semiotics, expanding on the analysis of language use to include gesture, use of space, dress, eye contact and so on. While at least some of these models and techniques are often taught in university Masters programmes, and are thus potentially available to teachers, for the most part participants in language classrooms do not have access to this kind of objectified understanding. Instead, they *intuitively* know and feel the quality of what-goes-on, as insiders (see Breen's discussion of Atkinson and Claxton's distinction between intuitive, rational/analytic and reflective ways of teachers' knowing, 2006, Chapter 10 in this volume). The introduction of the idea of *felt* understanding leads us to the role of affect, which is central to the humanistic tradition in language teaching.

The humanistic tradition (Gattegno, 2002; Moskovitch, 1978, 1981; Rinvolucri, 1999; Stevick 1980, 1990) is devoted to engaging the 'whole person' in learning, by which is meant a combination of cognitive and affective aspects, and harnessing intuition, creativity, aesthetic sensibilities and other dimensions sometimes associated with the right side of the brain (Rinvolucri, 1999). It sometimes explicitly espouses personal development as a goal of language teaching (for example, Moskovitch, 1999), as it seeks to engage the learner as a person in the learning process rather than as solely a cognitive processor, on the grounds that 'the better students feel about themselves and others, the more likely they are to achieve' (Moskovitch, 1999: 178). Arnold and Brown (1999) include under *affect* the feelings, emotions, dispositions, preferences and attitudes conditioning behaviour. A concern for QoCRL must surely include these considerations as central. There is a tension in the humanistic literature, however, between paying attention to affect as an end in itself and using this attention as an aid to effective teaching and learning – that is, it becomes an instrumental, technicist approach to quality. Arnold (1999), for example, addresses the idea of *affect management* – approaches and procedures devoted to harnessing affect to the goal of learning. Similarly, while Arnold and Brown (1999: 4, emphases in the original) state that 'From the point of view of affective language learning, *being* is just as important as doing; a good language teacher *knows* and *does* but most essentially *is*', this is not as radical as it might seem. Teachers' 'being' is immediately reduced to a concern with 'their own emotional intelligence' (though also later their 'personal qualities, vision and sense of mission'), and this allows their teacherly knowledge and skills to be 'much more effective' (1999: 4).[1] It may be helpful here to refer to Heidegger's distinction between the ways of Being associated with *zuhanden* (the 'ready-at-hand') and *vorhanden* (the 'present-at-hand), as discussed by Donnelly (1999). By introducing Being into their consideration of teaching, Arnold and Brown are perhaps trying to promote the significance of what Donnelly casts as 'concernful being-with children' (or here, learners), but the rest of their edited volume reflects an instrumental attitude, one which Donnelly characterizes as resulting from a deficiency of a form of Being that is having-to-do with the world concernfully. Locating the theoretical justification of humanistic activities in effectiveness of learning in either a cognitive (second language acquisition) sense or a personal transformation sense misses the essence of dwelling in the present that the notion of Being concerns.

A model of language that illuminates the relationship between linguistic interaction and life rather than pedagogical work, and allows a link between *classroom work, classroom life* and *the lives* of classroom participants, can be found in the work of Bakhtin. 'After all,' as Bakhtin (1986: 63) puts it, 'language enters life through concrete utterances (which manifest language) and life enters language through concrete utterances as well'. As we have anticipated earlier, we suggest that QoCRL emerges in moment-by-moment situations as each classroom participant responds, in a Bakhtinian sense, to the *other* in the every-dayness of the learning community. In classrooms, as in other communicative situations,

> when the listener perceives and understands the meaning (the language meaning) of speech, he [*sic*] simultaneously takes an active, responsive attitude toward it. He either agrees, or disagrees with it (completely or partially), augments it, applies it, prepares it for execution, and so on. And the listener adopts this responsive attitude for the entire duration of the process of listening and understanding, from the very beginning – sometimes literally from the speaker's first word. (Bakhtin, 1986: 69)

We speculate that, even in highly asymmetrical pedagogic situations oriented by a knowledge-transmission model or by expectations of learners' 'echoic' performance (Stevick, [1976] 1996: 194), the teacher-as-speaker

> does not expect passive understanding that, so to speak, only duplicates his own idea in someone else's mind. Rather, he expects response, agreement, sympathy, objection, execution and so forth (various speech genres presuppose various integral orientations and speech plans on the part of the speakers or writers). (Bakhtin, 1986: 69)

The three fundamental notions of *specific authorial intent, the speaker's speech plan or speech will,* and *the choice of a particular speech genre* that are in Bakhtin's view inseparably linked in the organic whole of the utterance, captures what, to us, seems to be the individual's process of sensing the QoCRL:

> In each utterance – from the single-word, everyday rejoinder to large complex works of science or literature – we embrace, understand, and sense the speaker's *speech plan* or *speech will*, which determines the entire utterance, its length and boundaries. We imagine to ourselves what the speaker *wishes* to say. And we also use this speech

plan, this speech will (as we understand it), to measure the finalization of the utterance. This plan determines both the choice of the subject itself (under certain conditions of speech communication, in necessary connection with preceding utterances), as well as its boundaries and its semantic exhaustiveness. It also determines, of course, the choice of a generic form in which the utterance will be constructed. (Bakhtin, 1986: 76–7, emphases in the original)

Bakhtin's description of how we process utterances appears to make explicit some of the subtle 'tools' that, within classroom walls (and also when we are away from them) allow us to understand and remember 'the people' (cf. Wenger, 1998: 47) in our classrooms – their salient psychological traits, our interpersonal and interactional relationships with them, and the social construction of what counts as 'classroom knowledge' (Manke, 2001: 26). Classroom interaction does not just consist of words being spoken in a cognitive process of meaning exchange; it is particular people expressing meaning (*milking* language to get meaning out of it) together with other people, who are anticipating their words. Two interrelated constitutive aspects of utterances are their *expressive intonation* (Bakhtin, 1986: 84) and their *addressivity* (Bakhtin, 1986: 95). The former is 'the speaker's subjective emotional evaluation of the referentially semantic content of his utterance' and is probably the most intimately connected to our 'quality' memories of the people in our school lives, because along with bodily characteristics and movements and particular favoured expressions they mark a person as an individual. Expressive intonation also carries a good deal of the weight of affect. With regard to addressivity, Bakhtin says:

the role of the others for whom the utterance is constructed is extremely great ... An essential (constitutive) marker of the utterance is its quality of being directed to someone ... Both the composition and, particularly, the style of the utterance depend on those to whom the utterance is addressed, how the speaker (or writer) senses and imagines his addressees, and the force of the effect on the utterance. (Bakhtin, 1986: 94–5)

An important characteristic of classrooms is that they have continuity over days, weeks, months and sometime even years of fairly consistent membership and, perhaps especially in language classrooms, that continuity is constituted in linguistic interaction. Over this time members come to know each other as people, knowing what can and cannot be said; they build up a shared repertoire of routines (both micro-routines and more extended speech genres) such that they predict the shape, length and purpose of interactional units; they build up a history of shared speech such that a continuity of connection between utterances may be maintained over extended periods of time; *intertextuality* (reference to, and the echoing or and repetition of words and wordings previously expressed in a shared history of chains of utterances) becomes a shared resource within the class (think of every time that teachers and learners say things like 'you remember when we were doing X?', or 'we were talking about Y last week'), though much intertextuality is not made explicit, and may not be conscious either. Bakhtin refers also to degrees of personal proximity of the addressee to the speaker, affecting 'confidence in the addressee, in his sympathy, in the sensitivity and goodwill of his responsive understanding' (Bakhtin, 1986: 97), which he associates with intimate speech. The use of this shared history of relationship and communication as a resource within a learning community contributes centrally to its perceived QoCRL. It can lead to a sense of bafflement by outsiders and newcomers when they drop into classes and find themselves cut out of this private shared knowledge, taken-for-granted assumptions, presuppositions and relationships, and are confronted with a 'smoothness' (Ikeda, 2004) that cannot be understood simply from listening in.

However, having said this, we must remember that each participant's memory, and interpretation, of the history of interaction, and their projection of this historical memory into the present, will be individual and different. Activity Theory (see, for example, Lantolf and Pavlenko, 2001) teaches us this, and reminds us that acts of negotiation (Breen and Littlejohn, 2000; Woods, 2006, Chapter 5 in this volume) or conflict – overt or underground (Canagarajah, 1993, 1999) – are part of classroom life, and that increasing the opportunities for overt, productive negotiation is to release possibilities for addressing QoCRL.

These concepts provide a framework for a discursive analysis of what a classroom feels like to live in: how care, affect and relationship grow alongside work on knowledge-construction. Awareness of the role of expressive intonation, intertextuality, addressivity and speech genres used in classroom communication may be a crucial element for teachers and learners to sense more or less 'betterness' in classroom life. In fact, much of the frustration or satisfaction experienced in foreign language classrooms may result from classroom participants' perceived incapability or capability of acting responsively to others' utterances.

Quality as process: practitioners addressing and creating 'betterness'

In this section we engage in 'global' thinking which, according to Allwright (2003: 123), allows us to 'extract from particular "local" experiences whatever might be of more global relevance and value'. Miller (2003b) has come to understand, based on her long-term involvement with practitioner-based research within the paradigm of Exploratory Practice in various educational settings (Allwright et al., 1994; Miller, 2001; Miller and Bannell, 1998; Miller and Cunha, 1997), that even when practitioners start from work-oriented puzzles, they soon allow the life-orientedness of their classroom issues to emerge.

Contributions of worldwide professional reflection (cf. the Exploratory Practice Centre website address in the References, p. 43) also illustrate that future or in-service teachers, public or private teachers, school or language institute teachers, older or younger professionals, teachers in degree or non-degree awarding contexts, coordinators or teacher–consultants, tend to ask themselves questions of professional identity. They wish to make sense of how they position themselves and others and how they are positioned by others as professionals – the others being society at large, the particular institution or institutions where they work, their peers and, last but not least, their students.

Taking 'work to be a part of life, or an attitude to it, not an alternative' (Allwright, 2003: 120), we find that issues related to the quality of classroom life tend to emerge both as motivating concerns as well as illuminating results in practitioner-based research. We support this proposition by bringing together some evidence of practitioner research – drawn from the context of teacher and learner development work carried out within the Exploratory Practice framework (Language Teaching Research, 2003) as well as from a small sample of non-Exploratory Practice teacher-based research conducted in the context of Post-Graduate studies in Language and Education at PUC-Rio, Brazil.

Practitioners working to understand QoCRL within Exploratory Practice

Exploratory Practice has been developed since the 1990s by Allwright and an expanding group of collaborators in Brazil and in other countries (Allwright, 2003, 2004b) as a professionally viable practitioner research paradigm. It is conceived 'as a way of getting teaching and learning done, not as a way of getting research done' (Allwright, 2006, Chapter 1 in this volume). Within this view, practitioners – teachers *and* learners – are seen as people trying to reach their locally helpful understandings by focusing on their perceived quality of *life* in the classroom, rather than by focusing directly on trying to achieve a high quality of *work*.

In our view, the value of Exploratory Practice (Allwright, 2003, 2004b) lies in recognising the key importance of engaging teachers and learners in discursive practices that enable them to explicitly address their intrinsic understandings of the 'quality of their classroom lives'. Since this exploratory work is integrated into pedagogic practice in a collegial way, it generates mutual and sustainable development among those involved. In this section, we review some published and on-going practitioner research work developed within Exploratory Practice. (More on the development of the Exploratory Practice paradigm can be found on the Exploratory Practice Centre website.)

Drawing on their initial experience as EP teachers and on their current involvement as multipliers of the Exploratory Practice Group in Rio, Lyra, Fish and Braga (2003) carried out their first investigation on EP in order to answer 'What puzzles teachers in Rio, and what keeps them going?' They present an interesting overview of their colleagues' concerns after working on a corpus of eighty-eight teacher puzzles documented by EP session organizers over six years of Exploratory Practice work. Through a careful process of grounded categorization, Lyra, Fish Braga and Braga (2003: 146) arrive at six categories of puzzle content, in the following order of mention: Motivation (31 per cent), Anxiety (27 per cent), Teaching (17 per cent), Institutional Lack of Interest (14 per cent), Discipline (7 per cent) and Exploratory Practice (4 per cent). The resulting proportion of recurrent puzzles surprised the authors. They were expecting a heavier focus on work-oriented concerns but discovered that teachers actually placed their work-related issues in broader life-related terms (2003: 144). These emergent categories appear to reveal at least two aspects worthwhile of mention. First, that the EP orientation towards 'puzzlement' rather than towards 'problem-solving' may have allowed teachers to go beyond 'technical' teaching aspects and plunge into more elusive issues of their classroom lives that they wish to understand. Secondly, that despite the difficulties involved in such categorization processes, the quantitative analysis brings out 'dramatically the fact that more than half (58%) of all the puzzles [we] analysed were concerned with motivation and anxiety' (2003: 150).

These results, allied to what the same informant teachers expressed to explain their sustained involvement in the EP process, show these teachers' strong interest in and awareness of the complexities of the

QoL both inside and outside the classroom. What appears to help keep participants going is *social involvement*, coming together with others who share similar problems and the resulting collegiality. According to the interpretation that Lyra, Fish Braga and Braga (2003: 153) gave to the teachers' own perceptions, the sustainability of teacher development processes also seems to be related to life issues such as the 'sense of belonging to a group' and to the realization that EP can become 'a comfortable routine in their [the teachers'] lives'.

Another example of practitioners' desire to probe into what goes on in their classrooms is offered by Kuschnir and Machado (2003) who, as practitioner researchers, share their own gradual movement from work-oriented puzzles to life-oriented understandings. Machado (Kuschnir and Machado, 2003: 164) explains how, during her MA research, her contact with EP helped her 'go from problem-solving to multiple understandings'. Initially concerned with her students' excessive use of the dictionary, she came to realize through her investigation that her beliefs did not have so much importance anymore. She says 'I am becoming more aware of students' beliefs and of the need to understand the negotiation of teacher–student beliefs' (2003: 167). Although the focus of Machado's questioning still remained on technical aspects of vocabulary teaching/learning, we find her critiquing her own beliefs and placing her puzzlement in the broader context of her 'life' as a professional inside and outside the classroom. She reveals her growing interest in understanding quality of classroom life – not only of classroom work – when she explains that 'the relationship between teacher and students becomes so important in EP that I realized that I had to try to improve my understanding of my context in class and of my activities'.

In Kuschnir's process we also notice that her initial puzzlement about 'why [her] students translate words even when they've already understood their meanings in English' (Kuschnir and Machado, 2003: 170) raised other more refined puzzles still related to students' insistence in translating but soon led her to a process of investigating such broader life-issues as 'embarrassment and competition among students' (2003: 171). Taking a reflexive stand towards their own practitioner puzzlement processes, Kuschnir also presents a preliminary proposal of *the puzzlement zone* (2003: 171–6) by relating it to Vygotsky's ([1930] 1984) zone of proximal development (ZPD). Based on the parallels that Kuschnir (Kuschnir and Machado, 2003: 176) and Lanziotti (2001) establish between EP and Vygotsky's ideas of *intrapersonal* and *interpersonal* relationships, Kuschnir and Machado jointly discuss how their own puzzlement affected their lives as teachers in the classroom, as colleagues in a Master's course and as human beings engaged in collaboratively understanding their own professional development processes.

Also within the framework of EP, we find Slimani-Rolls (2003), Gunn (2003) and Perpignan (2003) working systematically through their pedagogic practice to understand their puzzles about the delicacy and the intricacy of classroom life and of the pedagogic relationship. Slimani-Rolls (2003: 221–39) exploits pedagogic activities, such as eliciting learner perceptions and group discussions, as investigative tools to pursue her puzzles about groupwork and about the possibility of developing a culture of inquiry. By stimulating brainstorming during normal classroom time, Slimani identified issues of teacher and learner responsibilities during groupwork (2003: 227–8), of positive peer support and constructive attitude (2003: 229) and of interference of learners' life in classroom events (2003: 229–30) as factors that affect perceived quality of life during groupwork and, more generally, during daily life in the classroom.

Gunn (2003: 420–58) also shows her search for deeper understandings of her students' communicative competence via the use of teacher and learner reflective sessions focused on pre-recorded student-led interviews. This joint guided reflection not only revealed to the author as teacher–researcher and to her student-researchers 'the complexity of communicative misunderstandings' but also helped 'the students help themselves understand their own mistakes' (2003: 249). It is interesting to note that in this investigative process the focus of the observation fell on how 'the degree of communicative interaction, and the development of rapport, can be influenced by the moods, personalities and participation of everyone involved' (2003: 249). The group's deeper understandings of the important role played by factors such as confidence, comfort level, culture and shared background information heightened their awareness of the quality of the conversational rapport built in their interviews and of their own quality of life in their classrooms.

Perpignan (2003: 259–78), researching written feedback in an EFL Academic Writing context, offers an excellent illustration of a practitioner researcher who acknowledges that her research 'began as a quest for a theory that could inspire guidelines for teacher effectiveness' but 'became a quest for an understanding of the conditions under which effectiveness could best be achieved' (2003: 259). When she expresses this in EP terms, she also succinctly clarifies her understanding that 'these conditions represent life in the classroom' and that the quest illustrates the aim of teacher research which, in her case, meant 'to strive toward improving the quality of life that will enable more effective use of feedback dialogue as a crucial element in the writing process' (2003: 259). By epitomizing the integration of pedagogic and research goals through 'the "Z" Activity' (2003: 268) as well as through other efforts to understand written feedback dialogue through actual manifestations of life in the classroom, Perpignan's conclusion acknowledges what she calls 'the research value of dialogue' (2003: 273).

Since variability in student preferences and use of strategies seemed to depend highly on beliefs about learning, about the role of the teacher in learning, on personal learning style and on growing understandings of the role of feedback, among others, Perpignan (2003: 271) concludes that the most telling conclusion to be drawn from her data is that 'it is not the mutual understanding that has the greatest potential to promote learning, but rather the knowledge by both parties that efforts are being made toward such understanding'. Perpignan emphasizes the centrality of 'the intentions that inspire them [conveyed messages] and the means which promote them' (2003: 272). In doing so, she echoes Bakhtin's notion of addressivity and the notion of QoCRL which concerns us here. Perpignan coherently suggests the importance for writers of feedback to transmit saliency, tone, intention and empathy. Furthermore, she insists that the quality of the dialogue promoted relies not only on the language being mutually understood and on the channels being kept open in both directions but, most importantly, on the special respect for the individual in all his or her idiosyncrasy and for the emotions involved in the receiving and giving of feedback (2003: 272).

Other researchers carrying out practitioner research at postgraduate level in Brazilian academic contexts have found in the principles of EP the methodological orientation they had been searching for. By allying EP to a discourse-analytic perspective on a longitudinal study of teacher development processes (Miller and Moraes Bezerra, 2005; Moraes Bezerra, 2003) and to a psychoanalytic interpretation of classroom participant relations (Sette, 2006), these doctoral theses, among other recently concluded MA research work (Azevedo, 2005; Falcão, 2005), illustrate how practitioners in different settings *care for* the quality of the personal professional lives they spend together.

In her pioneering EP work with learners over the 1990s, Cunha (2004) shows that her Brazilian learners in primary and secondary schools can bring to language classrooms and to language learning clinic discussions a desire to express puzzles about their lives – both inside and outside the classroom. 'Who invented homework?', 'Why don't I know how to study English?', 'Why are there so many languages in the world?', 'Why do we need to learn English?', are but a few of the questions about language learning and study, language evolution, motivation and globalized world markets that Cunha's learners have posed and investigated through locally managed pedagogic practice. Working within EP paradigm, the classroom becomes the locus for teachers *and* learners to address their puzzles about interpersonal relationships, identity, meta-cognition and meta-communication, among many other issues of school life. This way we do not need to struggle to bring 'life' to the classroom but allow space for classroom participants to work to understand their own 'classroom lives' by using pedagogic activities such as texts, exercises, tests, games, narratives, diaries and debates, among many others, as investigative tools.

Teacher-based academic research oriented towards QoCRL

Among other teacher–researchers who have been investigating discourse in pedagogic contexts for their postgraduate research work, we find Junqueira (2003) and Siqueira (2003) unearthing interesting connections between classroom life and the teaching of Portuguese as a first language (L1) in Rio de Janeiro school contexts.

Working with the Bakhtinian notions of *voice, dialogism* and *polyphony*, Junqueira investigates the teaching of L1 grammar in Rio de Janeiro private and public schools. Her data revealed a much stronger connection than she had expected between student motivation for the study of grammar, methodological frameworks, classroom interactional aspects and significant learning. By confronting the participating voices of learners, teachers, school directors and parents, Junqueira's results reinforce the centrality of 'a teacher–student relationship in creating a climate favorable to learning' (2003: 194) and of 'conceptualizing grammar-teaching as a way of educating discursively competent human beings for life' (2003: 64). Based on her study, Junqueira makes a strong plea for researchers and teachers to rethink the teaching of Portuguese as L1 in schools in order to consider 'life and pedagogy conjointly' (2003: 194).

A similar concern with the quality of life in the L1 grammar classroom motivated Siqueira to illustrate the pedagogic confusion generated by unhelpful definitions used in structurally-oriented grammars. Siqueira's most original contribution for our purposes here, however, lies in the pedagogical implications she draws from her study. By suggesting that teachers and learners should reflect *together* on the deficiencies identified in the definitions available in pedagogic grammars, Siqueira reveals in a special way her teacher-based respect for teachers' and learners' intellects as well as their self-esteem. Her prioritization of these aspects of 'quality of classroom life' and their potential for teacher/learner empowerment and for the enhancement of learning opportunities is reminiscent of Palmer (1998), who proposes to engage students and teachers in a community of truth by putting *a third thing* – the subject – at the centre of the pedagogic circle. In doing so, Palmer (1998: 117) envisions a situation in which 'teacher and students have a power beyond themselves to contend with – the power of a subject that transcends our self-absorption and refuses to be reduced to our claims about it'.

The subtlety and complexity of co-constructed student–student and student–teacher relations also emerge in Spitalnik's (2004) micro-analytical study of a computer science university course. In her ethnographic investigation, which focused on interpersonally constructed humour and conflict, multiple participant interpretations of their classroom lives were centrally placed. This is how as non-participants we discover, among other things, the interactionally paradoxical ways in which humour and conflict can be locally co-constructed and interpreted by the specific members of the researched classroom culture. This doctoral investigation offers insightful empirical evidence to support our belief that quality of classroom life can best be perceived and understood by its agents. Furthermore, Spitalnik's positioning as a researcher also illustrates our view that one of the most productive roles for researchers may be that of creating opportunities for participants to reflectively express their interpersonal lived experience and, thus, collaborate in the process of broader understandings.

This sample of practitioner research, which attempts to understand attitudinal, emotional and personal professional issues, among others, suggests that teachers, learners and reflection facilitators puzzle about issues that unveil a stronger integration between life and work than appears to be 'globally' acknowledged in academic research or 'institutionally' expected and admitted by themselves, their peers, or their superiors. With respect to our concern with 'quality', such empirical evidence also echoes our position that practitioners in the educational contexts studied tend to be mostly oriented towards understanding issues of 'life' than towards issues of 'work'.

Conclusion

The discussion of QoCRL in this chapter has clear connections with the directions for Applied Linguistics proposed by Allwright (2006, Chapter 1 in this volume). Our conception of QoCRL emphasizes its subjective, relative nature and local specificity. It will be understood differently by educational actors in different settings, and what might be considered highly amenable in some contexts would not be valued by other classroom participants elsewhere. We recognize also the complexity of classroom life and that, while participants' interpretations of speakers' intentions are built on a shared history of interactions over the life of a class, because of the multiplicity of goals actors bring to it the life of a class cannot be simply read off its surface. We have argued against an instrumental, technicist understanding of QoCRL, and voiced our concern that thinking about the life of school and classrooms has been appropriated by concern for the quality of educational outcomes, which are to do only with 'work'. In schools and classrooms, life has become subordinated to teaching and learning, instead of learning being part of life; our lives do not end when we enter institutional contexts. We live our lives in classrooms as much as outside classrooms; we bring our identities with us to our lives within the classroom, and construct new local identities; we have collective, communal classroom lives (Breen, 1985) that are different from our 'life-world' lives, because they are institutionally framed (Wenger, 1998).

We have emphasized, too, the value of practitioners – teachers and learners – working for their own understandings through Exploratory Practice (EP). Teachers and learners are the people best placed to appreciate what constitutes the quality of their classroom lives; this is experiential knowledge, and not readily transferable from one class to the next, never mind across contexts. We propose that this appreciation is developed in the search for understanding: quality is felt as process not product, experience not outcome. In the act of addressing and working to understand their classroom puzzles as they go about their teaching and learning teachers and learners are (re)creating their own QoCRL; we propose that the quality of classroom life is discursively constructed within the classroom as classroom practice is enacted. In this process approach, quality derives from the act of participants working towards a deeper understanding of the nature of classroom as an institutionally recontextualized part of our lives. This applies to both parts of the meaning of quality as *nature* and *betterness*.

Recognition of Bakhtin's (1986: 84) view of 'the utterance as a link in the chain of speech communication' leads us to propose that classroom participants can have a dynamic and developmental sense of the quality of their classroom lives. It is particularly in relation to the historicity of classroom living that we would like to reinforce our belief that QoCRL can best be internally 'recognized' or established by insiders to the particular setting – that is, by the practitioners themselves. The QoL in classrooms may be poor if there is a lack of possibilities for person-to-person addressivity in the pedagogic relationship: we talk not to each other but to a generalized group perhaps, or we underestimate each others' or the learners' capabilities, or for other reasons. It is through our perceptions of the intention of the speaker that we sense, define and interpret the quality of each moment. Contrary to the position held by the humanistic school it follows that if the QoL is good, then we can 'suspend disbelief' about content, and about the peculiar inauthentic or unnatural nature of pedagogic discourse willingly, and submit to pedagogical constraints. When participants are engaged in a search for an understanding of it, the QoL in the classroom may be renegotiated and enhanced, because addressivity is perceived more clearly, sensed, verbalized and reconstructed.

Through teachers and learners searching together for understandings and articulating them to each other they are developing an enriched 'classroom awareness', by which the nature of the experience of classroom life becomes qualitatively enhanced. This has been born out by the experience of the Exploratory Practice Group in Rio de Janeiro (see the Exploratory Practice Centre website address in the References). Classroom awareness can be understood as an appreciation of how the fact of being in a classroom both constrains and provides opportunities for various kinds, including learning. It includes an appreciation of the constraints on classroom life imposed by external conditions and factors that are necessarily shared by all participants, as well as the opportunities or affordances (van Lier, 2000) provided by them. This means those constraints that apply to the teacher as well as to learners. Classroom awareness includes a shared appreciation of how the affordances can be utilized to address the constraints. It provides the ground for learners' awareness of themselves as individuals with their own learning styles, goals, attitudes, motivations, strategies and degrees of dependence or autonomy. A technologising approach that starts from expert formulations (such as we find in coursebook exhortations to learners to reflect on their learning processes, or Crabbe's (2003) insertion of quality of learning opportunities into curriculum statements) is as likely to flounder as it is to succeed when it arises out of teachers' and learners' own appreciations of what place these learning technologies have in their lives. We suggest that there is an empowerment effect in teachers and learners *doing it for themselves* which can both endure and transfer to other parts of their lives.

Note

1. Ehrman and Dörnyei's (1998) discussion of interpersonal dynamics in the language classroom has an even stronger technicist orientation; while drawing attention to the importance of relationship in groups this is solely its relevance as a form of learning technology to improve learning (work, not life).

References

Allwright, D. 2002. Putting quality of life first: principles of and for Exploratory Practice. Unpublished manuscript drafted for the EPCentre, Lancaster University, 24 January.

Allwright, D. 2003. Exploratory Practice: rethinking practitioner research in language teaching. *Language Teaching Research 7*, 2:113–41.

Allwright, D. 2004a. Innovation: going beyond 'success'. Paper presented at the RELC Seminar, Singapore, April.

Allwright, D. 2004b. Developing principles for practitioner research: the case of Exploratory Practice. Paper presented at the AAAL Colloquium, Portland, Oregon, USA, May.

Allwright, D. 2006. Six promising directions in Applied Linguistics. In: *Understanding the language classroom*, eds S. Gieve and I.K. Miller. London: Palgrave Macmillan, Chapter 1 in this volume.

Allwright, D. and K.M. Bailey 1991. *Focus on the language classroom: an introduction for language teachers*. Cambridge: Cambridge University Press.

Allwright, D., R. Lenzuen, T. Mazzillo and I.K. Miller 1994. Integrating research and pedagogy: lessons from experience in Brazil. CRILE Working Paper 18. Lancaster University, UK.

Arnold, J., ed. 1999. *Affect in language learning*. Cambridge: Cambridge University Press.

Arnold, J. and H.D. Brown 1999. Introduction: a map of the terrain. In: *Affect in language learning*, ed. J. Arnold, 1–24. Cambridge: Cambridge University Press.

Azevedo, D.M. 2005. 'Você vai ser nossa professora no ano que vem?' Trabalhando para entender a sensação de prazer e sucesso vivenciada por alunos de língua inglesa e sua professora. Unpublished MA disscitation, Pontifical Catholic University of Rio de Janeiro (PUC-Rio), Brazil.

Bakhtin, M.M. 1986. *Speech genres and other late essays*. Trans. V.W. McGee, eds C. Emerson and M. Holquist. Austin: University of Texas Press.

Ball, S.G. and I. Goodson 1989. *Teachers' lives and careers*. Lewes: Falmer Press.

Benson, P. and D. Nunan 2004. *Learners' stories: difference and diversity in language learning*. Cambridge: Cambridge University Press.

Bernstein, B. 1996. *Pedagogy, symbolic control and identity*. London: Taylor & Francis.

Breen, M.P. 1985. *The social context for language learning: a neglected situation? Studies in Second Language Learning* 7:136–58.

Breen, M.P. 2006. Collegial development in ELT: the interface between global processes and local understandings. In: *Understanding the language classroom*, eds S. Gieve and I.K. Miller. London: Palgrave Macmillan, Chapter 10 in this volume.

Breen, M.P. and A. Littlejohn 2000. *Classroom decision-making: negotiation and process syllabuses in practice*. Cambridge: Cambridge University Press.

Canagarajah, A.S. 1993. Critical ethnography of a Sri Lankan classroom: ambiguities in student opposition to reproduction through ESOL. *TESOL Quarterly* 27, 4:601–26.

Canagarajah, A.S. 1999. *Resisting linguistic imperialism*. Oxford: Oxford University Press.

Cazden, C.B. 1988. *Classroom discourse: the language of teaching and learning*. Portsmouth, NH: Heinemann.

Celani, M.A.A. 2006. Language teacher educators in search of 'locally helpful understandings'. In: *Understanding the language classroom*, eds S. Gieve and I.K. Miller. London: Palgrave Macmillan, Chapter 11 in this volume.

Chang, C.-W. 2004. Teacher motivation: factors affecting English teachers' motivation and teaching enthusiasm in Taiwanese senior high schools. Unpublished MA dissertation, University of Leicester, United Kingdom.

Christie, F. 1993. Curriculum genres: planning for effective teaching. In: *The Powers of literacy: a genre approach to teaching writing*, eds B. Cope and M. Kalantzis, 154–178. London: The Falmer Press.

Coleman, H. 2006. Darwin and the large class. In: *Understanding the language classroom*, eds S. Gieve and I.K. Miller. London: Palgrave Macmillan, Chapter 6 in this volume.

Crabbe, D. 2003. The quality of language learning opportunities. *TESOL Quarterly* 37, 1:9–34.

Csikszentmihalyi, M. 1997. Intrinsic motivation and effective teaching: a flow analysis. In: *Teaching well and liking it: motivating faculty to teach effectively*, ed. J.L. Bess, 72–89. Baltimore, MD: Johns Hopkins University Press.

Cunha, M.I.A. 2004. Clínica de aprendizagem de Língua Inglesa. *Pesquisas em discurso pedagógico: práticas de letramento* 3, 1:101–6. Rio de Janeiro: Instituto de Pesquisa e Ensino de Línguas, Departamento de Letras, PUC-Rio, Brazil.

Donnelly, J.F. 1999. Schooling Heidegger: on being in teaching. *Teaching and Teacher Education* 15:933–49.

Dunham, J. and V. Varma 1998. *Stress in teachers: past, present and future*. London: Whurr Publishers.

Ehrman, M.E. and Z. Dörnyei 1998. *Interpersonal dynamics in second language education: the visible and invisible classroom*. London: Sage.

Epstein, J.L., ed. 1981. *The quality of school life*. Lexington, MA: Lexington Books.

Evans, L. 1998. *Teacher morale, job satisfaction and motivation*. London: Paul Chapman.

Exploratory Practice Centre. http://www.lehras.puc-rio.br/epcentre/epcentre. htm

Fairclough, N. 1995. *Critical discourse analysis*. Harlow: Longman.

Falcão, E.S. 2005. 'My teacher... He is a mirror for [sic] me.' A construção da identidade profissional de um aluno-professor. Unpublished MA dissertation, Pontifical Catholic University of Rio de Janeiro (PUC-Rio), Brazil.

Fanselow, J.F. and R. Barnard 2006. Take 1, Take 2, Take 3. A suggested three-stage approach to Exploratory Practice. In: *Understanding the language classroom*, eds S. Gieve and I.K. Miller. London: Palgrave Macmillan, Chapter 9 in this volume.

Gattegno, S. 2002. Teaching – a way of relating. *Humanising Language Teaching* 4, 4, http://www.hltmag.co.uk/jul02/mart1.htm

Gerson, E.M. 1976. On 'quality of life'. *American Sociological Review* 41:793–806.

Gieve, S. 1999. What makes thinking critical? What makes for critical thinking? Discourse analysis of episodes in teacher education. In: *Theory in language teacher education*, eds H. Trappes-Lomax and I. McGrath, 156–66. Harlow: Pearson Education.

Goffman, E. 1974. *Frame analysis: an essay on the organization of experience.* Harmondsworth: Penguin.

Goodson, I. 1991. Sponsoring the teacher's voice: teachers' lives and teacher development. *Cambridge Journal of Education* 21, 1:35–45.

Gunn, C. 2003. Exploring second language communicative competence. *Language Teaching Research Journal* 7, 2:240–58. London: Arnold.

Hargreaves, A. 1988. Teaching quality: a sociological approach. *Journal of Curriculum Studies* 20, 3:211–31.

Huberman, M. 1988. Teacher careers and school improvement. *Journal of Curriculum Studies* 20, 2:119–32.

Huberman, M. 1989. The professional life cycle of teachers. *Teachers College Record* 91, 1:31–57.

Huberman, M. 1993. Burnout in teacher careers. *European Education* 25, 3:47–69.

Ikeda, M. 2004. Towards an understanding of classroom ecology. Unpublished MA dissertation, University of Leicester, UK.

Junqueira, F.G.C. 2003. Confronto de vozes discursivas no contexto escolar: percepções sobre o ensino de gramática da língua portuguesa. Unpublished MA dissertation, Pontifical Catholic University of Rio de Janeiro (PUC-Rio), Brazil.

Karatzias, A., K.G. Power and V. Swanson 2001. 'Quality of school life: development and preliminary standardisation of an instrument based on performance indicators in Scottish secondary schools'. *School Effectiveness and School Improvement* 12, 3:265–84.

Kuschnir, A.N. and B.S. Machado 2003. Puzzling, and puzzling about puzzle development. *Language Teaching Research* 7, 2:163–80. London: Arnold.

Language Teaching Research 2003. 7, 2. London, Arnold, May.

Lantolf, J. and A. Pavlenko 2001. (S)econd (L)anguage (A)ctivity theory: understanding second language learners as people. In: *Learner contributions to language learning*, ed. M. Breen, 141–58. Harlow: Longman.

Lanziotti, M.G. 2001. Prática Exploratória e 'glimpses' do pensamento Vygotskiano: uma possível interface. Retrieved 18 April, 2005 from http://www.ling.lancs.ac.uk/groups/crile/epcentre/epcentre.htm

Lumsden, L. 1998. Teacher morale. *ERIC Document ED422601.*

Lyra, I., S. Fish Braga and W.G. Braga 2003. What puzzles teachers in Rio, and what keeps them going? *Language Teaching Research* 7, 2:143–62. London: Arnold.

Manke, M.P. 2001. Defining classroom knowledge: the part that children play. In: *Developing pedagogy: researching practice*, eds K. Collins and J.S. Kinsley, 26–38. London: Paul Chapman and The Open University.

Mercer, N. 1995. *The guided construction of knowledge: talk amongst teachers and learners.* Clevedon : Multilingual Matters.

Miller, I.K. 2001. Researching teacher-consultancy via Exploratory Practice: a reflexive and socio-interactional approach. Unpublished PhD thesis, Lancaster University, UK.

Miller, I.K. 2003a. Researching teacher-consultancy via Exploratory Practice, *Language Teaching Research* 7, 2:201–19. London: Arnold.

Miller, I.K. 2003b. Exploratory Practice: working to understand our everyday classroom lives. Plenary paper presented at the XIII Encontro da Associação de Professores de Inglês do Espírito Santo (APIES), Vitória, Espírito Santo, Brazil.

Miller, I.K. and R.I. Bannell 1998. Teacher education, understanding and Exploratory Practice. *IATEFL Teacher Trainers SIG Newsletter* 22:20–27, September, Canterbury, UK.

Miller, I.K. and M.I.A. Cunha 1997. Exploring our classrooms – and our teacher development sessions. In: *Perspectivas: o ensino da língua estrangeira*, ed. E. Taddei, 54–72. Prefeitura da Cidade do Rio de Janeiro, Brazil.

Miller, I.K. and I.C.R Moraes Bezerra 2005. Discurso da reflexão e da conscientização profissional: A contribuição da Prática Exploratória. In *Língua Portuguesa: reflexões sobre a descrição, pesquisa e ensino*, eds C.C. Henriques and D. Simões, 147–159. Rio de Janeiro, Brazil: Editora Europa.

Moos, R.H. and T.G. David 1981. Evaluating and changing classroom settings. In: *The quality of school life*, ed. J.L. Epstein, 59–80. Lexington, MA: Lexington Books.

Moraes Bezerra, I.C.R. 2003. Prática Exploratória: um caminho para o entendimento. *Pesquisas em Estudos Pedagógicos* 2, 2:58–72.

Moskovitch, G. 1978. *Caring and sharing in the foreign language class: a sourcebook on humanistic techniques.* Boston, MA: Heinle & Heinle.

Moskovitch, G. 1981. Effects of humanistic techniques on the attitude, cohesiveness, and self-concept of foreign language students. *Modern Language Journal* 65, 2:149–57.

Moskovitch, G. 1999. Enhancing personal development: humanistic activities at work. In: *Affect in language learning*, ed. J. Arnold, 177–93. Cambridge: Cambridge University Press.

Norton, B. 2001. Non-participation, imagined communities and the language classroom. In: *Learner contributions to language learning*, ed. M.P. Breen, 159–71. Harlow: Pearson Education.

OECD 1994. *Quality in teaching.* Paris: OECD Center for Educational Research and Innovation.

Palmer, P.J. 1998. *The courage to teach: exploring the inner landscape of a teacher's life.* San Francisco: Jossey-Bass.

Pennington, M. 1995. Work satisfaction, motivation and commitment in teaching English as a Second Language. *ERIC Document ED404850.*

Perpignan, H. 2003. Exploring the written feedback dialogue: a research, learning and teaching practice. *Language Teaching Research* 7, 2:259–78. London: Arnold.

Pirsig, R.M. [1974] 1989. *Zen and the art of motorcycle maintenance: an inquiry into values.* London: Bodley Head/Black Swan.

Poppleton, P. and G. Riseborough 1990. Teaching in the mid-1980s: the centrality of work in secondary teachers' lives. *British Educational Research Journal* 16, 2:105–24.

Ramsay, P. and D. Oliver 1995. Capacities and behaviour of quality classroom teachers. *School Effectiveness and School Improvement* 6, 4:332–66.

Rinvolucri, M. 1999. The humanistic exercise. In: *Affect in language learning*, ed., J. Arnold, 194–210. Cambridge: Cambridge University Press.

Rogers, R., ed. 2004. *An introduction to critical discourse analysis in education.* Mahwah, NJ: Lawrence Erlbaum.

Seedhouse, P. 2004. *The interactional architecture of the language classroom: a conversation analysis perspective.* Oxford: Blackwell.

Sette, M.L.D. 2006. Prática Exploratória e Psicanálise: para entender a relação pedagógica. PhD thesis, Pontifical Catholic University of Rio de Janeiro (PUC-Rio), Brazil.

Sinclair, J. and M. Coulthard 1975. *Towards an analysis of discourse.* Oxford: Oxford University Press.

Siqueira, C.L. 2003. A tradição gramatical e a ótica funcionalista: um estudo das definições de sujeito. Unpublished MA dissertation, Pontifical Catholic University of Rio de Janeiro (PUC-Rio), Brazil.

Slimani-Rolls, A. 2003. Exploring a world of paradoxes: an investigation of group work. *Language Teaching Research* 7, 2:221–39. London: Arnold.

Spitalnik, M.N. 2004. Conflitos em sala de aula: relações construídas entre professor e alunos em um curso universitário. Unpublished PhD thesis, Pontifical Catholic University of Rio de Janeiro (PUC-Rio), Brazil.

Stevick, E. [1976] 1996. *Memory, meaning and method.* Rowley, MA: Newbury House.

Stevick, E. 1980. *Teaching languages: a way and ways.* Rowley, MA: Newbury House.

Stevick, E. 1990. *Humanism in language teaching.* Oxford: Oxford University Press.

Tarone, E. 2006. Language lessons: a complex, local co-production of all participants. In: *Understanding the language classroom,* eds S. Gieve and I.K. Miller. London: Palgrave Macmillan, Chapter 8 in this volume.

Tuffs, R. 1995. Language teaching in the post-Fordist era. *System* 23, 4:491–502.

van Lier, L. 2000. From input to affordance: social-interactive learning from an ecological perspective. In: *Sociocultural theory and second language learning,* ed. J.P. Lantolf, 245–59. Oxford: Oxford University Press.

Vygotsky, L.S. [1930] 1984. *A formação social da mente.* São Paulo: Martin Fontes.

Wenger, E. 1998. *Communities of practice: learning, meaning and identity.* Cambridge: Cambridge University Press.

White, R. 1998. What is quality in English language teacher education? *ELT Journal* 52, 2:133–9.

Winch, C. 1996. Quality and education. Special issue of *Journal of the Philosophy of Education* 30, 1.

Woods, D. 2006. Who does what in the 'management of language learning'? Planning and the social construction of the 'motivation to notice'. In: *Understanding the language classroom,* eds S. Gieve and I.K. Miller. London: Palgrave Macmillan, Chapter 5 in this volume.

Wright, T. 2006. Managing classroom life. In: *Understanding the language classroom,* eds S. Gieve and I.K. Miller. London: Palgrave Macmillan, Chapter 4 in this volume.

3
What Happens between People: Who We Are and What We Do

Adrian Holliday

I am writing in a climate of change in TESOL which is perhaps unprecedented for the way in which ESOL educators are seeing themselves and others. The change is, of course, gradual; but it is given texture by events which mark our professional and personal lives. An example of this change is that each year my Masters students are more worldly and intelligently sensitive to this need. They indulge less in reducing Other cultures and in partisan views about particular classroom methodologies. All of this is underpinned by a general movement in the social sciences and educational research towards a postmodern view of knowledge. I do not wish to get into a discussion of postmodernism here. I will simply say that a postmodern sensibility helps me to understand that practices and technologies *are* embedded in ideologies – systems of ideas that influence beliefs, interests and actions of social groups. Usher and Edwards (1994: 10) describe this postmodern 'moment' as characteristic of:

> A world where people have to make their way without fixed referents and traditional anchoring points. It is a world of rapid change, of bewildering instability, where knowledge is constantly changing and meaning 'floats' without its traditional teleological fixing in foundational knowledge and the belief in inevitable human progress.

I do not see this realization as a slippery slope to intellectual anarchy, but rather as an imperative to reassess in ideological terms what we have always seen as right and efficient. Whether or not he himself subscribes to postmodernism, I find Fairclough's work (for example, 1995) in looking at how ideology is embedded in everyday discourses very helpful here, as well as the more critical elements of qualitative research. Examples of this type of investigation can be seen in my own work and that of my students and colleagues, where we look at the way in which the everyday discourses of our professionalism reveal our beliefs and prejudices about the people we teach and work with (Ainscough, 2001; Anderson, 2003; Baxter, 2003; Delikurt, 2006; Ge, 2004; Grimshaw, 2002; Holliday, 1997, 2001; Hyde, 2002; Kullman, 2004; Palfreyman 2001; Tong 2002).

The first move in this discussion is inspired by Allwright (1988:51), when he urged applied linguists to consider 'what really happens between teacher and class' in order to understand the wider contexts of language learning and teaching as a social as well as a psycholinguistic activity, bringing part of applied linguistics research within the domain normally inhabited by mainstream educational studies. My concerns, however, are slightly different to those of Allwright's and those other researchers who have investigated language learning as it is contextualized in the culture of the classroom. I am interested in what happens between people, both students and their teachers, and other involved professionals, within the broader context of the whole profession of TESOL, as conceptualized by ESOL educators.

Getting away from a native-speakerist narrative

I have therefore been involved over the years in looking at the classroom and TESOL as small cultures (for example Holliday, 1999, 2005a). Very recently I have arrived at the conclusion that the most important feature of this TESOL culture is a long-standing division between 'non-native speakers' and 'native speakers' which, following the work of Phillipson (1992), Pennycook (for example, 1994, 1998), Canagarajah (1999) and Kubota (1999, 2001, 2002), is irrevocably coloured by issues not only of imperialism, but also of how the 'native speaker' Self finds the 'culture' of the 'non-native speaker' Other problematic and in need of 'correction'. I use inverted commas liberally to indicate that terms which are found commonly in the everyday discourse of TESOL are 'so called' and ideologically problematic. A major location of where this correction takes place is 'the learning group ideal' which emphasizes learning though classroom talk in small class groups which are organized to allow oral interaction (Holliday, 1994:167–71). In Holliday (2005a) I trace native-speakerist thinking within the profession back to audiolingualism, which, not unlike Foucault's notion of corrective training (1991), saw the cultural behaviour of the 'non-native speaker' students as something which had to be corrected. The residues of this still remain in current practice within the culturally corrective discourses of learner training and learner autonomy, and the support and confinement of supposedly culturally infirm language learners within the strictures of PPP and 'the four skills' (see also Anderson, 2003 and Baxter, 2003). This native-speakerist narrative colours much of the dominant discourse of TESOL. I define *native-speakerism* as the chauvinistic belief that 'native speakers' represent a 'Western culture' from which spring the ideals both of the language and of language teaching methodology. Although TESOL native-speakerism originates in a specific set of educational cultures in the English speaking West (Phillipson, 1992), and is an easy position to adopt, particularly for those who conceptualize themselves as 'native speakers', it has had a massive influence and exists to a greater or lesser degree in the thinking of *all* ESOL educators.

This 'us' – 'them' division has been brought into sharp focus by the destruction of the World Trade Centre in New York on 11 September 2001, and the events that followed. Particularly significant in this connection was the opening speech at the 8th International TESOL Arabia Conference in Abu Dhabi, 2002, by His Excellency Sheikh Nahyan. At a conference which had a very large majority of expatriate delegates, many of whom were from the English-speaking West, he requested that they do their professional best and strive to ensure the ability of the young people in their charge to appreciate the richness of cultural diversity and to avoid the prejudice and divisions that had brought about the possibility of the 11 September disaster. How different ESOL educators see each other across cultural divisions is not just to do with the internal issues of TESOL, but parallels how people see each other across cultural divisions in world politics. Sheikh Nahyan was alluding to the fact that ESOL educators are particularly confronted by cultural divisions between the English-speaking West and the rest of the world, either with culturally Other students, colleagues or texts and curricular content. By addressing these differences, with the backdrop of English as a global influence, ESOL educators can indeed contribute seriously to the divisions which surrounded the 11 disaster September. I also noted that at the 2002 TESOL convention in Salt Lake City there was a significant group of papers that specifically addressed what ESOL educators could do about 11 September; and, for the first time at such a conference, I saw a marked opposition to the traditional culturist presentations about how to package cultural difference and deal with it as though it were a problem. I use the term 'culturism' to relate to any thought or act which reduces a person to something less than what she is according to an essentialist view of culture. It is similarly constructed to racism and sexism (Holliday, 1999; Holliday, Hyde and Kullman, 2004). Although culturism is widespread in late modern society, it is a major element of native-speakerism. It hides itself beneath the liberal thinking of what Kubota (2004) and others term 'liberal multiculturalism'. By appearing to 'celebrate' 'other cultures', 'we' in effect commodify, collect and reduce 'them'; and 'they' always appear less democratic, complex and modern, and more hierarchical, collectivist and exotic than 'us'.

With this new discourse against culturism, and a parallel discourse problematizing the native–non-native speaker divide (for example, Braine, 1999, and the work of the NNEST Caucus to 'create a nondiscriminatory professional environment for all TESOL members regardless of native language and place of birth', www.unh.edu/nnest/purpose.html), I feel therefore that there is hope for a mutually inclusive world community of *all* ESOL educators, despite its great diversity and its many worlds with many types of people in every type of educational institution. The forces of native-speakerism, however, remain strong, as I shall demonstrate below.

Allwright's work continues to help me to make sense of these issues. I shall therefore organize elements of this discussion around directions 1–4 in Allwright (2006, Chapter 1 in this volume): *From prescription to description to understanding; From simplicity to complexity; From commonality to idiosyncrasy;* and From *precision to scattergun.* Other elements of Allwright's chapter will emerge throughout my discussion. I shall draw piecemeal on email interview data from thirty-six informants – colleagues I have worked with, taught, or met at conferences – who represent all TESOL sectors across fourteen countries, and include twenty colleagues from outside the English-speaking West. These informants comprise a major source of evidence for the larger discussion of native-speakerism and cultural chauvinism in Holliday (2005a). In conclusion, I shall summarize their views on what can or cannot be done about native-speakerism in TESOL.

From prescription to description (direction 1)

In order to overcome culturist, native-speakerist prescriptions on how TESOL should be carried out it is important to understand how colleagues and students in diverse milieux across the span of World TESOL see themselves and get on with the business of educating and learning. The key to this is ethnographic description of what happens in classrooms, which can often speak against what we are led to believe and also what we *think we see* in front of our eyes in our own classrooms.

One example of ethnographic description is Tong's study of the classes of two teachers in Hong Kong secondary school's which reveals that the students are not the 'passive' people they at first appeared to be, and do not lack autonomy. He concludes that the students are sufficiently autonomous to motivate themselves to carry out a wide range of self-directed study activity. This involves both private study and classroom activity which includes answering and asking questions, interacting with the researcher and, overall 'confidence, creativity and feeling' and 'were not all the time conforming to the will of their seniors' (Tong, 2002: 254). He supports his study with detailed descriptions of classroom life. The following exemplifies their autonomy in the way they press their teacher for more information:

> Some students asked the teacher for the meanings of the words they had found in the dictionary. The teacher looked at the words in the dictionary. He then went back to the front and said: 'I'm not your walking dictionary. I don't want to explain this.' The student kept on asking the teacher: 'Sir, what's the meaning of these words?' The teacher kept saying: 'I don't know.' One student told another student: 'That's enough. I think the teacher in fact knows the meanings but he doesn't want to tell us.' (Tong, 2002: 179, citing lesson observation)

Significantly, this may not be the specific type of autonomy expected by the teacher and defined by the formally stated curriculum. It shows how the social autonomy the students bring with them may also exist away from, and on some occasions in opposition to, the agenda of the teacher. In another description the students are seen to form groups and pairs spontaneously. From his position as observer, Tong is able to see the detail of how they 'discussed the choices of the answers, the meanings of words' turn to consult other students and 'refer to their coursebook or exercise books' (Tong, 2002: 151, citing lesson observation). A major point he makes is that whereas they were expected by their teachers to conform to the 'filial piety' expected of Confucianism, this was in fact a cultural resource which they could choose, along with their teachers, to take up or not.

Hayagoshi, in her Masters study of why Japanese adult language students were quiet in the classroom in Britain when they were always noisy in her classes in Japan, presents the following description which hints at how it was somehow the strange régime of the British classroom that led them to behave, in a sense, culturally out of character:

The quietness of these seven Japanese definitely dominated the atmosphere of the classroom. There was nobody to throw a stone into this quietness.

> They were very slow to react and rarely express their opinions... The teacher went out for a while... I felt that the tense (hard) atmosphere... suddenly changed dramatically to a mild gentle one. Actually, I heard one Japanese student sigh with relief. However, this mood vanished when the teacher returned. They were quiet, tense and stressed, again. (Lesson observation)

> After the class, these quiet Japanese became *normal* students... friendly and, of course, quite talkative! (Hayagoshi, 1996, emphasis in the original)

My own study of video sequences of high-school classes in Japan confirms this image of talkative students and leads me to hypothesize that Japanese silence in British classes may be influenced by the way in which talk is controlled by the teacher. Whereas in the Japanese classes, talk is often allowed within the 'underlife' of the classroom, and which is controlled by the students, in British language classes there is a tendency, probably due to the native-speakerist desire to control, for talk not to be allowed at any time unless authorized in teacher-designed tasks – a régime which drives the students to silence (Holliday, 2003).

The notion of 'underlife' comes from Canagarajah (1999: 92), which he terms 'the vibrant' aspect of the lesson, often out of sight of the teacher, where students 'collaborate in providing social, emotional, and psychological sustenance' and 'solidarity'. A very poignant example of this is his description of Tamil students writing their own stories and identities into their American textbooks, changing characters and dialogues, in an attempt to authenticate them. In contrast, the immense control with which British teachers manage their lessons is recorded in Anderson's ethnography of a university language centre. He describes how:

> The teachers controlled the lesson structure, content, the way the tasks were taught, when each task was taught, the classroom interaction for each task, as well as the teaching materials used: the *what, how,* when and *with whom* of the teaching. This was clearly in evidence in the task setting part of the stages where the instructions explicitly stated the *what, how,* when and *with whom*... but it was also implicit to every other part of a stage. (Anderson, 2003: 46, emphasis in the original)

Description of this nature enables us to look beyond the common native-speakerist prescription that 'non-native speaker' students from 'Asian cultures' lack autonomy and that it is the 'learner-centredness' of English-speaking Western TESOL methodologies that can 'correct' this. I share Allwright's conviction (2006, Chapter 1 in this volume) that the more one investigates the 'more layers of complexity' are revealed. I also increasingly see that what prevents us from a deeper *understanding* of what we see is connected to the professional ideologies we bring with us. This is demonstrated in this statement from one of my informants. Lydia, a Ugandan academic, confirms that certain dominant views originate from the English-speaking West and exclude her colleagues and ESOL educators like them:

This historical legacy of how English 'should be taught' has plagued English language teaching the world over. The British government through the British Council has perpetuated the notion that the way English ought to be taught is a domain that they are experts in. It is true that this has done a lot to advance English language teaching but in the same breath this feeling of ownership has paid no attention to the knowledge held by TESOL educators in the colonies. The colonies have therefore only been exposed to practices that have been funded by the British Government and documented by British based scholars. Even if the periphery has had its own ideas on methods and practices in English language teaching the Centre would not fund the dissemination of such an idea in terms of publication and dissemination especially if it means that it takes away the legacy of control of 'what ought to be taught'. The feeling has been 'If you feel bright enough to come up with your own ideas that exclude me from the equation, then you better be ready to fund it as well', therein lies the powerlessness. (Email interview)

Despite the critical writing on the imperialism issue which has come from the English-speaking West (for example, Holliday, 1994; Pennycook, 1994, 1998; Phillipson, 1992), Lydia remains cynical when she adds that 'The Centre is not more critical of its practices in terms of the service that it needs to offer to English language learners, but more for the control that it seems to be losing with the changing of ownership of the language and the subsequent loss of authority over 'how things should be done' (email interview).

This lack of faith in the critical approaches from the English-speaking West is further evidenced in this angry response by Kuo, a Taiwanese teacher, to Jenkins' (2000) argument for what Jenkins presumes to be the anti-imperialist notion of an international English

> Although I did feel comfortable to be told that I did not have to be native-speaker like, I would definitely feel upset if I could not reach my own expectation in pronunciation...I just wanted to draw attention to the psychological part, the feeling, how people feel about themselves in terms of speaking...If we take Jenkins's view and tell them to stay where they are – you don't need to twist your tongue this way and that and it's perfectly all right to keep your accent – at some point, we would terribly upset the learners because they might want to...It's been clear that I'm a language learner from the periphery and – listen to this – I prefer to speak for myself! (Email interview)

Returning to the issue of 11 September, Esmat, an Egyptian academic, presents a description of how she sees its impact on the ownership of English, which is in direct opposition to the very new English-speaking Western prescription that this ownership is now being shared:

> I think that after [11 September] there is a resurgence of nationalism, particularly in the US and in the West in general and in the process, English speakers are reclaiming and reasserting their own, including their language. I think you have to revisit your assumption by perhaps recognizing that the process is going circular. We are in an anti-global trend where cultures are setting up '*boundaries*' and it is 'us' or 'them' the good and the bad, soldiers and robbers and of course terrorists and this must be reflected in many facets of life. (Email interview, emphasis in the original)

It is descriptions such as these, of what is going on and how people feel, which make even the new 'truths' presented by English-speaking Western academics and researchers, in Esmat's words, a prescriptive 'assumption' which seriously needs to be 'revisited'.

From simplicity to complexity; from commonality to idiosyncrasy (directions 2, 3)

There is hence no way that we can return to a simplistic view of the TESOL world in which classrooms which incorporate the 'learning group ideal' can train or teach 'non-native speaker' students to behave in certain ways. The real narrative is more complex than that perceived by native-speakerism and reveals that the views that come out of the English-speaking West, rather than having common application, are indeed ideologically idiosyncratic. Some of my thirty-six informants speak of a range of issues which are both negative and positive in their conceptualization. These can be summarized as follows, and indeed in some part reflect the formation of new discourses in opposition to native-speakerism:

- The struggle for teachers outside the English-speaking West to deal with the derogatory 'non-native speaker' label and to assert identity, professional status and employability
- The struggle for teachers from the English-speaking West themselves to fight their own prejudices, avoid reducing the foreign Other, to appreciate the meanings their students bring to the classroom and to deal with the changing, global ownership of English
- The struggle for language students and teachers to deal with the cultural dilemmas implicit in language learning.

My informants support their comments with varying degrees of detailed qualitative descriptions of professional life, as already seen with Lydia and Esmat above. This is not 'new knowledge' about 'how' students learn, but greater detail about how things already are, which brings deeper reflection and analysis which can help us rationalize how to behave. It suggests that what we need is deeper understanding of who we are and what we do to each other.

Esmat counters the 'simple' notion that English-speaking Western TESOL is always higher status by describing the 'complex' éliteness of Egyptian university English departments as 'the "keepers" of a language that can raise the social and economic standards of those who know it' (email interview). Lama counters the 'simple' view that English-speaking Western TESOL is always 'commonly' applicable by telling a story of marked independence from its influence in Syria. She explains that students often initially prefer to be 'taught English by its native speakers' and 'rush to the English or American cultural Centres' even though 'they often employ non-specialist native speakers to teach English'. However, many of them become disillusioned with foreign teachers and return to Syrian language institutes, which they find have higher standards. Although they encounter a globalized foreign culture through the learning of English, many of the students develop 'their own method of internalizing the language and devising it to suit their culture and traditions thus developing a new genre of English...and culture specific vocabulary' (email interview). The students thus, in one sense, grow to understand the cultural idiosyncrasies of the English-speaking Western mode of teaching while, in another sense, developing their own idiosyncratic style of language use.

Danai, a Greek language school owner, expresses strong opinions about how her Greek colleagues need to struggle to assert their professionalism and defend their jobs against the tide of 'native-speakers' with their twenty-hour Cambridge Certificates. She talks of the 'hypocrisy' of the 'British exporting teachers system' which claims such high professional standards (email interview).

Laila, another Egyptian academic, speaks forcefully on the way in which TESOL outside the English-speaking West can acquire its own idiosyncratic momentum in its own locations. She explains that she 'would not call the ideas and practices' from the English speaking West 'superior', but 'different':

> In my experience as a teacher and – I think – in many of my colleagues', there is a feeling that some of those practices do not suit the Egyptian context due to the difference in facilities and the structure of the education system...Lately, there has also been resistance to the use of computers and technology in general in the Egyptian classroom, not because it is 'superior', but because of our 'different' context that makes such use rather difficult and in many cases ineffective. (Email interview)

Mona, who has long insider experience of working in Pakistan, tells us the following:

> My experience of teaching English in Pakistan has been very different to what I see in other countries where the divide between native and non-native speakers is much wider. In Pakistan, a lot of emphasis is placed on learning English and all private and most government institutions have English as the medium of instruction. The medium of instruction in higher education is mainly English. Native speakers are valued but are not considered 'custodians' of English language instruction and the teaching approaches that they bring to Pakistan are welcomed but not followed blindly. Non-native speakers who are able to adapt such 'best practices' to the context in Pakistan are highly favoured. A recent example (from personal communication) is of a university in Pakistan that did not outsource

its language programme to a leading British language centre because past experience of the centre's programmes proved that its language enhancement programmes could not relate to the learners' context in Pakistan. Though these programmes were based on sound theory and latest methodology, they could not relate to the learners' needs and context. (Email interview)

Aliya, a British teacher with an Asian heritage, has a professional biography and views which demonstrate the complexity of the 'us' – 'them' issue:

I am expatriate when I teach in Pakistan because I have to live there on a visa and that's what qualifies one as an expatriate. After September 11 I was asked to leave Pakistan by the British High Commission just like other expatriates... I studied there and worked there but as a foreigner. Many would not classify me as a 'native speaker' of English, maybe because for one I lived in the UK for only seven years and then lived in a third neutral country (UAE, which is not my country of descent) for 16 years before studying and working in Pakistan for seven years. Second, I think its more than language; it's a little more racial – the colour of the skin that matters. My husband was born and raised in England and lived all his life there. He is monolingual (understands only English) but at work he is still treated like an Asian. (Email interview)

She continues to describe how she has been marginalized within the 'us' – 'them' distinction while working in the UAE:

I'm a certified examiner and applied at a university to examine for them. They did not rely on Cambridge University's judgment. I received an e-mail after a month asking me to send my CV to see if I was 'suitable to be hired' since I had a foreign name and may not be an appropriate candidate. I am still looking for a decent teaching job because I seem to have been trapped in the us–them issue. In the Middle East I'm 'them' although English is my first language. This makes me feel that it is more complex than a simple native versus non-native issue here at least. (Email interview)

These descriptions of the complexity of local conditions and preferences reveal the naïvety of the English-speaking Western view that its approaches could ever find common application, showing them to be as ethnocentrically idiosyncratic as any other.

From precision to scattergun (direction 4)

The examples presented so far in this chapter paint a complex and sometimes politicized picture of TESOL across the world. This makes the precision one sees in the native-speakerist notion of a 'learning group ideal' seem limited and naïve. The sort of precision one often sees, based on the calculation of what students from specific 'cultures' can or cannot do, is encapsulated in these notes from a teachers' meeting in Anderson's ethnography:

> PPP was directly promoted in the summer syllabus where teachers were encouraged to provide 'clear opportunities for practice and production' and where this 'method' was particularly suitable for 'Asian' students (Document 6.3). In a broader sense the teaching day could be conceptualized as the paradigm writ large with the Language Focus lessons equating with *presentation* and *practice*, while Skills Focus lessons and Options generally equating with *production*. (Anderson, 2003: 203, emphases in the original)

This approach inherits the notion of discipline from the staged structure of audiolingualism, as described at the beginning of this chapter; and is designed to limit and train rather than to expand and educate. It is of course culturist in its essentialist image of the stereotyped 'Asian' student.

A similar native-speakerist phenomenon is seen in this extract from Baxter's qualitative study of British teacher training. She explains how students are conceptualized:

> in discriminatory and culturist ways...as a constraint to the methodology, and positioned within the discourse in relation to 'problems'...I suggest that this discursive positioning is largely based on persistent perceptions about national groups and ethnicities...I have seen this come from both tutors and participants, suggesting that this cultural orientation within the profession towards the essentializing of learners may begin in the training process, or is, at least, reinforced there. The following examples illustrate my point:

>> The trainees were asked to suggest what kind of students would have problems with such a text. It was stated by the trainer that

the text would be problematic for Arabs as they 'wouldn't be tuned in to it', and maybe don't read much even in their own script. (Baxter 2003: 179–80, citing observation)

I feel there is a sharp contrast between this type of narrow thinking, which seeks to confine and limit, and the following summary of how to address the issue of native-speakerism which comes from my email informants. These eleven strategies represent an opening up and an expansion:

1. There needs to be as deliberate a move to undo native-speakerism as there has been from the English-speaking West to impose it.
2. Teachers must be valued for their professional ability and academic qualifications regardless of 'speaker' status and nationality – with equal opportunities exercised by employers. All teachers should be accredited equally in English for International Communication.
3. 'Non-native speakers' must continue to assert themselves to become more prominent.
4. The teaching ideology and methodology must be recognized as more important than the origin of the teacher, with increased understanding of the nature of the profession. This must be supported by concerted, decentralized research into situation-specific methodologies.
5. The image and discourse of the profession needs to be changed, learning from other movements in widening inclusion. Teachers should be labelled positively for who they are in terms of nationality, not in terms of what they are 'not'.
6. We should all recognize our positioning in Self and Other discourses, scrutinize attendant norms in everyday life and be aware of the nature of the 'native speaker' myth.
7. Reform can be carried out through the process of training. This should involve educating ESOL educators to value themselves and their skills in ways which are not aligned with native-speakerism, and to see all ESOL educators as their peers. We should not model 'best practice', which is ideologically embedded, but encourage spaces for reflection on and scrutiny of existing practice. There should be equal opportunity for all ESOL educators to be trainers and trainer-trainers.
8. The deep-rooted beliefs held by millions of people, within diverse audiences and mediated by uncontrollable political, economic and ideological factors, need to be countered with deeper, mutual understanding of Other cultures.

9. The image of English and its speakers as multicultural and multinational needs to be promoted in curricula by: making the issues part of the content, de-emphasizing cultural and country-specific aspects, broadening source material to include texts written by 'non-native speakers' and translations from other languages, presenting 'native' English cultures as ethnically diverse and, along with many others, teaching English for International Communication in schools in the English-speaking West.

10. We must heed existing movements against native-speakerism by being aware of: attendant ideologies and debates, the fact that 'non-native speaker' teachers are beginning to work in other countries and are valued at the classroom level in many milieux, the undisputed role of English as a world means of communication and the image of 'native speakers' as a race of undesirable imperialists after 11 September and the Iraq war.

11. We must recognize people's aesthetic preferences for types of English and types of speakers, and the possibility that they may prefer flavours from the English-speaking West over indigenous' flavours for a multiplicity of reasons.

Perhaps 'scattergun' is the wrong term to be used for this form of radical opening and recognition of diversity. As Allwright admits, it is too militaristic a term. What we need is to recognize *diverse action for diverse locations* and the huge diversity of ESOL educators and their students.

Messy realities

The tone of this chapter has been qualitative and subjective. It has not been neat in either its presentation or conclusions. Using Allwright's (2000) terms, it has avoided solving the 'problem' of how to do something, and instead tried to open up to a range of possibilities, observations and opinions from colleagues and students who are themselves struggling with the puzzles of their professional lives. The qualitative studies cited all try hard to look at the broad span of social life within professional contexts, and to stand outside professional discourses.

But standing outside one's own professional discourses may be difficult. This raises the question of who *I* am in this narrative. In my (2005a) book I employ a lot of personal narrative – deconstructing my own professional discourses in a long autobiography of TESOL life. I do this because it is difficult for someone like me, from the English-speaking

West, trying to shake off a native-speakerism which I have spent my career being socialized into. I make an explicit statement about not speaking *for* any of the informants who give me email data. It would be too presumptuous to imagine that I understand their points of view sufficiently to be able to do this. Instead, I see them as voices which inform my own professional struggle. I therefore speak only for myself (see also Holliday, 2005b). I say this here because I know that Allwright in his writing and thinking as a researcher is sensitive to the issues of the power held by English-speaking Western academics.

In fact I have very little power to speak outside my own professional discourse. This came home to me in a recent email discussion with Suresh Canagarajah about the way he wrote about *me* in his (2002) paper. There he challenged me for presenting the 'learning group ideal' as *the* communicative norm, whereas in fact I have always distanced myself from it, as inappropriate in most world contexts; and I have argued instead for broader, more universal communicative principles (Holliday, 1994). Suresh apologized for making the mistake, but, nevertheless made the point that despite my apparent rejection of the 'learning group ideal', what I had to say was '*still* influenced' (Canagarajah, 2005, personal communication) by this dominant native-speakerist pedagogy.

Moving away from simplicity, commonality and precision cannot help but take us into a messier world, where the very neatness of what we say becomes questionable. In trying to understand the complexity, idiosyncrasy and scattergun of the cultural nature of TESOL classrooms and the broader profession, we need therefore to heed Geertz's (1993: 17–18) warning:

> Coherence cannot be the major test of validity for a cultural description ... There is nothing so coherent as a paranoid's delusion or a swindler's story. The force of our interpretations cannot rest on the tightness with which they hold together, or the assurance with which they are argued. Nothing has done more, I think, to discredit cultural analysis than the impeccable depictions of formal order in whose actual existence nobody can quite believe.

References

Ainscough, V. 2001. Who decides how language learners learn? The importance of teachers' and students' expectations in the acceptance or rejection of ELT materials and methodologies. Unpublished PhD thesis, Canterbury Christ Church University College, UK.

Allwright, R.L. 1988. *Observation in the language classroom*. London: Longman.

Allwright, D. 2000. Exploratory practice: an 'appropriate methodology' for language teacher development? Unpublished paper presented at the 8th IALS Symposium for Language Teacher Educators, *Politics, Policy and Culture in Language Teacher Education*. Edinburgh, UK.

Allwright, D. 2006. Six promising directions in Applied Linguistics. In: *Understanding the language classroom*. eds S. Gieve and E.K. Miller. London: Palgrave Macmillan, Chapter 1 in this volume.

Anderson, C. 2003. The dominant discourse in British EFL: the methodological contradictions of a professional culture. Unpublished PhD thesis, Canterbury Christ Church University College, UK.

Baxter, A. 2003. The reproduction of professional culture through teacher education for ELT. Unpublished PhD thesis, Canterbury Christ Church University College, UK.

Braine, G. 1999. Non-native educators in English Language Teaching. Mahwah, NJ: Erlbaum.

Canagarajah, S. 1999. *Resisting linguistic imperialism*. Oxford: Oxford University Press.

Canagarajah, S. 2002. Globalization, method and practice in periphery classrooms. In *Globalization and language teaching*, eds D. Block and D. Cameron, 134–50. London: Routledge.

Delikurt, P. 2006. Revolution or evolution in educational change: the intended policy – actual policy — policy in use continuum revisited. A case study in the English language teaching and learning context of the Turkish Republic of Northern Cyprus. Unpublished PhD thesis, Canterbury Christ Church University College, UK.

Fairclough, N. 1995. *Critical discourse analysis: the critical study of language*. London: Addison-Wesley Longman.

Foucault, M. 1991. *Discipline and punish: the birth of the prison*. Trans. A. Sheridan. Harmondsworth: Penguin.

Ge, J. 2004. Discursive struggle and change – an investigation of the lived experiences of language teachers in a Chinese higher education institution. Unpublished PhD thesis, Canterbury Christ Church University College, UK.

Geertz, C. 1993. *The interpretation of cultures: selected essays*. London: Fontana.

Grimshaw, T.A. 2002. Discursive struggle: linguistic imperialism and resistance on Chinese university campuses. Unpublished PhD thesis, Canterbury Christ Church University College, UK.

Hayagoshi, H. 1996. British teachers' perceptions of Japanese students in contrast with Japanese students' perceptions of their own needs and wants. Unpublished MA dissertation, Canterbury Christ Church University College, UK.

Holliday, A.R. 1994. *Appropriate methodology and social context*. Cambridge: Cambridge University Press.

Holliday, A.R. 1997. The politics of participation in international English language education. *System* 25, 3:409–23.

Holliday, A.R. 1999. Small cultures. *Applied Linguistics* 20, 2:237–64.

Holliday, A.R. 2001. Achieving cultural continuity in curriculum innovation: dealing with dominant discourses. In: *Innovations in English Language Teaching*, eds D. Hall and A. Hewings, 169–76. London: Routledge.

Holliday, A.R. 2002. Teachers' and students' lessons. In: *Enriching ESOL pedagogy: readings and activities for engagement, reflection, and inquiry*, eds V. Zamel and R. Spack, 17–34. Mahwah, NJ: Erlbaum.

Holliday, A.R. 2003. Japanese fragments: an exploration in cultural perception and duality. *Asia Pacific Journal of Language in Education* 5, 1:1–28.

Holliday, A.R. 2005a. *The struggle to teach English as an international language.* Oxford: Oxford University Press.

Holliday, A.R. 2005b. How is it possible to write? *Journal of Language, Identity, and Education* 4, 4:304–9.

Holliday, A.R., M. Hyde and J.P. Kullman 2004. *Intercultural communication.* London: Routledge.

Hyde, M. 2002. The mobilization of culture in professional discourse within the international ELT profession. Unpublished PhD thesis, Canterbury Christ Church University College, UK.

Jenkins, J. 2000. *The phonology of English as an international language: new models, new norms, new goals.* Oxford: Oxford University Press.

Kubota, R. 1999. Japanese culture constructed by discourses: implications for applied linguistics research and ELT. *TESOL Quarterly* 33, 1:9–35.

Kubota, R. 2001. Discursive construction of the images of US classrooms. *TESOL Quarterly* 35, 1:9–37.

Kubota, R. 2002. (Un)ravelling racism in a nice field like TESOL. *TESOL Quarterly* 36,1:84–92.

Kubota, R. 2004. Critical multiculturalism and second language education. In: *Critical pedagogies and language learning,* eds B. Norton and K. Toohey, 30–52. Cambridge: Cambridge University Press.

Kullman, J.P. 2004. Cultural identity and cultural values in the UK-published ELT coursebook. Unpublished PhD thesis, Canterbury Christ Church University College, UK.

Palfreyman, D. 2001. The socio-cultural construction of learner independence in a tertiary EFL institution. Unpublished PhD thesis, Canterbury Christ Church University College, UK.

Pennycook, A. 1994. *The cultural politics of English as an international language.* London: Longman.

Pennycook, A. 1998. *English and the discourses of colonialism.* London: Routledge.

Phillipson, R. 1992. *Linguistic Imperialism.* Oxford: Oxford University Press.

Tong, W.M. 2002. 'Filial piety': a barrier or a resource? A qualitative case study of English classroom culture in Hong Kong secondary schools. Unpublished PhD thesis, Canterbury Christ Church University College, UK.

Usher, R. and R. Edwards 1994. *Postmodernism and education: different voices, different worlds.* London: Routledge.

4

Managing Classroom Life*

Tony Wright

Classroom life is what teachers and learners make it. At the same time, classroom life is what they make *of* it, and what it makes them. These apparently simple observations capture both the inherent contradictions of classroom life and its complex, systemic nature. As a teacher and teacher–educator living and working with such contradictions, I am concerned with enabling as high a quality of educational experience for my learners as I can in and around both my own and others' classrooms. However, I know that this is not easily attained; my work is a constant process of adjustment, and any feeling of completion or satisfaction rarely lasts for long. Today's good educational experience can be tomorrow's minor disaster. Our actions as teachers can have unintended negative consequences which can cancel out any transitory pedagogic satisfaction we may feel or threaten the sense of security which we and our learners often crave. Uncertainty and even disappointment are facts of life in classrooms. Not everyone sees this in a positive light, though, and one person's positive experience may be another's nightmare. Classroom life is thus no more or no less problematical than life itself.

This chapter is an attempt to make some sense of the complexity of classroom life in order to guide my own and other teachers' efforts at enhancing the quality of classroom experience (see Allwright, 2006, Chapter 1 in this volume). I intend to examine the neglected, but potentially rich construct of *classroom management* as a way of trying to understand complexity, and enhance the chances of achieving valuable learning experiences. I shall propose an alternative to the prevailing view of classroom management, one which characterizes what teachers and learners do in classrooms as a combination of ways in which they directly attempt to initiate and regulate events and processes, how they interpret what happens as classroom life unfolds and how events and processes themselves can shape the ways in which participants think, feel and act. This perspective I term *managing classroom life*; it includes the coping sense of *managing* in addition to the initiating and responding senses. I believe that this expanded sense of 'managing' comes closer to the daily experiences of teachers and learners and the realities of classrooms than a view of classroom management based on organisation and control of learning groups (for example, Ur, 1996). It is also in tune with contemporary views of pedagogy which characterize it as more than the implementation of methods, or 'methodology' (Brumfit, 2001; Kumaravadivelu, 2001). Briggs and Moore, outlining a systemic view of classroom life, capture this view as follows:

> At the classroom level, we have interaction between the presage factors, *students*, and their characteristics, individually and collectively, and *teaching context*, comprising the teacher and the school-determined constraints (curriculum, rules of interaction between teachers and students, and so on) which together focus on the central *process* issue of how students go about learning and what the *product* or outcome of learning is. (1993: 450, emphases mine)

The first part of the chapter argues for a revised view of classroom management. It draws on our knowledge of classrooms as complex contexts in order to explore the current, restricted view of classroom management which is centred on control. This will be contrasted with a *complexity* view of classroom management which includes control, and which views the social and pedagogic strands of classroom life as intertwined rather than separate. The second part of the chapter explores the implications of the revised conceptualization of classroom management for classroom research. It advocates a view of research which reflects participants' experience of classrooms and which contributes towards an improved quality of classroom life. The final part of the chapter examines the implications of managing classroom life for language teacher education. Language teacher education may, as a consequence, become more inquiry-oriented as well as striving to provide a context in which teachers acquire and develop skills and knowledge as language teachers.

Classroom complexity

Classrooms are both simple and complex contexts. They are simple when we assume, quite reasonably, that they are places where teaching and learning happen. After all, that is the primary reason for their existence;

they are at the very heart of the educational process, the *business end*, where education is *done*. The reality is very different, as any person directly involved in classroom life will attest. Few would argue that classrooms are anything but complex and problematical. As Larsen-Freeman (1991: 269) puts it, (language) teachers are 'confronted with the complexity of language, learning and language learners every day of their working lives', a complexity 'they must grapple with on a daily basis'. Presumably these complexities are also experienced by learners who also deal with the additional complications of having to form effective relationships with their teachers in order to learn. There appears to be consensus that classrooms are complex along three main lines.

Pedagogic and institutional

The work of Doyle (1986: 394–5) has identified specific 'properties' of classrooms which are to be treated as 'givens' 'already in place when teachers and students arrive at the classroom door'. These are:

- *Multidimensionality* – the quantity and variety of tasks in the classroom
- *Simultaneity* – many things happen at once in classrooms
- *Immediacy* – the rapid pace of events in the classroom
- *Unpredictability* – classroom events often go in unforeseen directions
- *Publicness* – classrooms are places where everyone is potentially a witness of others' actions
- *History* – classes have a temporal history of activity together.

These characteristics will doubtless resonate with teachers and learners, and are readily observable and relatively easily confirmed. They are a useful starting point in attempting to understand classrooms in that they provide the basis for observation, but they tell us little about the deeper social and psychological realities of people gathering in a classroom to engage in learning.

Sociocultural and psychological

In contrast with Doyle's descriptive categories, drawn from the observation and experience of classroom life, Breen (2001a) sees the classroom as a 'culture' with the following characteristics:

- *Interactive* – all participants interact verbally and non-verbally
- *Differentiated* – classroom events are interpreted differently by different participants at different times

- *Collective* – a learning group has a collective psychological reality
- *Normative* – there is continual evaluation of participants as learners and often as people
- *Asymmetrical* – teachers and learners have different rights, duties, roles and identities
- *Inherently conservative* – classrooms tend to be resistant to change because of the need for security and regularity of life there
- *Jointly constructed* – content and process in classrooms are jointly constructed by teachers and learners
- *Immediately significant* – participants accord immediate significance to classroom events as part of ongoing activity.

Breen's main claim is that greater understanding of classroom life in social and psychological terms is possible using this set of descriptors, which work at a deeper level than those provided by Doyle (1986). The characteristics he identifies add depth to the notion that classrooms are complex. It is questionable to what extent teachers and learners would immediately recognize them, however, and this poses a problem for teacher education and research alike. As participants in a complex social and cultural world, it is unlikely that teachers and learners have articulated these features in any meaningful way, although they are likely in their different ways to be very aware of, for example, the power dimension in classrooms.

Different goals and pressures in classroom activity

Recent attention has been given to the idea that classrooms are unavoidably complex because goals are in potential conflict. Allwright (1996) has discussed the idea that classroom life inevitably brings about conflict between what he terms *pedagogic and social* goals. He notes that the pedagogic goal of providing *new* learning material can often conflict with the social goal of avoiding embarrassment to both teachers and learners. However, he also notes that in many cases, pedagogy includes other social considerations.

> [P]art of the teacher's job, in many if by no means all situations, is perhaps that of helping the classroom group to learn to act in a socially responsible way, both inside the classroom and outside it. If we accept this, then we can properly say that at least some of the social pressures of classroom life are fundamentally pedagogic in nature, since they arise directly from part of what it is intended that the learners should learn. Allwright (1996: 211)

Prabhu (1992) also notes the potential dualism of pedagogic and social goals in the classroom. He reminds us that the social dimensions of classroom life, such as a sense of security and protection of self-image, are central concerns for both teachers and students. These, he points out, are likely to be prioritized in the event of any conflict between pedagogic and social goals (Gieve and Miller, 2006, Chapter 2 in this volume; Prabhu, 1992: 233). Prabhu (1995) identifies four further components of pedagogy – operational, managerial, ideational and ideological – and emphasizes the importance to teachers of the operational and managerial components which connect teachers and their learners and pedagogy to institutional life. This enables him to make a connection between teachers' knowledge and professional life, and also enables us to see when pressures from institutions can lead to a preoccupation with specific aspects of pedagogy which may interfere with what Allwright (1996) has termed 'pedagogic goals'. A common example is the institutional goal of maximizing examination success, which may inhibit other types of learning – managing the social aspects of learning, for example.

The picture emerging from this brief survey of sources, primarily theoretical and to some extent speculative, is borne out by a growing body of empirical work which attests to the inherent complexity of language classroom life and the multiplicity of internal forces at work in these contexts. Additionally, studies by Chick (1996), Shamim (1996), Lin (2001), Razianna Abdul Rahman (2003) and Nigussie (2004) illustrate how *external* influences are reflected in the ways in which classroom participants experience lessons. For example, Razianna Abdul Rahman's (2003) study of learners' perceptions and experiences of language learning in Malaysia illustrates how secondary students treat the classroom as a context with the specific purpose of assisting them to pass their examinations. This contrasts strongly with their experience of learning English outside the classroom, an activity which for them has much wider significance in a social sense. Classroom learning tends, for good reasons – notably security for both learners and teachers – to be highly routinized; it appears to be more broadly meaningful for the students only when the teacher allows them 'discussion time' and a chance to express themselves, or as they see it, 'to practice' what they already can do. They experience the classroom as closer to 'real life' outside the classroom on these occasions.

Nigussie's (2004) study of his attempts to innovate at tertiary level in Ethiopia raises significant issues about the potential for innovation in highly routinized didactic language classrooms. The story of how his innovatory teaching is 'socialized' into existing classroom patterns, and how he is compelled to move towards a way of teaching more in tune with learners' collective interpretations illustrates the complexity of these classrooms despite their apparently 'traditional' or conservative character. (There is a tendency to see 'traditional' classrooms as unproblematically simple: teacher talks, students listen.) Both these studies in classroom contexts of varying degrees of transmission orientation feature teachers and students managing classroom life as a complex interplay of sociocultural, psychological and institutional forces.

Classroom management: efficiency, order and control

The account of classrooms and classroom life above challenges the conventional view of classroom management as the maintenance of control. Classroom management has tended to be concerned with the creation of an orderly environment in which instruction can take place rather than ways in which teachers and learners can live with complexity – managing (or coping) – in classrooms. Richards (2001: 170) defines classroom management, among other dimensions of teaching – structuring, task and grouping – as:

> [T]he ways in which student behaviour, movement and interaction take place during a lesson are organized and controlled by the teacher to enable teaching to take place most effectively.

Richards goes on to note that good managerial skills contribute to teaching and learning experiences which are characterized by good discipline and the active engagement of learners in tasks and activities. Classroom management is thus seen as a series of teacher activities to organize, direct and control classroom life in order to meet instructional and curriculum goals. There is a linear logic behind this view that sees classroom management as a means of creating the necessary conditions for teaching to take place. *Management* and *teaching* are thus seen as separate activities. Jones (1996: 514), criticizing this perspective, notes that:

> Classroom management has too often focused on mechanical methods rather than on viewing the classroom environment as a complex interactive system of personal, social and cognitive demands.

Jones and Jones (1986) (see Jones, 1996: 507), prefer the notion of 'comprehensive classroom management', consisting of five teacher skills and general functions:

- Understanding of current research and theory in classroom management and students' psychological and learning needs
- Creation of positive teacher–student and peer relationships
- Use of optimal instructional methods which respond to individual and group needs
- Use of organisational and group management methods which optimize on-task behaviour
- Use of a range of methods for assisting students with behavioural problems.

Doyle (1986: 393) in his wide-ranging review of research into classroom management, notes that there is some debate about whether 'instructional methods' should be included in classroom management. He also notes that because classroom management studies tend to focus on 'the texture of the environment in which teachers work', it is inevitable that they should include discussion of classroom interaction. However, he maintains his position that the creation and maintenance of order is the main focus of classroom management.

Towards opportunity

There are, then, a number of potential criticisms of the 'order view' of classroom management which hint at a less teaching-focused view, which I shall term an *opportunity* view:

1. Order in itself is a necessary, some might say vital condition for classroom life, but it is not a prerequisite for learning to take place. Order might indeed inhibit learning – we cannot, for example, assume that because every learner in a group is *on-task* that they will learn. They may learn as much or more from the chance opportunities which disorder or randomness present.
2. There is an assumption that only *teachers* can control events in classrooms. The fact that teachers may have to impose order is evidence enough that learners too have a role in controlling events, initiating and responding to ongoing activity.
3. Evidence from studies of classroom talk (Mercer, 1995; van Lier, 1996) indicate that *instruction* and *management* are intimately bound, and that a great deal of classroom talk is incidental, even accidental,

even when order has been established. It is also often decidedly non-instrumental. Learning opportunities can emerge from open-ended 'social' talk as well as strictly controlled 'instructional talk', and not only about language, but also about how language is used (Wright and Bolitho, 1993). Breen and Littlejohn (2000) also show how discussion of learning and the organisation of classroom activity can lead to learning on several levels.

4. The order view assumes that teaching leads to or even causes learning in the classroom. A constructivist stance on learning, in which learners actively construct knowledge and negotiate meaning intra – and inter-personally, questions the extent to which direct instruction can lead to learning. I would add that there is no guarantee either that inductive, 'discovery'-based instructional strategies lead to learning. No cause and effect link appears to connect *learning* with *teaching* (Breen, 2001b).

5. Classrooms are *contested domains* in the sense that they mirror the wider society's tensions and complexities. The order metaphor may be untenable if classroom teaching and learning are seen as part of, not separate from, wider sociocultural trends and practices.

An opportunity view of classroom management allows for a wide range of instructional and social strategies to engage students with learning opportunities, and can tolerate creative 'disorder' or unstructured activity as part of the learning process. Opportunity can also occur within a 'traditional' classroom context of acknowledged and sanctioned teacher power and authority, as Sullivan's (2000) study of Vietnamese classrooms demonstrates, as well as in apparently more 'progressive' Western classrooms: the notion of opportunity should not be equated with 'communicative' or 'learner-centred'.

Towards care

A further criticism of the order school, but of a different nature, comes from McLaughlin (1991, 1994). Recognising the emotional dimensions of classroom life (singularly absent from many discussions of classroom management, despite the emphasis on 'good' and 'bad' behaviour), McLaughlin proposes that classroom management based on control and obedience is limited. He argues for a closer connection between instruction and management in a *caring* atmosphere, promoting responsibility rather than obedience. It finds its strength in positive classroom relationships and draws its moral power from a position of caring for learners, and is founded on the processes of negotiation between teachers and learners. As McLaughlin (1994: 78) puts it: 'There is no sense in divorcing how one establishes and nurtures classroom relationships from how one teaches; the former is part and parcel of the latter.'

The negotiation idea is coincidentally very close to the types of 'negotiated curriculum' reported by Breen and Littlejohn (2000) (and see Gieve and Miller, 2006, Chapter 2 in this volume), although the essence of negotiation is to promote learning opportunity rather than caring in the majority of studies they report. McLaughlin's views on classroom management add an important emotional dimension to the discussion, lacking in many discussions of practice, and yet central to any practices of discipline and control. Following its logic may indeed lower the stress for teachers, which comes from either the requirement or the perception of the need to impose obedience. It is also a view that teachers and learners may instinctively recognize, and perhaps value.

As our knowledge of classrooms gradually develops, both from *outsider* research and the gradual recognition of teachers' and learners' insights and practices in accounts of classroom life, so views on classroom management have shifted, from order to opportunity and from control to care (obedience to responsibility). At the same time, some believe that teaching has become less a question of efficiency and more a question of promoting significant learning (Allwright, 2006, Chapter 1 in this volume; van Lier, 1996) (Figure 4.1).

The shifts represented in Figure 4.1 are intimately bound to the changes in our characterizations of classrooms discussed in earlier sections of this chapter. They contribute to a different way of conceptualising classroom management, which emphasizes the *managing* aspects of what teachers and learners do in classrooms as part of a dynamic system. This invariably *includes* the need for relative order in which teachers and learners can contribute and take advantage of learning opportunities. Such a system also includes the social and emotional dimensions of classroom life and cannot be divorced from pedagogic goals, while at the same time recognizing learning goals. This is the

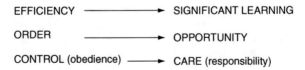

EFFICIENCY ⟶ SIGNIFICANT LEARNING

ORDER ⟶ OPPORTUNITY

CONTROL (obedience) ⟶ CARE (responsibility)

Figure 4.1   Shifts in thinking about pedagogy and classroom management

opportunity view of classroom management – or, more dynamically, *managing classroom life*.

Managing classroom life: opportunity, care and community

The *opportunity* view of classroom management takes as axiomatic that a classroom is best understood from a sociocultural perspective (Allwright, 1996; cf. Breen, 2001a; Mercer, 1995, 2001; van Lier, 1996). Not only is the classroom an inherently complex and unpredictable context, it is like this because it is a context where social, cultural, psychological and institutional forces interact. Simply to see classroom management as a means of keeping the lid on these forces so that instruction can take place is not only a narrow strategy, it is also potentially a risky strategy. We cannot assume that because a classroom is under control that people are going to learn. The evidence is contradictory at best (see, for example, Jones, 1996). Teachers may teach (or 'tell', or 'direct students through stages of activity') under these circumstances, but there is no guarantee that they will be followed by or influence learners.

An opportunity view of classroom management is the basis for action which enhances the *quality of experience* in classrooms and also provides a means of illuminating our understanding of classroom life. The conceptualization has three main aims:

- To provide a means for examining the relationships between teaching and learning as they are forged and recast in classroom life. To provide the basis for classroom research that aims to provide a more *holistic* account of classroom life and to understand the nature of pedagogy (see the section on Researching classroom life, below).
- To provide a way for trainee and serving teachers to frame their growing understanding of classroom life as they think about what happens in their own and others' classrooms by way of providing learners with *opportunities to learn* (see the section on Teacher education: preparing to manage, below).
- To provide the basis for *reducing conflict* in classroom life, and thereby lowering stress levels for all concerned. In this way, action is aimed at providing the sort of caring environment that McLaughlin (1991, 1994) refers to. This is not, in passing, a 'new humanism': it is a view of caring that sees responsibility for order negotiated. In short, a more 'open' classroom predicated on care and self-discipline.

Elements of an opportunity view of classroom management

The opportunity view of classroom life has five main elements (Figure 4.2) which are in constant interrelationship during classroom activity. These are:

- *Time* – the temporal dimension
- *Space* – the spatial dimension
- *Engagement* – the emotional or affective dimension
- *Participation* – the social dimension
- *Resources* – what teachers and learners bring to classroom life, materially and cognitively.

Time and space: the constants of classroom life

Unlike learning in more informal settings, classroom learning is deliberately and emphatically time- and space-bound. Teachers and learners gather in particular spaces for specified periods of time for particular purposes. The temporal and spatial architectures of formal education are thus powerful and fundamental influences on classroom life, and, although they are *obvious*, they are most often ignored in discussions of

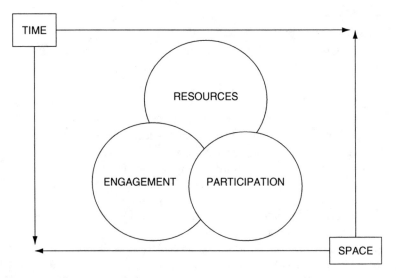

Figure 4.2 Elements of classroom life
Note
The element of 'resources' in Figure 4.2 has been absorbed into the elements of engagement and participation in a more recent discussion of classroom management (Wright, 2005, forthcoming).

classroom life (although see, for example, Breen, 2001a). To teachers and learners, though, these are the boundaries of their world for long periods of time: for the lifetimes of many teachers, and increasingly for learners, for long periods of their lives as the concept and practice of lifelong learning gains currency. Lessons in educational institutions have time limits; courses and programmes are time-bound. School learning and higher education run to temporal rhythms (the higher-education year in the UK still largely follows the medieval agricultural calendar, for example). Classroom time itself is segmented by teachers as they plan lessons, and it is these decisions which create the rhythms for lessons, unless learners contest the time frame. Traditionally, the temporal dimension of formal education is extended with homework. North and Pillay (2002) analyse the influence of homework on the educational experience of Malaysian undergraduates. When traditional time limits are removed, as in many forms of distance education, their absence enables designers to create new forms of programme, and frees learners from having to be in formal learning at a particular time. Time is also, as Hargreaves (1994) and Lemke (2002) among others point out, a hidden force which has the power to create pressure and stress for teachers and learners. For example, where a curriculum has to be completed in a given time, teachers will terminate or curtail activities which are not achieving their immediate objectives. Wright (1992a) terms this phenomenon 'the completion imperative'.

Classrooms are typically enclosed physical spaces, although the *virtual classroom* in cyberspace is now commonplace in technologically rich contexts. At the other end of the scale of educational opportunity, a classroom is a gathering with a teacher under a tree or in a bombed-out building. Again, unlike most informal learning, which tends to happen in the context in which the learning will be of immediate value, formal learning institutions have created buildings dedicated to teaching and learning, and divided them into classrooms. Once inside a classroom, a learning group will have to accommodate itself to furniture layouts and orientate itself towards major physical features of the classroom such as a chalk board or similar. (Holliday, 1997, provides several rich examples from different contexts.) The amount of choice over these quite funda-mental decisions is a major factor in understanding classroom life. Institutions deem that certain layouts of furniture are unchangeable, and even bolt down desks to the floor to signal their intent (and perhaps guard against theft, too). Where we are positioned – at the front or back, for example – as we sit together in a classroom is a major social marker – of status, and of relative intimacy – and who may stand

and who must sit may be of equal importance to participants in their experience of the classroom world.

Engagement: the emotional dimension

Classroom learning and teaching is an emotional activity. First, the very act of attempting to learn something exposes us to the risk of potential ridicule, and is thus infused with emotions. Failure to learn can bring on frustration and anger. Success after effort can bring satisfaction and increased self-esteem. Secondly, the challenges and emotional risks of learning may lead us to withdraw from learning. On the other hand we may decide to meet the challenge. We may thus possess the quality that Claxton (1999) calls 'resilience': the capacity to initiate and persevere with learning have everything to do with positive emotions. Withdrawal, bad behaviour, open rebellion and even violence are related to the negative emotional aspects of being a 'captive' learner.

What is usually referred to as 'motivation', an issue of great import-ance for teachers, is, as Dörnyei (2001) points out, intimately linked to the emotional domain. Vygotsky's (1978) work links cognition with the affective domain through the channel of 'meaning' (learners' responses to language are essentially emotional) and the ways learners perceive, experience and process emotional aspects of social interac-tion. The act of learning itself thus has important emotional overtones, especially in its social context, where learning in zones of proximal development can be enhanced by caring and support by teachers and peers (Mahn and John-Steiner, 2002). Taking all these elements together we can begin to create a picture of the emotional domain of classroom life and how it might interrelate to the other domains. The emergent view is a picture of *engagement*, and the ways in which teachers and learners are engaged at an emotional level in classroom life, and what the quality of this engagement is. Teachers and learners alternatively seek and withdraw from direct engagement in classroom activity; how conditions for engagement are created by teachers and learners is the essence of classroom climate, or 'atmosphere', the emotional tone of classroom proceedings (Allwright and Bailey, 1991). Because of the all-pervasive influence of classroom climate, an opportunity view of classroom management sees engagement as a key element of managing classroom life.

Participation: the social domain

Since Barne's, Briton and Rosen's (1969) and Barnes' (1976) work on classroom communication it has become axiomatic to our thinking about classrooms that they are *talk-rich* contexts. Classroom discourses are key indicators of modes and patterns of participation in classroom life. Numerous studies have described patterns of talk in classrooms since the work of Sinclair and Coulthard (1975) became established in the public domain. More recent work has gone further in seeking an understanding of the discourses of classroom life as they reveal underlying conversations about the purposes of classroom activity and the value of different types of knowledge. Seedhouse (1997, 2004), for example, has shown how classroom discourse is a form of *institutional discourse*, constrained by social and institutional views of classrooms (presumably 'control' views). Mercer (2001) provides a full range of tools for analysing classroom language to illustrate the essentially social and cultural nature of classroom discourse, and to try to understand classroom talk with reference to its contexts of occurrence and how teachers and learners create meaning through the construction of 'common knowledge'.

Of particular significance to the opportunity view of classroom management is the ways in which different types of participation enhance or inhibit learning opportunity. Participation is not only accessible through talk or silence, and the ways in which participants manage these. It also connects to physical, temporal and emotional elements of classroom life. Learners may participate because they are positioned near a teacher, or because the teacher has given them a particular time in which to lead class activities. Lack of participation may be an emotional sign of boredom or disaffection. Denial of participation may lead to negative emotional responses. Maximum participation for the maximum number of learners does not mean the creation of a multitude of learning opportunities if the cognitive challenge of the activity is too great for the learners or the levels of engagement are inhibited by a *cold* climate. Understanding the ways in which participation contributes to managing classroom life is central to understanding how learning opportunity is created.

Resources: what's in the classroom and what we bring with us

Classroom life utilizes and creates a wide range of resources. From a teacher's point of view, the key resources may be their teaching materials – books, visuals, technological aids, realia and so on. These may or may not be important for learners. Other teachers regard their students as the most important resources in terms of what they bring with them in terms of life experience to contribute to classroom activity. What learners already know, what they have done, what they have not done, what they prefer and dislike are all resources in the same way as cognitive capacities – intelligence, 'problem-solving ability', 'learning styles' and a host of other constructs exhaustively listed in second language acquisition theory. Classroom life itself may be seen as a resource – that is, the social relationships and emotional world of a classroom group as they engage in learning activities are a legitimate source of discussion, conjecture, dispute and learning.

An opportunity view of managing classroom life sees resources and their management as an integral aspect of the classroom world and regards anything that contributes to the creation of learning opportunity, *including the teacher*, as a resource. Resources are constructed through their use in activity and the ways in which they are referred to during activity. Thus resources and participation patterns are connected in the same way that participants' moods and states can also be regarded as something to learn from and learn about if such learning can contribute to the development of the capacity to learn. The appearance in recent years of new material resources such as computers and the internet have the capacity to change patterns of participation, and pose new challenges to learners worldwide as they come to terms with learning both with and about the new resources. Acknowledging how discussion of and reflection on classroom climate are potential sources of learning opportunities provides further impetus to the idea that an opportunity view of classroom management can change our perceptions on what can be achieved in classroom settings.

Researching classroom life

The five 'elements' of classroom life that have been identified above are in constant interplay during classroom activity, generating the 'ecology' of classroom contexts described by van Lier (1996). At times classroom life is directly managed – there is a deliberate intention to change the course of events. A basic example is when a teacher initiates a new sequence of activity. At all times, whatever participants (or non-participants such as curriculum designers, materials designers and other 'players' in the classroom game) are doing, the classroom is 'managing itself'. It is self-regulating in the same way that an ecosystem is; it is dynamic and yet static, working to rule-governed rhythms. Experienced classroom participants intuitively know this. They do not necessarily need to articulate what they do, and are likely to be unaware of the 'rules' in any conscious ways.

The 'managing classroom life' metaphor generates new research issues and puzzles:

1. Most fundamentally, how do the various elements of the classroom system *interact* and how are they *connected*? This entails both a description of how the elements work – we now have a large number of descriptions of classroom life, mainly from the point of view of talk, but also ethnographic descriptions of classrooms (Canagarajah, 1999; Holliday, 1997, for example). Understanding one element – participation, for example – is, in the first instance, possible only with reference to the other elements. How talk is used to provide support to learners is an example of where *engagement* overlaps with *participation*. At the same time we need to understand how an awareness of time or a response to space influences participation or engagement or the use of resources. Further, we can explore ways in which the classroom is *contested* and how this influences the creation of learning opportunities.

   Ultimately an understanding of how the complex classroom system generates learning opportunities, stores and creates resources, invites or discourages participation and engagement may enable us to see in greater depth what happens in classrooms, and why. But it should not be another means of looking at the 'effectiveness' of teaching or the efficiency of learning. Understandings will be of value as a point of departure for discussion or thinking about classrooms and their role in learning, not as a means for methodological (or 'technological') 'improvement'. How classrooms provide opportunities for learning is of more importance ultimately to educators and to above all learners than how classroom life can be controlled and directed, as Allwright (2006, Chapter 1 in this volume) argues.

2. Understanding of classroom life cannot emerge solely from *in-classroom research*. Recent work by, for example, Chick (1996) and Lin (2001), has shown that much of what happens in classrooms can be understood with reference to broader sociocultural currents in operation outside the classroom. How classroom elements interact may be understood with reference to how certain behaviours are valued in the wider society. How participation patterns work may be influenced by a learner's out-of-class identities, and there may be conflict between these and desired in-class identities or non-identities. Enough compelling evidence has already accumulated to suggest that understanding classrooms as contexts governed only by pedagogical imperatives is misguided and partial.

What I have discussed here by way of research directions and potential action is research *on* classrooms (see Wright, 1992b for a discussion of the distinction between research in and on classrooms). There is a place in educational research for this type of work, which has the primary advantage of being objective to the point of being conducted by 'outsiders' (who are neither teachers nor learners). However, I would also argue that understandings generated by such research are of value to educationalists only if they have *resonance*. This implies sensitivity at least, and collaboration of the sort discussed by Mercer (1995: 120) at best, where classroom participants' concerns and lives are addressed directly and *they* are enriched and informed by what outsider researchers find out:

> the kind of applied action research which has most potential, in a whole range of fields as well as education, is socio-cultural research in which practitioners and external researchers work in research partnership, each contributing their expertise and experience. The gathering and analysis of data must take account of the different and potentially conflicting perspectives and agendas of each partner. For this to happen there has to be some negotiation of what aims and agendas are being pursued, and of course the relationship has to be one of mutual trust.

Issues regarding, for instance, the interaction between the elements of classroom management as teachers and learners go about managing classroom life may form the basis of an agenda for research on classrooms. Inquiry may also be more closely embedded in the fabric of classroom life, as a means of teachers and learners understanding their world and also as a way of understanding *learning* better. And by so doing, teachers and learners may create and take advantage of more opportunities for learning, learn about the processes of learning itself and contribute directly to classroom climate by opening and pursuing dialogues on learning.

In order to exploit the possibilities afforded by this agenda, it is essential that the classroom is described and understanding attempted from the *participants'* perspectives. How teachers and learners experience the emotional, social and cognitive worlds of the classroom and how this experience contributes to or impedes learning opportunity will provide insights into educational processes that can help participants and other concerned outsiders make more of their daily classroom experience. Much descriptive work on classrooms is of what one might term, to extend a metaphor of Breen (2001a) after Malinowski, 'archipelagic' – classroom life could be likened to a stretch of open ocean with clusters

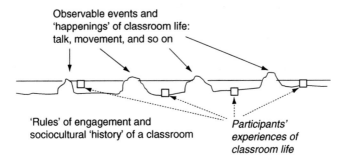

Observable events and
'happenings' of classroom life:
talk, movement, and so on

'Rules' of engagement and
sociocultural 'history' of a classroom

Participants'
experiences of
classroom life

Figure 4.3   Points of reference in research on classroom life

of islands representing the 'observables' of classroom activity about which accounts are written. Seeking participants' perspectives is akin to exploring the underwater areas and the sea bottom between the islands, which connects them, because their experiences are not simply on the surface – they are also only partially remembered, or forgotten, but still present as part of their tacit knowledge. In this way we can build up our knowledge of the deep psychology – building knowledge of the rules of engagement and sociocultural history – of the classroom as a step towards understanding its complexity, and building on the episodic and fragmented accounts that we have so far managed to generate (see Figure 4.3).

A final point on research is that managing classroom life is not responsive to a set of formulae or even maxims (tips). It is unpredictable and ultimately 'messy'. The approach to research advocated above is a means of beginning to comprehend *from the inside* the messiness of classrooms, their complexity and how they are managed by teachers and learners. Outsiders have a particular role in this process, in assisting insiders to articulate their experiences, as a way of assisting insiders in enhancing the quality of their classroom experiences.

Teacher education: preparing to manage

On many teacher education programmes for language teachers, 'classroom management' is an insignificant sideshow to the main events of methodological training and the development of linguistic knowledge. 'Classroom management' typically involves sessions on 'group and pair work', discipline and classroom language (often use of the target language for all aspects of classroom activity). It occupies a minute proportion of the time available for training. If managing classroom life is a question of gradually perfecting the art of living with uncertainty and complexity, of managing the five elements of classroom life, it would thus appear that current teacher education practice is inadequate. Teacher education on the other hand could assist teachers to become more adept at exploiting the potential of classrooms as contexts where opportunities for learning can be generated, to see control as a potentially limited and limiting strategy for managing classrooms and classrooms in which there is more open-ended (contingent – van Lier, 1996) activity as sources of opportunity.

Teacher education for managing classroom life would focus on the five main elements of classroom life. In other words, classroom management, rather than being an appendix to other more 'technicist' concerns, should be a central theme in learning pedagogy. Methodology would become one aspect of such an approach rather than a central component. Space does not permit a full discussion of the implications of this reconceptualization. However, there are two linked principles which ought to inform teacher education for managing classroom life.

Focus on the realities of classroom life through immersion in experience

Stage 1

Classroom management skills are learned *in context*. They are the bedrock of pedagogy and learned through actual experience in the classroom as a learner and a teacher. It is well established that student teachers begin their induction into the teaching profession after a lengthy exposure to and contribution to classroom life as learners (John, 1996; Lortie, 1975). Their task is to draw upon this experience to transform themselves into teachers. Teacher education may best begin from the perspective of a learner and an exploration of student teachers' learning history and mental models of teaching and classroom life. Learning is built upon what the student teacher already knows. Combining this with extensive periods of attachment to classes, in the company of supportive teachers and peers, provides a platform from which to view classroom life, with the choice of becoming as directly involved as one wishes.

Stage 2

This stage links periods of attachment in schools with subsequent periods of review and reflection at a training institution. These focus on how the main elements of classroom life were managed and at the same time interacted and influenced what went on. This provides the basis for beginning to think about the ways in which pedagogy is embedded in classroom management. Instructional procedures which aid students in their learning can then be introduced and practised in the safe environment of the training institution before being practised under supervision in real classes, again with the support of mentors or supervisors. Awareness gradually develops of patterns of participation, the conditions of engagement and how resources contribute to classroom life within temporal and spatial constraints.

Stage 3

The final phase of learning in this early part of teacher education, following periods in the training institution focusing on content and methodological issues, would be a period of 'internship' – again under supervision, but on this occasion less directive – in which the student teacher starts to become a 'real' teacher. The intern would be well aware of such issues as classroom climate, resistance to learning and the effect of particular participation patterns on student learning opportunity by this stage, and be able to begin practising their pedagogy in earnest.

An inquiry focus

Teacher education in the hands of experts in education and pedagogy has a tendency to become didactic – the passing on of a view of pedagogy and of learning that can conflict with the student teacher's experience as a learner and as an apprentice. The framework for managing classroom life is well suited to the use of inquiry methods during these learning periods. Student teachers in effect become researchers of classrooms as they learn about engagement, participation and resources by engaging in observation, dialogue with teachers and learners and each other. Because the elements themselves are not closely defined there are ample opportunities for exploring their meaning, and understanding that patterns of activity are not always consistent – for example, that a particular procedure works differently on different occasions. The combination of pedagogic experience and critical review of this experience is the basis of an 'inquiry-centred' approach to teacher education (Matei, 2001, is a good example of this practice). Classroom research thus becomes a *learning* tool and an educational process rather than an abstract, distant set of procedures, in ways very similar to those of

Exploratory Practice (Allwright, 2003). Perhaps this is the real value of classroom research – as a central *modus operandi* of teacher education. Understanding classrooms rather than simply trying to control them is likely to lead to pedagogic contexts which encourage engagement, afford different participation patterns and make use of a range of resources – classrooms in which the positive quality of experience contributes to a healthy learning climate.

Final comments

I have argued that an opportunity view of classroom management – managing classroom life – is a natural outcome of a reconceptualisation of classroom life, acknowledging the complexity and systemic nature of all classrooms. Quality in classrooms is thus an emergent property of complexity. However, while it has become fairly widely accepted that classrooms are complex, the response to complexity has not always been to regard it as a source of potential for learning, for both students and teachers. Control, (if it is required) as McLaughlin (1991, 1994) points out, has to be *negotiated*, not imposed. Our learners are more aware about their learning and are more deeply concerned about learning than is often portrayed. How they experience classroom life, and how they contribute, are indicators of the quality of classroom life. Engagement must be understood, as the emotional dimensions of learning are as important as participation (and non-participation). The range of resources in the classroom extends far beyond coursebooks if learners' lives, and teachers' explicit modelling of learning are viewed as sources of learning. If teachers can make this explicit, then passing awareness has the chance of being transformed into real learning and understanding. It is highly unlikely in our lifetimes that classrooms will be done away with. But their role and function will change as the role and function of education changes – networked learning communities working online are already a reality for many teachers and learners and pose new problems in classroom management. How to create opportunity for learning while managing classroom life under conditions of change remains the most pressing challenge for today's and tomorrow's learners and teachers. The framework presented in this chapter may go a small way towards helping us maximize the quality of classroom life, and simultaneously to understanding and meeting the challenges. Exploratory Practice, as conceived by Allwright (2003), has the potential to provide a practical working framework for achieving both of these aims in our own classrooms.

Note

* I am very grateful to my colleague Gabi Matei for her helpful comments on an early draft of this chapter, and to the editors for their valuable suggestions and comments on later drafts.

References

Allwright, D. 1989. Interaction in the language classroom: social problems and pedagogic possibilities. *Language Teaching in Today's World* 3. Paris: Hachette.

Allwright, D. 1996. Social and pedagogic pressures in the language classroom: the role of socialisation. In: *Society and the Language Classroom*, ed. H. Coleman. Cambridge: Cambridge University Press.

Allwright, D. 2003. Exploratory Practice: rethinking practitioner research in language teaching. *Language Teaching Research* 7, 2.

Allwright, D. 2006. Six promising directions in Applied Linguistics. In: *Understanding the Language Classroom*, eds S. Gieve and I.K. Miller. London: Palgrave Macmillan, Chapter 1 in this volume.

Allwright, D. and K.M. Bailey 1991. *Focus on the language classroom*. Cambridge: Cambridge University Press.

Barnes, D. 1976. *From communication to curriculum*. Harmondsworth: Penguin.

Barnes, D., J. Briton and H. Rosen, eds 1969. *Language, the learner and the school*. Harmondsworth: Penguin.

Breen, M.P. 2001a. The social context for language learning: a neglected situation. In: *English language teaching in its social context*, eds C.N. Candlin and N. Mercer. London: Routledge.

Breen, M.P. 2001b. Overt participation and covert acquisition in the language classroom. In: *Learner contributions to language learning*, ed. M.P. Breen. Harlow: Longman.

Breen, M.P. and A. Littlejohn 2000. *Classroom decision-making: negotiation and process syllabuses in action*. Cambridge: Cambridge University Press.

Briggs, J.B. and P.J. Moore 1993. *The process of learning*. 3rd edition, Sydney: Prentice Hall.

Brumfit, C.J. 2001. *Individual freedom in language learning*. Oxford: Oxford University Press.

Canagarajah, A.S. 1999. *Resisting linguistic imperialism in English teaching*. Oxford: Oxford University Press.

Chick, K. 1996. Safe-talk: collusion in apartheid education. In: *Society and the language classroom*, ed. H. Coleman. Cambridge: Cambridge University Press.

Claxton, G. 1999. *Wise up*. London: Bloomsbury.

Dörnyei, Z. 2001. *Teaching and researching motivation*. Harlow: Pearson.

Doyle, W. 1986. Classroom organisation and management. In: *Handbook of research on teaching*, ed. M.C. Wittrock. 3rd edition, New York: Macmillan.

Gieve, S. and I.K. Miller 2006. What do we mean by 'quality of classroom life?'. In: *Understanding the language classroom*, eds S. Gieve and I.K. Miller 2006. London: Palgrave Macmillan, Chapter 2 in this volume.

Hargreaves, A. 1994. *Changing teachers, changing times*. London: Cassell.

Holliday, A. 1997. Six lessons: cultural continuity in communicative language teaching. *Language Teaching Research* 1, 3.

John, P.D. 1996. Understanding the apprenticeship of observation in initial teacher training: exploring student teachers' implicit theories of teaching. In: *Liberating the learner*, eds G. Claxton, T. Atkinson, M. Osborn and M. Wallace. London: Routledge.

Jones, V. 1996. Classroom management. In: *The handbook of research on teacher education*, eds J. Sikula, T.J. Buttery and E. Guyton. 2nd edition, New York: Macmillan.

Kumaravadivelu, B. 2001. Toward a post-method pedagogy. *TESOL Quarterly* 35, 4: 537–60.

Larsen-Freeman, D. 1991. Second language acquisition research: staking out the territory. *TESOL Quarterly* 25, 2: 315–42.

Lemke, J.L. 2002. Becoming the village: education across lives. In: *Learning for life in the 21st century*, eds G. Wells and G. Claxton. Oxford: Blackwell.

Lin, A.M.Y. 2001. Doing-English: lessons in the reproduction or transformation of social worlds? In: *English language teaching in its social context*, eds C.N. Candlin and N. Mercer. London: Routledge.

Lortie, D.C. 1975. *Schoolteacher: a sociological study.* Chicago, IL: Chicago University Press.

Mahn, H. and V. John-Steiner 2002. The gift of confidence: a Vygotskyan view of emotions. In: *Learning for life in the 21st century*, eds G. Wells and G. Claxton. Oxford: Blackwell.

Matei, G.S. 2001. Student teachers as researchers: an inquiry-oriented to initial teacher education. Unpublished PhD thesis, University of Exeter, UK.

McLaughlin, H.J. 1991. Reconciling care and control: authority in classroom relationships. *Journal of Teacher Education* 42, 3: 182–96.

McLaughlin, H.J. 1994. From negation to negotiation: moving away from the management metaphor. *Action in Teacher Education* 16, 1.

Mercer, N. 1995. *The guided construction of knowledge.* Clevedon: Multilingual Matters.

Mercer, N. 2001. Language for teaching a language. In: *English language teaching in its social context*, eds C.N. Candlin and N. Mercer. London: Routledge.

Nigussie, N. 2004. Exploring new teaching/learning procedures in EAP classrooms at the Ethiopian Civil Service College. Unpublished PhD thesis, University of Exeter, UK.

North, S. and H. Pillay 2002. Homework: re-examining the routine. *ELT Journal* 56, 2: 137–45.

Prabhu, N.S. 1992. The dynamics of the language lesson. *TESOL Quarterly* 26, 2: 232–48.

Prabhu, N.S. 1995. Concept and conduct in language pedagogy. In: *Principle and practice in Applied Linguistics*, eds G.Cook and B. Seidlhofer. Oxford: Oxford University Press.

Razianna Abdul Rahman 2003. Learners' understandings of the experiences of learning English: a Malaysian perspective. Unpublished PhD thesis, University of Exeter, UK.

Richards, J.C. 2001. Beyond methods. In: *English language teaching in its social context*, eds C.N. Candlin and N. Mercer. London: Routledge.

Seedhouse, P. 1997. Combining form and meaning. *ELT Journal* 51, 4: 149–56.

Seedhouse, P. 2004. *The interactional architecture of the language classroom: a conversation analysis perspective.* Oxford: Blackwell.

Shamim, F. 1996. Learner resistance to innovation in classroom methodology. In: *society and the language classroom,* ed. H. Coleman. Cambridge: Cambridge University Press.

Sinclair, J.McH. and M. Coulthard 1975. *Towards an analysis of discourse: the language of pupils and teachers.* Oxford: Oxford University Press.

Sullivan, P. 2000. Playfulness as mediation in communicative language teaching in a Vietnamese classroom. In: *Sociocultural theory and second language learning,* ed. J.P. Lantolf. Oxford: Oxford University Press.

Ur, P. 1996. *A course in language teaching.* Cambridge: Cambridge University Press.

van Lier, L. 1996. *Interaction in the language curriculum: awareness, autonomy and authenticity.* Harlow: Longman.

Vygotsky, L.S. 1978. *Thought and language.* Cambridge, MA: Harvard University Press.

Wright, T. 1992a. Critical moments in the second language classroom: towards an understanding of second language classroom culture. Unpublished PhD thesis, University of Lancaster, UK.

Wright, T. 1992b. L2 classroom research and L2 teacher education: towards a collaborative approach. In: *Perspectives on second language teacher education,* eds J. Flowerdew, M. Brock and S. Hsia. Hong Kong: City Polytechnic of Hong Kong.

Wright, T. 2005. *Classroom management in language education.* Basingstoke: Palgrave Macmillan.

Wright, T. and R. Bolitho 1993. Language awareness. a missing link in language teacher education? *ELT Journal* 47, 2: 292–304.

5

Who Does What in the 'Management of Language Learning'? Planning and the Social Construction of the 'Motivation to Notice'*

Devon Woods

Introduction

An important issue in the thinking of teachers in many second and foreign language classrooms, although often implicit, is the issue of who is going to do what – how much of the responsibility and the decision-making and work is going to be done by the teacher, and how much is going to be done by the learners? The language teaching literature also reflects this concern: the movement to *learner autonomy* (Benson, 2001; Riley, 1988) and *learner training* (O'Malley and Chamot, 1990; Wenden and Rubin, 1987) is based on the idea that it is beneficial to teach learners to take more responsibility for their own language learning. Allwright's concept of the 'management of language learning' (Allwright, 1984) was originally developed with reference to this issue. When the question stated in the title of this piece – 'who does what?' – is examined closely, it begins to become clear that it is not in principle answerable. The process of deciding appears more and more as a *dynamically evolving interaction*, with constantly changing rules. More appropriate questions might be:

- Who is expected to do what, and what happens to and results from such expectations as language classes proceed?
- How does the negotiation of who is supposed to do what evolve?
- What are the factors and constraints that affect the process of negotiation?

This chapter examines these questions both theoretically and empirically through analysis and interpretation of data collected by Dick Allwright and myself during his stint as visiting lecturer at Carleton University in 1991. The research and this discussion embody Allwright's 'six promising directions' (2006, Chapter 1 in this volume): especially the directions of 'understanding', of 'complexity', of 'idiosyncrasy', and of 'teaching/learning as life', with my argument being that these directions and the concepts central in Allwright's work from the 1980s to the present have been essentially constructivist and intepretivist.

What is the 'management of language learning'?

The term 'management of language learning' was coined by Allwright (1981) to refer to the process of strategic thinking, decision-making and acting made with the intent to achieve certain language learning goals (and is distinct from the notion of 'classroom management'). As Allwright has noted, we cannot actually 'do' learning or 'see' the learning itself taking place (in the same way, to use another organic metaphor, we cannot 'see' a tree grow). We can tell, after the fact, that learning (like growing) has taken place, and we can also observe the things that people have decided to do that seem to enhance it. From this, we can speculate, and perhaps come to some conclusions, about the conditions under which learning seems to have taken place.

Allwright's point is that the term 'management of language learning' removes any *a priori* assumptions about the traditional distinction between 'learning' – what the learner is supposed to do – and 'teaching' – what the teacher is supposed to do. It therefore makes the question of 'who does what' an empirical one. It is clear that this concept, as well as the others noted in Allwright's 'six promising directions' (Allwright, 2006, Chapter 1 in this volume) is essentially a constructivist one.

The management of language learning involves actions, but through what learners and teachers (and other participants in the process) say about what they do, we can postulate that there is a process of *decision-making* underlying these actions. This process includes planning (decision-making about actions in the light of goals), and the interpretation and evaluation (in the light of perceived goals) of the events which take place as a result of the actions (Woods, 1996). These decisions and actions occur over time and are interrelated. However, it is not easy to track the thinking that underlies the decisions because, although the term 'decision' has the connotation of consciously thought-out deliberation, the process is not entirely conscious. Any decision may be more or less deliberately carried out, with fewer or more factors (goals, prior experiences, prior decisions) being attended to and explicitly taken into account at any particular moment in any decision (Woods, 1996).

The management of language learning, then, is goal-directed decision-making, intended to lead to learning – towards an explicitly or implicitly conceived state of 'knowing how to speak the target language'. The conceptions of this above-mentioned state of 'knowing . . . the language' can vary from individual to individual. In addition, there can be different conceptions of the conditions that lead to this state, and different conceptions of how to best create those conditions. As a result of these differing conceptions, we can expect there to be some negotiation among different individuals involved in the process, and between the two categories of participants: on the one hand the learners themselves, and on the other hand the teachers, whose profession it is to make decisions that will lead the learners to the goal state. We may also find, then, that there are differences in conceptions about participant roles in the process – that is, whose job it is to do what.

Most people have a general conception, based on their own classroom experiences, of who is supposed to do what, under normal circumstances, in the process of classroom language teaching and learning. We can all easily imagine a teacher standing in front of a class, giving instructions for students to follow, giving samples of the language, demonstrating meanings, giving explanations of how certain elements of the language work, and making corrections to the learners' utterances.

Traditionally, in many approaches to language teaching, an explicit distinction was made between *learning* the language and *using* the language. Learning the language happened first, through explanations, through drills and exercises; once the learning was done, the individual could then begin to use the language and at that point was no longer considered to be learning but practising what had been learned. With the evolution of communicative teaching, the distinction between using the language and learning the language became blurred. The notion of learning by doing, or learning the language *through* using the language became a legitimate way of considering the process. Because of this development, the teacher's role shifted from one of explicitly teaching the language to one of setting up conditions that demanded the *use* of the language. As a result, our conception of what is normal in a language classroom has broadened. The teacher may stand at the front of the class speaking in the target language, but discussing a topic far removed from the features of the language being learned. The teacher may ask the students to get into groups to solve a problem unrelated to the characteristics of the target language, but in the target language. This breakdown in the traditional conception of whose job it is to do what meant that we suddenly found classroom situations where the learners were asked (by the teacher) to make decisions usually reserved for the teacher, or where the teacher expected the students to take the initiative in deciding what they wanted to learn and how they could best do it. This would lead to an actual manifested curriculum (and the learning opportunities which result) which is different from the one planned by the teacher or laid out in the curriculum.

In addition, my own research (Woods, 1996) has illustrated how the individual teacher's own beliefs, assumptions and knowledge (BAK), or 'personal theory', will influence the decisions that he or she makes and the classroom actions that he or she takes. Teacher decisions about responsibility for motivation, for attendance and attention, for correction of errors, for deciding on and planning themes, topics and classroom activities can vary dramatically from one teacher to another depending on the teacher's beliefs about the best path to success. Similarly, learners can have very different beliefs about whose role is it to do what in the classroom, and these different beliefs can cause classroom clashes (Woods, 2003).

These differing approaches and beliefs open up the possibility for negotiating whose job it is to do what. However, this negotiation may not always be cooperative. For example, learners from a traditional education system may question why the teacher is talking about endangered species rather than about English, or asking them which topics they would like to discuss in class or write a paper on. As one learner once said to me angrily when I asked a class what they were interested in learning: 'Why are you asking us? That's your job!'

As a result, our conception of instructional decision-making takes on an *interactional complexity* that reflects Allwright's discussion of promising directions. To move towards an understanding of this complexity, we need to examine the notion of instructional decision-making a little more closely.

Decision-making in the 'management of language learning'

Teacher cognition and teacher decision-making

Woods (1996) described a model of the teacher's decision-making process in the management of language learning, treated as part of what is now termed 'teacher cognition' (Borg, 2003; Woods, 1996). An important feature of this model is that it does not produce a categorization and taxonomy of the individual decisions themselves, but rather a description of the *relationships* among decisions. Decisions do not occur independently of other decisions, and understanding decision-making as a process involves examining these relationships. In the model, two kinds of relationships were posited.

The first type of relationship is *process-focused and dynamic*. It involves the relationships among *phases* in the decision-making process. Decision-making in this model is seen as cyclical and recursive. The first phase involves planning, which may be explicit or implicit, and done in light of certain background information and explicit or implicit goals. The second phase involves action, organized units of activity carried out in order to create certain events intended to accomplish certain of the planned goals. The third phase involves interpretation of the events that resulted from that action (which may or may not have turned out as planned), and evaluation in terms of the goals. This evaluation then feeds into the background information used in subsequent planning. Decisions can thus be seen as having a kind of internal dynamic pattern: a series of decisions occurs through cycles of this pattern and involves several further researchable relationships. For example, the relationship between what the teacher plans and the actions he or she carries out is an essential relationship in teaching. The relationship between the actions he or she carries out and the interpretations and evaluations of the events that occur as a result is another crucial relationship. And the relationship between the interpretations and evaluations of the events and the formulation of the next plans is a third important relationship.

The second type of relationship is *structural and product-focused*. It relates to the structure of perceived events that is produced by actions issuing as a result of decisions. The structure includes a logical dimension and a chronological dimension. Each of these dimensions also involves a certain type of relationship, the understanding of which is key in conceptualizing the management of language learning.

Decisions do not produce events at a single level of logical structure; rather, the resulting actions and events have a perceived quasi-hierarchical structure (actually involving multiple hierarchies, 'tangled hierarchies' – or, to use a term I have adapted from de Mey (1977) – 'heterarchies'). In this heterarchical view, an event includes or subsumes other sub-events. In other words, from the point of view of a teacher (since all events are 'situated' and seen from a particular perspective), a decision to teach a particular course (let's say ESL 1001) will produce an event – the course

ESL 1001 – that can be treated as a unit: referred to, planned, partaken of and completed (and perhaps appear on a student's transcript or certificate). This decision will imply a certain set of sub-decisions that must be made as a part of the major super-ordinate decision, and will produce events and sub-events that will occur and be included in the period of time 'governed' by the event issuing as a result of the super-ordinate decision.

The important characteristic of this relationship of decisions is that, since decision-making is goal-directed, successfully realizing the super-ordinate decisions is the reason for, or function of, carrying out the subordinate actions, and carrying out the subordinate ones can be seen as the means or method for achieving the super-ordinate one. In other words, planning decisions/actions are related in the following logical way: I will achieve X, by doing a, b and c. Interpretations are similarly related: The reason for doing a, b and c was to achieve X. In both cases, there is further embedding: the a, b and c each can function as an 'X' with their own a, b and c.

The other dimension of the structural relationship is chronological. It includes the sequential and temporal relationships among the events produced by the decision-making process. This set of relationships includes both sequence and timing: decisions (and the events issuing from them) occur in a sequence spaced out in time. What is significant, therefore, is both the ordering of the events and their relationship to each other in that order (certain ones must come before others), as well as the spacing of events in time, since the duration of pauses in language learning events can be significant to teachers and learners (for example, for reasons of 'rest' or 'incubation', as well as the scheduling of classes or lessons through a term).

Learner cognition and learner decision-making

Woods (1997) used the terms 'learner cognition' and 'learner decision-making' to integrate a number of previously separate theoretical notions in the second language acquisition literature – namely motivation, learning strategies and learner beliefs – and to add a dynamic perspective to the analysis. From a discussion of a hypothetical set of decisions made by a learner about his or her language learning, we can see that the relationships operating for the teacher's decision-making, discussed above, also operate on the part of the learner.

Learners do not typically think of the issue of their decision-making process as having a structure. However, a learner's decisions – especially in cases where the learner is self-directed – produce a structure with essentially the same characteristics as a teacher's. The actions (and resulting events) that are a product of the learner's decision-making process have a relationships which are logical (heterarchical) and chronological (sequenced though time), just as noted above for teachers. To exemplify this in the abstract, we can imagine an initial decision to learn the language which may be the learner's, although it could well be made by a ministry of education, a school board, a parent, or an employer. Once the initial decision to learn the language has been taken, further decisions ensure. The decisions are subsequent in terms of the chronological structure and subordinate (in that they occur within the overall event of 'learning the language' and function as a means to accomplish that decision) in terms of the logical structure. Subsequent and subordinate decisions can include, for example, the decision to take a course, the decision to move to a location where the language is spoken, the decision to socialize in that language, to initiate a conversation, to buy a grammar book, to read and memorize and so on. For example, a higher-level decision to socialize in the new language results, let's say, in a sub-decision to initiate a conversation with a speaker of the language, which leads to an embarrassing misunderstanding that the learner interprets as unfriendliness on the part of the target culture or incompetence on his or her own part, which leads to a re-evaluation of the decision to socialize and the subsequent decision to go to the library with a grammar book and study verb tenses.

Although these decisions are taken by the learner, they usually interact with decisions made by other individuals. In the case where a learner decides to take a course, for example, in effect hiring a teacher to take on some of the responsibility for some of the decisions related to the management of his of her language learning, a number of subsequent decisions will be made by the teacher. These include curricular decisions about how the course is organized and what learners will be engaged in at different points during a semester, decisions about a textbook to buy, decisions about exercises to do and phrases to memorize and to whom to answer questions in class.

In the classroom, the learner's decisions contribute to events that occur and, as with the teacher, the learner then interprets these events and evaluates them (in the context of all the other life decisions being made), and these interpretations and evaluations feed into subsequent decisions.

Negotiated cognition and decision-making

However, many decisions seen as the learner's – for example, to go to class, to put up a hand and ask or answer a question, even to pay attention – can be shown to be shared at micro levels through an intricate process of negotiation. Similarly, many decisions seen as the teacher's – for example, to use a particular activity in class, or to ask a particular student a question – can be shown to be shared at micro levels through this same process of negotiation. In other words, when we put these two aspects of decision-making side by side, we see that there is another set of *researchable relationships*: the relationship of teacher decisions and learner decisions, and the notion of negotiated and shared decision-making. In this perspective, decision-making is seen as socially constructed, with each side of the process playing a role in what possibilities are available for subsequent decisions made by the other. The purpose of the sections that follow is to sketch out some of this dynamic, theoretically and practically, in a very preliminary way.

Research on the negotiation of decision-making

In the work that Dick Allwright and I did together, we were interested in understanding how the negotiation of decision-making takes place, and what kinds of things are barriers to or constraints in the process of negotiation. We initially decided to investigate one specific phase of the decision-making process, that of planning. Using the model described above as a lens to look at observational and interview data from the teacher and learners of a course in academic English being taught at Carleton University, we attempted to get a sense of learner and teacher perspectives on their roles, and how these affected their decision-making.

Subsequently, out of this analysis, and out of both Dick's on-going concern about 'exploratory teaching', 'classroom life' and creating 'learning opportunities' for learners (Allwright, 1992; Allwright, 2006; Allwright and Bailey, 1991) and my emerging interest in the interaction of teacher and learner cognition (discussed in Woods, 1997, 1998, 2003), came an analysis of two areas of theoretical interest: *motivation* and *focus of attention*. Our research was focused on how responsibility is negotiated in each of these areas and how from a decision-making perspective they are related.

The data presented here was collected as part of an on-going research programme on learner and teacher interactive processes initially framed by Dick and myself. The initial data-collection stage draws from a number of university ESL courses – one credit EAP class, one academic writing class and one writing process component of an intensive non-credit ESL program – each of which was treated as a separate case study. This initial work was followed up by individual studies undertaken by graduate students in a course in Second Language Classroom Research in Carleton's Master's Program in Applied Language Studies (taught in its inception by Dick in 1991, and by myself many times since), and reported in the *Carleton Papers in Applied Language Studies* (1996, 1998). This chapter reports observational and interview data from the initial study, and in particular the initial case of the credit EAP class, labelled here as Case A. The conclusions drawn below, however, have emerged from the overall research programme.

The research methodology used for this study was inspired by ethnographic approaches and 'participant-based research'. The initial data collection for Case A included classroom observation, semi-structured teacher interviews (weekly over four weeks of the course), learner interviews (weekly over four weeks with eight learners), videotaped lessons (twice for three hours), stimulated retrospective commentary with learners (once each with two learners) and stimulated retrospective commentary with the teachers (twice). The loose structuring of the interviews is illustrated by the list of questions in the Appendix (p. 111). However, the ideas listed were not asked outright, but rather kept in mind by the interviewers as they elicited narrative recounting of 'episodes'. The analysis of the data involved examining the transcripts of the classes and interviews for recurring themes (tentatively taken from my previous work on teacher decision-making, but evolving in light of the new data), for relationships among themes (relationships sought included relationships of contextual synonymity and contextual contrast, relationships of inclusion and causality and temporal and collocational relationships), and for evaluative statements about 'success' or 'failure' in the learning–teaching process. This investigation assumed that events are interpreted rather than objective, and that researching interpretations of events can be only a collaborative process. As a consequence, the patterns in instructional interactions that emerged appear much more subtly structured than most discussions of teaching practices give credit for, and are illustrative of Allwright's 'directions'.

Planning: whose role is it?

Our initial questions about decision-making were framed in terms of the notion of 'planning'. The rationale was that neither in the teaching literature (for example, in the literature on tasks) nor in the language learning literature (for example, in the literature on learner strategies) was the *process* of planning investigated. Language teacher education programmes often have practical assignments around 'lesson planning', in which teachers must produce, for evaluation, a document which demonstrates that they *have* a structure for a language lesson that they will teach. However, the notion of a 'planning process' – in other words, what a teacher does on a cognitive level while developing a 'lesson plan' in the context of a course that they are actually teaching – has scarcely been broached in the language teaching literature (the education field has made a more thorough exploration of this concept). In one attempt to do this (Woods, 1996), I used teacher interview data to construct a descriptive process model of teacher planning, following the lead of research into the process of composing written texts undertaken in the 1970s and 1980s.

Meanwhile, the notion of 'learner planning' for the language classes in which they are participants has not been discussed at all in the literature. As noted in Woods (1997), learner planning has been examined in terms of strategies but as a decontextualized and taxonomous product rather than a process of decision-making. Within the model of decision-making described above, where decisions are dynamic, embedded and recursive, the term 'planning' denotes the forward-looking emphasis in the learner's decision-making cycle. And so, it was this question – 'how do learners plan?' – that sparked this research. More specifically, the investigation focused on 'role negotiation' in the planning process. We began by asking whose role is planning, and how do teacher and learner planning processes differ?

During the process of collecting data, an important methodological result emerged: that there are important differences between 'learner data' and 'teacher data', which reflect the different conceptions of roles. In the interviews, teacher turns were generally much longer than interviewer turns (which were generally prompts or questions). Teachers more often nominated topics, or reframed question to bring in another topic. In contrast, learner turns were much shorter, often equal to or shorter than the interviewer turns. Learners less often took initiative to nominate or reframe topics. There are a number of factors that are possibly relevant in accounting for these differences:

- First, the learner interviews were carried out in the L2 for the learners, while teacher interviews were carried out in L1 of the teachers, presumably allowing them to express themselves more easily.
- Second, learners are in more of a power differential *vis-à-vis* researchers than are teachers, they are younger and more reticent, and they are in a situation of being evaluated by the institution that the researchers may represent.

- Third, and most important for our research, learners do not actively invest in, think through and rationalize classroom activity in the way teachers do, and therefore have less to say about it.

These factors are important to take into account in evaluating conclusions stemming from such interview data, especially on the part of learners.

In the first class that we investigated (Case A), we attempted to locate the classroom within the set of plans and choices on the part of the participants that produced it. The situation that we were looking at was one where a group of (adult) learners and a teacher at a particular moment found themselves in the same classroom at the same time (schematized in Figure 5.1). We found a larger general picture in which both the teacher and learners had (more or less explicitly formulated) general overall 'plans' for their lives, in which one component was a plan for their careers. In this plan for both, there was a learning or training component (in which the focus was either the learning itself, or some kind of certification representing the learning). For the teacher, it included a career path that involved professional training and experience gained as a result of their teaching. In other words, the teachers had some preferences and made some choices about where to teach, about the institution and perhaps about the course for reasons of professional development. For learners, the learning or training component included

Levels of planning

Learner	Teacher
Life 'planning'	Life 'planning'
Career planning	Career planning
Language learning planning	Professional development plan
Programme choice to learn	Programme choice to teach

Course planning
Lesson planning
Activity planning
Transaction planning
Exchange planning
Move planning
Utterance planning
Phrasal/lexical planning
Articulatory planning

Figure 5.1   Levels of planning

language learning for personal or professional reasons. They made choices about where to learn (at home or abroad), about taking a course, about the institution and, to some extent, about the course and teacher (although there was a placement test for level, there was a choice as to which section of the course to register in). The amount of choice was often seen to be restricted by circumstances, in the case of both learners and of teachers, but that does not affect the basic finding that they had *goal-related* preferences, and that they tried to formulate and pursue plans in all these respects. The planning process mirrors and reflects the two structural dimensions (logical and chronological) of decision-making posited above; the hierarchical dimension is shown in Figure 5.1. Figure 5.1 assumes that the planning process at its extremes extends from 'life planning' to 'articulatory planning'. Although it may seem irrelevant to include the two extremes, the points I wish to emphasize are that life plans become interactive when two participants meet in a shared venture, and that there is a 'context for every tongue movement' (where even articulatory planning can be shared and negotiated – for example, in the case of the corrected pronunciation of a vowel in a technical term used in a student's major field of study).

It is at the level of the 'course' – and specifically in the first lessons of the course – that the teacher and learners meet in the classroom. Typically, there is an important difference when this happens. At the level at which they come together, the teacher is being paid to think of the learners' 'learning needs' while the learners are paying in one form or another to have their learning needs thought about. The usual construction of the classroom events (through teacher and learner roles and actions in structuring these events) is based on this assumption. It is theoretically possible for learners to continue to take the lead in making decisions at the more 'local' end of the hierarchy (planning classroom activities and having teachers acting as informants to fill in the appropriate aspects of the language to be learned). (This would be easier with one-on-one classes or very small classes where different learners' needs can be negotiated and synthesized.) In practice, however, this occurs rarely. In our data, as well, it was evident that by the time the learners got to the classroom, they seemed to feel that they had done enough decision-making. They (or their parents) had paid for the job to be taken over by a person acting in the role of an expert. They expected the teacher to have planned for them what was to happen in the classroom and outside the classroom (in terms of home-work) between meetings. Meanwhile the teacher seemed to feel a sense of responsibility and obligation (as well as power) to be the primary high-level decision-makers for the classroom, although at more local levels, the teacher made frequent attempts to engage the learners in active decision-making.

To this point in the planning process, the decisions had been made separately between learners and the teacher (although the teacher's decision-making process was strongly influenced by interactions with students in previous similar courses). However, at the event level of *course*, specifically in the first class, learners and teacher met and began to co-construct instructional events in light of their goals through a complex negotiation of planning activities. In the case studied here, the classroom was the primary focus for events from the course level down (although not all courses take place in classrooms, and not all activities from classrooms take place in classrooms). Yet classroom decision-making reflected these higher-level plans on both the learner side and the teacher side.

In theory, the learner can play a more or less active role in planning for classroom lessons and in the negotiation of classroom decisions. However, there can be different perceptions or expectations of this role by teachers and learners. These perceptions themselves become part of the negotiated process. Figure 5.2 indicates, theoretically, a potential for conflict in teacher and learner roles. In the upper left-hand quadrant, the teacher expects the learner to play a passive role in classroom decision-making (represented by $T = P$), and the learner also expects to play a passive role (represented by $L = P$). This symbolizes a traditional 'transmission of knowledge' classroom, where the teacher is the expert and the decision-maker, and the learners listen to and follow the teacher's instructions. The lower right-hand quadrant is where both teacher and

Teacher expects . . . Learner expects . . .	. . . the learner as a passive participant **(P)**	. . . the learner as an active participant **(A)**
. . . the learner as a passive participant **(P)**	$L = P$; $T = P$	$L = P$; $T = A$
. . . the learner as an active participant **(A)**	$L = A$; $T = P$	$L = A$; $T = A$

Figure 5.2   Teacher and learner roles in classroom decision-making

learner expect the learner to play an active role in co-constructing the classroom events (T = A and L = A). This would represent an 'autonomous learner' perspective where the learner takes initiative in making decisions about what will be done, and takes an active role in being responsible for contributing to the success of the classroom, as well as being creative and initiative-taking in deciding on and using his or her own strategies. The other two quadrants are where conflict typically occurs. In the upper right-hand quadrant, the teacher expects the learner to take an active role (T = A) while the learner expects to take a passive role (L = P). This is the example described in Woods (2003) where learners from traditional education systems meet teachers in classrooms which are structured according to principles of communicative language teaching, and face what has been termed 'pedagogical shock' by Soucy and Gray (1999) – the classroom aspect of culture shock. The lower left-hand quadrant represents the case where the learner has clear ideas about how he or she wants to proceed with learning the language, and wants to be very active in the process (L = A), but the teacher has a more traditional view about roles and decisions (T = P). My attempt to learn tap dancing in Harlem, described in Woods (1998) exemplifies this quadrant.

Because it is what normally occurs in classrooms, this traditional set of roles shown in the upper left-hand quadrant becomes the 'default setting' for planning. This 'script' for role participation will make it difficult for teachers who want students to be the managers of their own learning, and develop 'autonomy' in their learning, or for learners who want to take this role over. It makes it also difficult for teachers who want to share their own sense of being 'learning-teachers' in the classroom and sharing this experience, because they are being paid by the learners to be the experts and to be responsible for planning.

An analysis of the planning decisions made by learners and teachers in the data revealed the following characteristics (Figure 5.3). The

Characteristics of teacher planning	Characteristics of learner planning
– Elaborated (many 'levels')	– Unelaborated (few 'levels')
– Relatively explicit	– Relatively implicit
– Proactive	– Reactive (expectancy based)
– Tentative	– 'Wait and see'
– Reliance on 'experienced structures'	– Based on 'experienced structures'
– Top-down and bottom-up	
– Constraints and resources	

Figure 5.3   Characteristics of teacher/learner planning

characteristics noted on the left-hand side of Figure 5.3 relate to the teacher, and also are consistent with Woods' (1996) discussion of the teachers' planning processes.

In the interviews with learners, there were some notable specific characteristics that emerged about learner planning. In terms of 'pre-course planning', the learners interviewed maintained a general policy of 'wait and see'. There was no mention in the interview data of a specific conscious plan for a course. Some learners had advance access to other students who had done the course previously, and had information about it and about the teachers (although it seemed more by chance than a deliberate strategy). Learners with no access did not seem to have done anything to get access. Some prepared for learning English in general by choosing to live with a homestay family, or by deliberately getting hold of reading material in English to warm up with. But most prepared only by getting to the first class with pen and paper. There was a sense that they have general expectations (not well articulated) about the course. But there was initially no sense that the students are in a position to contribute to success or failure of a course, let alone to the its design, shape or priorities.

In terms of planning for individual lessons, the 'wait and see' policy continued to operate, as indicated in the following excerpt taken from a learner interview in Case *A*:

> **Dick:** ... *I'm interested in what you do when you have those questions or problems when you're doing the homework.*
> **Lila:** *First I try to understand by myself. If I can't then I wait to the lesson.*
> **Dick:** *If you wait to the lesson then what can you do to make sure you get an answer?*
> **Lila:** *I make sure I pay attention about the topic when the teacher mentions. If she didn't mention I would ask her after class.*

There was a general resistance to taking over the overall planning initiative related to several factors, including:

1. Lack of knowledge and ability:

> **Dick:** ... *she's teaching a course which involves asking you to make plans about what you want to learn. So she must be interested in what you want out of it.*
> **Aisa:** *Right. But I guess other problem is, I don't really know what to do with my skills. How can I improve my writing skills. I have no idea what is the best way to improve my writing skills*

2. Lack of knowledge of teacher's plan:

> **Dick:** *Before today's lesson did you do anything to get ready for it?*
> **Lili:** *I did last class homework only. I don't know what we are doing this class, in this class. So I just do homework.*

and

> **Dick:** *Do you know what will happen in the next lesson?*
> **Aisa:** *Learn some reading strategies that help you.*
> **Dick:** *Do you think you'll get that?*
> **Aisa:** *Next time?*
> **Dick:** *Next time.*
> **Aisa:** *Do I think I will?*
> **Dick:** *Yeah.*
> **Aisa:** *Yes and no.*
> **Dick:** *Well what does it depend on.*
> **Aisa:** *Well, I don't know. Maybe something to do with my attitude or my strategies. What's she gonna do? I'm confused.*

During the lessons themselves, there was a general feeling that it was the job of the teacher to make classroom decisions. This seemed to be related to:

1. The educational system of origin of the students:

> **Aisa:** *But this is not our way. I got used to in Japan, we're just sitting...students are supposed to sit and keep quiet and do their work. They're not supposed to argue with the teacher or discuss what they're gonna teach.*

2. An awareness of other learners' differing agendas:

> **Dick:** *Could you ask during the class?*
> **Lila:** *Usually I ask after class, because I think maybe it's my individual problem.*

3. Shyness:

> **Dick:** *Are there other reasons?*
> **Lila:** *Maybe, well, too shy to speak up.*

However, there are exceptions to this generalization that are important to note. One of the learners interviewed in Case *A*, a graduate student from Iran, had very well-articulated views about his language learning, not just in terms of autonomous strategies and their relationship to his 'life plans', but also in terms of his classroom planning process and his contribution to the learning of others in the class. This example illustrates the complexity of the negotiation with regard to the concept of planning. One of the highest-order goals of the teacher in this course was to help the learners become autonomous learners, and to take a major role in the shaping of the course. She did this by not imposing a strict set of materials (for example, a textbook) for the course. Instead, she attempted to draw out from the students their interests and academic needs to inform her curricular choices. As a consequence, the course was intended to evolve organically, based on her carefully planned and very intricate choices of activities, in response to what students indicated was important to them. Ironically, and surprisingly, it was precisely this set of decisions on the part of the teacher that made it difficult for this student to exercise his own choices. He indicated, in terms of his planning procedures for classroom activity, that he preferred to have a textbook and a clearly laid out curriculum that would allow him to prepare for future lessons and to design his own learning plan. In this circumstance, contrary to the goals of the teacher, he had to become more passive than he would have liked in terms of his planning. If, instead, she had taken choices away from him on one level (by using a pre-planned curriculum with a course textbook), it might have allowed him more choice on another level – to play an active role in the classroom interactions that made up the course. On the other hand, however, it might also be that once he got used to the fact that he was able to play the role of a contributor on a much higher level, co-creating the course with the teacher, his ability to actively plan and direct his learning might be enhanced. This example illustrates the importance of the theoretical notion of *hierarchy* and *levels* in the event structure in the analysis of classroom teaching/learning, and is consistent with Allwright's direction 2, 'From simplicity to complexity'.

The social construction of the motivation to notice

The concept of motivation in language learning has for the most part been treated as an isolatable, decontextualized and independently researchable concept. In the research literature, it has traditionally been treated as a relatively static trait inherent in the learner (as noted by Crookes and Schmidt, 1991; Dörnyei, 2001; Oxford, 1996; and others).

Research has generally attempted to categorize motivation into distinct types and then to correlate the presence of each category with success in language learning. More recent discussions and critiques of motivation theory have argued that motivation has a dynamic dimension that must be part of the theory. Dörnyei (2001), for example, has argued that there are different types and levels of motivation, and that teachers can affect certain of these levels.

In a similar vein, the concept of attention, or 'noticing' (and its related concept, 'focus on form') has become a researchable concept, one that is also treated as an important factor in acquisition (Schmidt, 1993, 1995). Crookes and Schmidt (1991) have argued that motivation and attention are related, although the nature of the relationship has not been explored in any depth.

The perspective that we wanted to take in carrying out this research acknowledges the complexity that underlies 'focus on form' as a process (also noted by Tomlin and Villa, 1994; and others) and the potential relationship of motivation to focus of attention. Our interest was with the roles of teacher and learner with respect to these areas, and how these roles are negotiated. An examination of the concept of *attending* as a process, through the lens of event structuring and negotiated decision-making, revealed a number of noteworthy relationships:

1. When we take into account the hierarchical nature of classroom events, we note that there is a relationship between 'attendance' (the decision to be physically present at the higher-level event of the lesson) and 'attending' (being mentally present for an activity or exchange during the lesson). We can see that deciding to 'attend' or 'not attend' on higher levels of event structure can pre-empt or provide the opportunity for lower-level decisions about whether or not to 'attend'. In other words, you cannot 'decide' to pay attention (to attend at a *local level*) in class if you have decided not to go to class (attend at a *super-ordinate level*).

2. There is also a relationship of *competition* for 'attention' on different levels. An attempt to put the focus of attention on more local levels of the event structure (such as grammatical structure of utterances and sentences, which is normally what is referred to by the terms 'focus on form' and 'noticing') can result in less attention to more global levels of structure (for example rhetorical organization of a text, or the overall communicative characteristics of an oral presentation). Similarly, placing a focus on these more global levels (on the part of the teacher) can result in the perception (on the part of the

student) that local levels (correction of grammatical errors) are being neglected.

3. The concept of 'attending' (both the physical and mental aspects) is intimately related to *motivation*. Decision-making about 'attending' is in essence decision-making related to motivational factors. Participants in the process can consider the source of motivation the responsibility of the teacher or of the learner. The motivation for 'attending' can be seen as intrinsic (created by the learner), extrinsic (created by the teacher); and, in the latter case, it can be an external appeal (by the teacher) to intrinsic factors (learner's interest), or it can be an external appeal to extrinsic factors (promise of reward, threat of punishment, or both).

4. Given the above three sets of relationships, we become aware of a potentially complex *negotiation of responsibility for decision-making* related to the learner's motivation to 'attend'. Figure 5.4 schematizes these relationships and roles.

In the teacher data, we found that decisions related to the learner's attending class (and the learner's punctuality) appeared as high-level explicit decisions in the teacher's *global course structuring* (in the course in question, the teacher kept a record of attendance and deducted marks for absence), and as well as more locally – for example, through comments made in classroom interactions. Ultimately, however, learners still made their own decisions to attend class and to be on time. Yet they frequently attributed responsibility to the teacher for their

Level	'Attending'	Responsibility
Course	Register	Usually learner
Lesson	Attend	Teacher or learner
Activity	Participate	Teacher or learner
Transaction	Engage	Teacher or learner
Exchange	Engage	Teacher or learner
Move	Initiate/respond	Teacher or learner
Utterance	Understand	Teacher or learner
Phrase/Word	Focus	Teacher or learner
Articulation	Focus	Teacher or learner

Figure 5.4 Decision-making related to the learner's motivation to 'attend'

actions. One learner (who was often late) stated that it was the teacher's responsibility to close the classroom door and not let latecomers join the class after the official 8.35 starting time, arguing that this would compel him to be on time.

Teacher decision related to the learner's participation in activities and engagement in exchanges were also made through global course structuring: the teacher made a number of explicit higher-level decisions related to the choice of course content, such choosing a wide range of themes, including themes about academic skills (related to the learners' purposes for taking the course) and allowing learners input into choices of themes and topics. At more local levels of event structuring, the teacher attempted to encourage engagement at the level of activity through the structuring of the group activities, and this was reflected in the procedural details of the group activity.

The learners also broached the issue of engagement and attention in class (as well as attendance), articulating it, negatively, with the term 'boredom'. Interestingly, the issue was frequently attributed to the (teacher's) choice of topics and themes. However, at the same time, the learners assumed that it was not their job to take an active role in negotiating themes, and sometimes were taken aback at this prospect when it was presented to them by the teacher.

From the learners' perspective, the responsibility for lack of engagement and attention was also placed on the teacher's structuring of individual activities:

The teacher give [sic] *us too much time. We always finish quickly and then have the same boring conversation.*

Sometimes, students' perceptions about their lack of engagement in the interactions during the activity were related to characteristics of the group:

The worst is when your partners are shy and don't speak.

And:

In Asian culture, silence is valued. It doesn't work in group work.

And:

He always interrupt and never listen [sic]. It makes me not interested.

Negotiation of attention to learner errors

In the literature on language teaching, the notion of attention is primarily related to 'focus on form', where a learner's acquisition is said to be enhanced by 'noticing' particular formal elements of the language while involved in using language for meaningful communicative purposes. One of the ways in which a learner's attention is focused on form is through error correction (Long and Robinson, 1998). However, typically 'error correction' is treated as a *concept* – usually decontextualized – rather than as a *process* (as noted by Woods, 1989). Arguments related to correction are generally framed as binary issues:

- Is correction necessary?
- Is correction helpful?
- Is correction a hindrance?

However, from the perspective of a socially negotiated structuring of classroom events, these questions over-simplify the issue. A learner's attention can be directed to a certain level of activity (whether related to a formal element or not), without it being explicitly pointed out, via a complex set of structured and negotiated activities, all of which can lead to attendance, engagement, attention and finally focus. For example, in Case *A*, it was clear that decisions on the part of the teacher related to local (grammatical) levels of attention were made in terms of global course structuring (the setting and articulating of course goals) and by what one teacher has called 'feedforward' – that is, the development of course units which prepare the learners in advance for handling different types of feedback (Librande, 2005).

Teacher feedback in the form of error correction relates to a teacher's indication to a student that a form the student has produced is non-targetlike. However, teachers also provide feedback in terms of appropriateness according to conventions of discourse within larger events in the target culture – in other words, effectiveness in terms of discourse goals. In this case, as noted above, there can be competition over where the learner is to place her or his attention.

In Case *A*, the teacher's feedback was usually intended to have the students focus their attention less on formal elements of grammar, and more on the rhetorical structure of the written academic texts that the students were producing. In the interview, the teacher revealed that her decision-making process was affected by two assumptions (both being important elements of her belief, assumptions and knowledge (BAK) about classroom language development). The first was that improvement comes primarily from extensive language use (both reception and production), which is hindered by *excessive attention to errors*. The second was that conscious knowledge of what these errors are has little effect on *correctness in performance*. These beliefs were based on both her interpretation of research questioning the effectiveness of correction, and her experience of learners' failure to use correction subsequently to improve their production.

The learners, on the other hand, expected to experience classroom events that were familiar to them from their previous courses, where the role of the teacher had been to draw their attention to their errors at a grammatical level. This expectation related to their own beliefs, assumptions and knowledge (BAK) about their language learning, which could be paraphrased as 'I need to (consciously) know about my mistakes in order to improve'. This assumption seemed to stem from their previous experiences with teachers and courses in which this practice was the norm, and from anecdotes they had heard from friends who claimed they had succeeded due to correction. As a result, there seemed to be a lack of trust in the teacher's attempts to have them experiment with what for them were new methods of learning. This perception on the part of learners led to a range of decisions and actions:

1. The most frequent response was to complain to friends (and the interviewers), but take no further action
2. On several occasions, the response was to make a more or less explicit request to the teacher to plan this type of corrective 'event' into the teaching
3. In one case, the response was to switch to another programme where this type of exchange was perceived to occur more frequently.

The teacher indicated that she was aware of this range of responses, not just from this course, but from a set of beliefs which had evolved over time through her previously 'experienced structures'

(Woods, 1996). Her resulting attempts to structure the classroom events included:

1. Giving a short lecture explaining the rationale for her approach to correction
2. Providing a 'pre-emptive' rationale for the type of classroom interactions that made up the program
3. Providing a structure whereby the learner became involved in taking responsibility for tracking and correcting their own errors.

For a detailed example of the negotiated evolution of a such strategies, see Woods (2003), which discusses a teacher's 'Krashen Unit', a thematic unit on Second Language Acquisition developed for her ESL students, including readings and a lecture explaining Krashen's theory of 'learning' and 'acquisition'. Her goal in creating this unit was to provide the reasoning for her approach to classroom procedures, as well as to expose her students to strategies consistent with this approach. In this case, the teacher is interpreting the teaching task with regard to error correction not as a focus on students' grammar, but rather about their *taking over responsibility for their own correction*. What is being negotiated between teacher and learners is not techniques: it is beliefs, and roles and responsibilities. In a sense, each is trying to negotiate change in the other, in light of the potential resources and constraints for doing this on different levels of the shared management of language learning.

Conclusion

The implications of examining classroom language learning processes through a constructivist lens can be framed in terms of Allwright's 'six promising directions'. I am going to use four of these to comment on the above models and examples:

1. *From prescription to description to understanding.* This direction implies a movement from a 'method orientation' in research into language teaching and learning (prescription) to a 'taxonomic orientation' (description), to an 'understanding orientation'. The above discussion makes clear the reasons why the field has evolved in a direction away from a 'method' and 'taxonomy' orientation. When we examine the interactions that take place in the management of

language learning, we can see that the most that a method can do is provide a starting point. The moment that teacher and learners step beyond this starting point, they engage in a reality which is not predictable from the method, nor from a set of abstract categories of instructional actions. It is a deeper situated reflective 'understanding' of the interactivity that plays the crucial role in decision-making.

2. *From simplicity to complexity.*
3. *From commonality to idiosyncracy.* These two directions imply an increasing acceptance of and appreciation for the situatedness of language learning. When we put an initial focus on the perceived individual realities and on dynamic interactive processes, rather than seeking an abstract concept of the universal, we are embracing complexity and idiosyncracy.
4. *From teaching and learning as 'work' to teaching and learning as 'life'.* This direction implies that local strategic action is typically framed in the light of larger life plans, and interpreted in terms of issues of personal beliefs about, identity with and investment in these plans. The framework and examples above demonstrate a way of conceiving of these relationships and developing new understandings of them. These three directions are closely related to the issue of 'understanding' noted above, and are quintessentially constructivist.

Appendix

Questions to teacher, as drafted for use on 16. 1. 91

1. What course are we talking about – in administrative terms – in other terms (e.g. has the course a history?)
2. Have you taught it before?
3. What were your thoughts on embarking upon this course?
4. How have you prepared for the course?
5. What have you planned, briefly?
6. What do you hope to get out of it yourself?
7. What do you hope the learners will get out of it?
8. What do you think they hope to get out of it?
9. Are there any learners with particularly clear expectations?
10. If a mismatch, what do you hope to result?
11. What are your plans for the next lesson?

Possible questions (or question topics) for use with learners

1. What course are we talking about? Tell me about the course, in general terms.
2. Have you taken this sort of course before?
3. What were your thoughts when you first knew you were going to take this course? (Were you pleased, sad, angry?)
4. How did you prepare for this course? (Did you do anything to make sure you were ready for the first class?)
5. What did you plan, briefly? (Did you think about what you wanted to get from the course? Did you think about how you were going to learn most effectively, or how you were going to get the most from the teacher, or from your fellow students?)
6. What do you hope to get out of it, personally?
7. What do you think your teacher hopes you will get out of it?
8. If your answers to 6 and 7 are not the same, what do you think will result?
9. What do you think the rest of the class want to get out of the course?
10. What do you think the teacher wants to get out of the course, personally?
11. What did you get from the last lesson?
12. What do you plan to get from the next lesson?

Note

* This chapter reports on the evolution of interpretations of data initially collected and analysed by Dick Allwright and Devon Woods in the winter term of 1991 when Dick was a visiting professor in the School of Linguistics and Applied Language Studies at Carleton University. Portions of this work were presented by Dick at TESOL Vancouver in 1992 and by Devon at RELC Singapore in 1997, JALT Hamamatsu in 1997, SLRF Hawai'i in 1998 and AAAL Seattle in 1998.

References

Allwright, D. 1981. What do we want teaching materials for? *ELT Journal* 36: 5–18.

Allwright, D. 1984. Why don't learners learn what teachers teach? The interaction hypothesis. In: *Language learning in formal and informal contexts*, eds D.M. Singleton and D.G. Little, 3–18. Dublin: BAAL/IRAL.

Allwright, D. 1992. Interaction in the classroom: social problems and pedagogic possibilities. In: Proceedings of the International Symposium of Language Teaching and Learning, 3: *Language teaching in today's world*, 32–53. Paris: Hachette.

Allwright, D. 2005. From teaching points to learning opportunities and beyond. *TESOL Quarterly* 39: 9–31.

Allwright, D. 2006. Six promising directions in Applied Linguistics. In: *Understanding the language classroom*, eds S. Gieve and I.K. Miller. London: Palgrave Macmillan, Chapter 1 in this volume.

Allwright, D. and K.M. Bailey 1991. *Focus on the language classroom.* Cambridge: Cambridge University Press.

Benson, P. 2001. *Teaching and researching learner autonomy in language learning.* London: Longman.

Borg, S. 2003. Teacher cognition in language teaching: a review of research on what teachers think, know, believe and do. *Language teaching* 36: 81–109.

Crookes, G. and R. Schmidt 1991. Motivation: reopening the research agenda. *Language Learning* 41: 469–512.

de Mey, M. 1977. The cognitive viewpoint: its development and scope. In: *CC77: International workshop on the cognitive viewpoint*, eds M. de Mey, R. Pixton, M. Poriau and F. Vandamme. Ghent: University of Ghent.

Dörnyei, Z. 2001. *Teaching and researching motivation.* London: Longman.

Librande, L. 2005. Feed-forward: scaffolding student writing. Unpublished paper for LALS 5204, Carleton University, Ottawa, Ontario.

Long, M. and P. Robinson 1998. Focus on form: theory, practice and research. In: *Focus on form in classroom second language acquisition*, eds C. Doughty and J. Williams, 15–41. Cambridge: Cambridge University Press.

O'Malley, M.J. and A. Chamot 1990. *Learning strategies in second language acquisition.* Cambridge: Cambridge University Press.

Oxford, R. 1996. New pathways of language learning motivation. In: *Language learning motivation: pathways to the new century*, ed. R. Oxford, 1–8. Honolulu: University of Hawai'i.

Riley, P. 1988. The ethnography of autonomy. In: *Individualization and autonomy in language learning*, eds A. Brookes and P. Grundy, 12–34. London: British Council.

Schmidt, R. 1993. Awareness and second language acquisition. *Annual Review of Applied Linguistics* 13: 206–26.

Schmidt, R. 1995. Consciousness and foreign language learning: a tutorial on the role of attention in foreign language learning. In: *Attention and awareness in foreign language learning*, ed. R. Schmidt, 1–63. Honolulu: University of Hawai'i.

Soucy, A. and A. Gray 1999. That's no way to teach a language. Paper presented at *Trends Conference*, Carleton University, Ottawa, Ontario.

Tomlin, R. and V. Villa 1994. Attention in cognitive science and second language acquisition. *Studies in Second Language Acquisition* 16: 183–203.

Wenden, A. and J. Rubin, eds 1987. *Learning strategies in language learning.* New Jersey: Prentice Hall.

Woods, D. 1989. Error correction and the improvement of language form. *TESL Canada Journal* 6: 60–72.

Woods, D. 1996. *Teacher cognition in language teaching.* Cambridge: Cambridge University Press.

Woods, D. 1997. Decision-making in language learning: a lens for examining learner strategies. Conference Feature Article. *JALT 97: The Language Teacher* 21, 10: 67–75, 115.

Woods, D. 1998. What do we mean when we say 'teaching'? *JALT 97: Trends and Transitions*, 1–20.

Woods, D. 2003. The social construction of beliefs in the language classroom. In: *New approaches to research on beliefs about SLA*, eds P. Kalaja and A. Barcelos, 201–29. Amsterdam: Kluwer.

6
Darwin and the Large Class*

Hywel Coleman

Introduction

This chapter takes the phenomenon of the 'large class' as a context in which to explore some of the issues raised by Dick Allwright in Chapter 1 in this volume (Allwright, 2006). The large class has often been perceived as a mundane problem which ought to lend itself to straight-forward technical solutions. However, the fact that such 'solutions' remain elusive indicates that this is an over-simplistic approach to the phenomenon. Efforts to understand the large-class phenomenon are under way, but these may be founded on unrealistic presuppositions regarding pedagogical efficiency. Alternatively, in our endeavour to make sense of the large class, a Darwinian metaphor may be more useful. This metaphor enables us to see that an individual classroom event, compared to other such events, possesses the characteristics of both *commonality* and *idiosyncrasy* (Allwright, 2006, direction 3). The Darwinian perspective also reveals that each classroom event represents the best available 'local adaptation' for the environmental niche in which it occurs.

Class size

The number of learners reported in language learning classes ranges from up to sixty in primary schools in Malaysia (Hashim, 1997: 121), sixty-two in state secondary schools in Pakistan (Shamim, 1993: 127), 309 in *yobiko* (cram schools for university entrance) in Japan (LoCastro, 1989: 9–10), 'about 500' in a university in Kenya (Mebo, 1995: 154), 5,000 at an open-access university in Thailand (Itzen, 1986: 27) and even 'up to 40,000' in public classes for young people in China (Jones, 1999: 24).

In the light of these figures, agreeing on a definition of 'large' becomes impossible.

Not only does actual class size vary. Extensive research since the late 1980s has demonstrated that teachers' *perceptions* of the point at which a class becomes large also vary. For instance, LoCastro (1989: 5) reported that a group of English teachers (both secondary and tertiary) in Japan claimed that they were beginning to experience problems because classes were getting too large when there were thirty-nine students (on average) in a class. However Coleman (1989a: 5) noted that university teachers of English in Nigeria felt that they did not begin to experience difficulties caused by excessive class size until there were fifty-two or more students in the class.

There appears to be some sort of relationship between the class sizes which teachers have experienced and their beliefs about whether certain numbers of learners can be considered to be 'large' or not. At first it was suggested that 'the larger a teacher's largest class is, the more tolerant of large classes that teacher is likely to be' (Coleman 1989a: 6). However, in a later though as yet unpublished study by Coleman and Parikesit it is argued that the experience–perception relationship is actually much more complex than this. There is probably no direct correlation between experience of class size and perceptions of class size. In fact it is more likely to be the case that the experience–perception relationship possesses similarities with the relationship which economists are beginning to explore between an individual's economic status and his or her sense of well-being (for example, Frank, 2000, Veenhoven et al., 1993). Just as increasing an individual's economic status does not provide a guarantee that that individual will enjoy increased happiness, so decreasing a teacher's class size does not guarantee that the teacher will believe their class to be 'small'. Nor does reducing class size ensure that the teacher will be more contented with their teaching than previously, except possibly in the very short term.

While teachers' perceptions of class size have been well researched, learners' views have received much less attention. Those studies which have looked at this question (an example being Embi, 1997) suggest that learners are rather less conscious of class size than are their teachers.

Prescriptivism and the large class

'Large' classes are frequently reported by teachers to be problematic (for example Carver, 1988; McLeod, 1989; Naidu, 1992; Sarangi, 1989; Wu, 1993). But, as we saw above, if teachers' experiences of class sizes vary considerably, and if there is no consensus as to what the parameters of a 'large' class are, it becomes almost impossible to think of 'large classes' as a homogeneous phenomenon.[1]

Despite this complexity, there has never been a shortage of suggestions for dealing with 'large classes'. My own bibliography on class size (see www.hywelcoleman.com) contains hundreds of offerings ranging from short articles in teachers' newsletters to book-length compendia of recommended 'solutions'. These suggestions tend to fall into three groups:

(a) Many have emerged from very specific large-class contexts and so they constitute accounts of *successful techniques* which individual teachers have come across, largely by chance.
(b) Other suggestions have been developed in contexts whose parameters are unspecified. Their authors simply assert that they are *appropriate* for use in 'large classes'.
(c) Yet others have been developed for contexts in which class size appears to be relatively modest, yet they are promoted as being *appropriate* for use in 'large classes' (despite the difficulty of achieving any agreement over the definition of this term).

Recommendations in category (a) are for the most part practitioners' reports, while those in categories (b) and (c) come largely from non-practitioners. This is a distinction to which we will return later in this discussion.

Few of these recommendations – even those in category (a) – are based on analysis of the characteristics and constraints of the contexts to which the label 'large' is being applied. Nor do they encourage teachers to undertake such analysis. All they do is offer solutions with either an unstated or an explicit assumption of universal applicability. In consequence, proposals that emerge from one (insufficiently described) 'large-class' context are of doubtful relevance for other (perhaps equally inadequately analysed) 'large-class' contexts. The only thing that two learning–teaching contexts have in common may be the fact that their respective teachers perceive that they have 'large' numbers of learners in their classes.

Borrowing techniques from one 'large-class' context and applying them to another 'large class' often leads to disappointment for the borrowing teacher. Indeed, unsuccessful attempts to implement recommendations borrowed from an inherently different large-class context may induce feelings of inadequacy and guilt in the borrowing teacher (Coleman, 1997).

What we have been discussing, then, is an approach in which the large class – regardless of context – is viewed primarily as a 'problem' which ought to be susceptible to immediate technical solutions. This represents an example of the *prescriptive* approach which Allwright (2006, direction 1) traces back to the 1950s and 1960s. The fact that the 'solutions' which are offered are generally unsatisfactory when applied in other contexts indicates how simplistic this approach is.

'Understanding' and 'improving' large classes

As we have seen, the class size literature has been heavily concerned with offering techniques as solutions to problems.[2] However, the large-class phenomenon has also been subjected to some attempts at *description* and *understanding* in Allwright's sense (2006, direction 1). One example is Shamim's careful analysis of teacher–learner interaction and classroom processes in large English classes in secondary schools in Karachi, Pakistan (Shamim, 1993).

However, writers – the present author included – have sometimes found it difficult to maintain a pure 'describe and understand' approach, and their analyses of large-class contexts have tended to be directed towards pedagogical improvement. Instances include a proposal to convert the 'teaching spectacles' of large university English classes in Indonesia into 'learning festivals' (Coleman, 1987), the use of a modified action research approach to a class of 115 learners in a junior college in India (Coleman, 1995) and an argument for taking into account the 'phenomenology of change' as part of a curriculum change project in universities in Egypt where classes have up to 450 students (Holliday, 1996).

These and similar efforts can therefore be thought of as examples of an 'appropriate methodology' or 'understand and improve' approach. They have two stages: analysis of a specific *context*, followed by recommendations for the introduction of *contextually sensitive change*. But it is interesting to note that even those of us who have argued in favour of such an analytic context-sensitive methodology have still had doubts about what we have been doing. So Coleman (1996: 81) worries that: 'Although our attempts at reform may be...well intentioned, our missionary zeal...may actually have unforeseen repercussions elsewhere in the academic ecosystem.'

Meanwhile Shamim warns that it is 'imperative that teacher educators take into account...the sociocultural background of both the teachers and the learners before recommending "solutions"' (1996: 143).

It is at this point that we remember Allwright's observation (2006) that achieving understanding of classroom life has value in its own terms without it necessarily having to contribute to *efficiency* – or, indeed, to change of any sort.

The problem we face is that underlying many discussions of 'large' classes – and of other types of class as well – there lies the unquestioned assumption that 'teaching' and 'learning' constitute the prime objectives of the participants in the classroom event. In fact, analyses of 'large' classes, especially in state educational institutions, are beginning to suggest that this may be an unwarranted assumption, as we shall see below.

What we require, then, in order to facilitate our understanding of classrooms and what happens in them, is a new way of *looking*. The purpose of this chapter is to propose that a Darwinian approach or metaphor may be useful. But first it is important to clarify what Darwinism is *not*.

What Darwinism is *not*

In despair, Gould (1978: 11) asks, 'Why has Darwin been so hard to grasp?' The theory that the history of the Earth is characterised by a process of gradual evolution (rather than providential creation) came to be widely accepted within the lifetimes of Darwin and his contemporary, Alfred Russel Wallace. Yet, according to Gould, Darwin's theory of natural selection is still frequently misquoted and misinterpreted.

It may come as some surprise to learn that Darwin himself rarely employed the term 'evolution'. His preferred formulation was 'descent with modification' since his prime objective was to explain how variation in nature came about. He had little interest in 'progress', saying, 'It would be absurd to talk of one animal being higher than another' (de Beer, 1960: Part I: 50; quoted by Howard, 1982: 81–2). Darwin consequently rejected the term 'evolution' 'because he was uncomfortable with the notion of inevitable progress inherent in its vernacular meaning' (Gould, 1978: 36).

In fact the terms 'evolution' and 'survival of the fittest' were introduced by Herbert Spencer, another of Darwin's contemporaries. Following Spencer, some of the most inaccurate and inappropriate interpretations of Darwin's thinking began to take hold. In particular, the concept of 'Social Darwinism' started to emerge. According to Bullock and Trombley, this is

the application of the concept of *evolution* to the historical development of human societies which lays particular emphasis on 'the struggle for existence' and 'the survival of the fittest'. Though not rooted in

Darwinism...such theories...provided a pseudo-biological justification for...imperialism and war. (1999: 800, emphasis in the original)

I want to emphasise, then, that in this discussion I am not using the term 'Darwinism' in this Social Darwinist way. 'Darwinism' is not employed here with any implication of progress, of improvement, of social development, of competition or of 'survival of the fittest'. So, in that case, what does Darwinism mean?

What Darwinism *is*

The theory of natural selection was first published in the jointly authored paper by Darwin and Wallace, 'On the tendency of species to form varieties' (1858). The theory was then developed further in Darwin's two major works, *On the origin of species* (1859) and *The descent of man* (1871) and in the contemporaneous work of Wallace (for example, *Contributions to the theory of natural selection*, 1871). The theory derives from observation of three phenomena:

- The *continuity of species* (that is horses always beget horses, never cats)
- *Variability within species* (that is, no two individuals are identical, despite being members of the same species)
- The *occurrence of occasional random mutations within species*.

Wallace summarises this as follows:

The grand feature in the multiplication of organic life is that of close general resemblance, combined with more or less individual variation. The child resembles its parents or ancestors more or less closely in all its peculiarities, deformities, or beauties; it resembles them in general more than it does any other individuals; yet children of the same parents are not all alike, and it often happens that they differ very considerably from their parents and from each other. This is equally true of man, of all animals, and of all plants. (Wallace, 1864: 160)

Mutations – which Darwin called 'modifications' and which Wallace termed 'variations' – occur rarely and even when they do occur the majority are either benign or disadvantageous. But just occasionally a mutation may occur in an individual in a particular environmental niche where it gives its owner a particular advantage. If this mutation is then inherited by the descendants of the first individual – and if further similar mutations occur in succeeding generations – then eventually we will see the emergence of a new species which is more specialised and better suited for this particular context. Gayon emphasises the gradualness with which evolutionary change occurs:

> In those rare cases where mutations chanced to be advantageous, natural selection was the only process that could guarantee their diffusion through the population...natural selection [is] a process that acts on *infinitesimally small differences*, producing a *gradual* trans-formation of species. (Gayon, 2003: 251, emphases in the original)

The essence of the theory of natural selection, then, is that organisms adapt to their local environments as those environments change, and this is the explanation for the variability of the natural world. As Gould (1978: 13) explains, 'evolution has no direction; it does not lead inevitably to higher things. Organisms become better adapted to their local environments, and that is all.' He adds:

> Natural selection is a theory of *local* adaptation to changing environments. It proposes no perfecting principles, no guarantee of general improvement...To Darwin, improved meant only 'better designed for an immediate, local environment'. Local environments change constantly: they get colder or hotter, wetter or drier, more grassy or more forested. Evolution by natural selection is no more than a tracking of these changing environments by differential preservation of organisms better designed to live in them. (Gould, 1978: 44–5, emphasis in the original)

Thus the very frequently misinterpreted concept 'survival of the fittest', from a Darwinian perspective, relates to the fact that it is those individuals – and ultimately those species – which are best adapted or best fitted to particular environmental niches which are likely to thrive in those niches. And so it is that polar bears are best fitted for survival in the Arctic, unlike giraffes, coconut trees and scorpions (which have their own niches elsewhere).

Core elements of a Darwinian approach for understanding large classes

So how can a Darwinian perspective be applied to the large-class phenomenon (or, for that matter, to any classroom)? We noted above that the theory of natural selection takes three phenomena as its starting point: the stability of species, variability within species and the occurrence of occasional random mutations or 'modifications' within species. Thereafter, the theory argues that species best adapted for specific contexts are most likely to survive in those contexts. Let us explore these elements one by one in relation to what happens in classrooms.

Stability of species

Just as a dog never gives birth to a dolphin, so the classes taught by Teacher X in a particular context with particular learners are similar to previous classes taught by the same teacher in the same context with the same learners, yet these classes are distinctly and recognisably different from those taught by Teacher Y in a different context with different learners. In other words, we can think of Teacher X's lessons in context X with learning group X as constituting one 'species' while those taught by Teacher Y in context Y with learning group Y constitute a separate species (though the two species may be related to each other and may even share certain characteristics).

Variability within species

No two individual members of the same species are identical. Similarly, no two lessons taught by Teacher X, even in the same context and with the same learners, will ever be absolutely identical to each other. Every single classroom event is a unique individual case, even though it will have many genetic similarities with all of its 'ancestors' which have been taught by Teacher X in context X and with learning group X on previous occasions. There may also be some similarities with events taught in neighbouring classroom contexts by different teachers. But as the distance between two different teaching contexts widens so the likelihood is that the two species of classroom event found in them will show less and less resemblance to each other.

Already, then, we can begin to appreciate why it is that the individual classroom event possesses the characteristics of both *commonality* and *idiosyncrasy* which Allwright (2006) identifies (direction 3). In fact, stability and variability in Darwinian theory exactly match Allwright's commonality and idiosyncrasy.

Mutations or modifications within species

From time to time Teacher X may deliberately or inadvertently introduce an innovation into his or her management of the classroom event. Or circumstances beyond the teacher's control (a power cut, the lack of availability of a book, external disturbance, etc.) may lead to change in the usual pattern of the event. Or the learners may unexpectedly influence the event (sudden enthusiasm for a particular issue, unpredicted requests for clarification of a problem).

Some of these innovations or 'mutations' will be benign; that is to say the modification may have no particular advantages or disadvantages in that context. Such innovations may or may not continue to make occasional appearances in future classroom events; they confer no especial benefits but at the same time they bring with them no negative consequences. Other modifications may have negative consequences. They may, for instance, be too time-consuming, confusing, face-threatening for participants in the event and so on. Such innovations are very unlikely to be incorporated into future classroom events.

There is a third possibility regarding planned or fortuitous innovation. This is that the modification – the mutation – brings with it distinct advantages, perhaps in making the teacher's life easier, in increasing learners' learning, or in some other way. It is then likely to become incorporated into other classroom events in the same context. If it continues to confer benefits then the mutation is gradually adopted as a standard feature in classroom events taught by Teacher X in context X with learning group X. In other words, in line with the theory of natural selection, just as species which are best fitted to specific ecological contexts are most likely to survive in those contexts so classroom modifications which make life more comfortable or more successful are likely to be maintained in future similar events in the same context.

At this point, we can refer back to the categorization of published advice for dealing with large classes presented earlier. It will be remembered that the first of the three categories consists of reports by practitioners on techniques which have been discovered largely by accident and which have turned out, fortuitously, to be useful. Though we can question the applicability of such recommendations for other contexts, it is clear that what we have in this part of the class-size literature is a corpus of teachers' accounts of how 'best fit' or local adaptation of classroom events for their particular context was achieved. This in turn reminds us of Allwright's argument (2006) that, increasingly, it is *practitioners* rather than *academics* who are knowledge-makers in the field (direction 6).

Two case studies

We can explore the relevance of this metaphorical borrowing of the theory of natural selection by looking at two case studies, one drawing on an observation of an English language lesson and the other making use of a recording of an English teacher talking about his/her work.

Case study 1

The following extract from my classroom observation diary was made after a visit which I made to a Year 5 primary class (age approximately eleven) in a large urban school for boys in a country in Asia. The observation lasted fifty minutes.

> The School was established...in the 1920s. However, in 1993 it moved to a brand new site with purpose-built buildings. The classroom was at the end of a long building, separated from the other classes only by an incomplete brick partition which did not reach up to the ceiling; there are no doors at all within the building. It was therefore very noisy because of the proximity of the other classes...There were 51 pupils in the class, packed together very tightly indeed.
>
> The teacher began by going through a dialogue from the Year 5 textbook, talking about it and asking a lot of highly repetitive questions about it. The teacher used English all the time and it was the teacher who was doing almost all the talking. The boys' role at this stage was just to shout out the names of the characters (for example, 'Meurig'[3]).
>
> The next stage – a brief one – consisted of choral chanting of the dialogue.
>
> In stage 3, the teacher asked for volunteers to read aloud the dialogue in pairs (across the room from wherever they were sitting, because movement to the front was so difficult)...Reading through the dialogue in this way was repeated several times. Many of the boys seemed keen to perform but others were restless and were obviously not paying much attention.
>
> At stage 4, the teacher said, 'Get out writing books' [and] then wrote on the board:
>
> *Monday the 27th of January in 1997*
> <u>*Fill in the blanks*</u>
> *1 Meurig is the ____ in the race.*
> *2 Gareth's number is number ____ .*
> *3 ____ is the second in the race.*
> *4 ____ and ____ are watching the race.*

The pupils closed their text books and copied these sentences into their exercise books. While they were working I talked quietly to those who were nearest to me (movement was impossible). I also looked at one boy's exercise book and transcribed the following from a page dated 20th January, that is, exactly a week before the date of my observation:

1) *Who are talking about the sprtsmeetx?*
   Hywel And Rhys
2) *At what time dous is start?*
   At 2.00 o'clock
3) *At what time is the first rase?*
   At two fifteen fifteen
4) *Is Owain ranning in the first rase?*
   Yes

This indicated that the class had been working on the same lesson from the textbook for at least one week.

I asked the boy next to me his name, age and where he lived. He was confident and friendly and understood everything almost immediately. Some of the other children seemed *very* confident, could answer my questions very easily and were obviously completely unchallenged by the lesson.

Once the children had finished the written task they had to make their way to the front to have their books checked. In many cases this meant crawling on hands and knees under rows of desks to get to the front. (Nobody went over the tops of desks, I noticed; perhaps this would be considered impolite?) It was clear that although the crawling under desks was necessary, it also provided a good opportunity to taunt friends out of the immediate eye of the teacher. Once the children had got to the front they stood in a jostling scrum waiting for their books to be checked. And once this was over they then had to crawl or squeeze their way back to their seats. Those who got back to their seats early had nothing to do while waiting for the rest of the class to have their books checked and settle down again.

The bell rang to indicate the end of the lesson. I am not sure that everyone had succeeded in getting their work checked.

Several issues emerge from this observation. By the end of the observation I wanted to know, most immediately, why so much time had been spent on checking the pupils' written work, even though this activity had been time-consuming and noisy. I also wanted to know why so many children were squeezed into such a small space and why teaching material which was apparently not challenging for the pupils was being used.

From discussions with the class teacher after the observation, with the school principal and with other professionals familiar with the context, I learnt that the school served an upper-middle-class community. Most parents spoke English and indeed several families used English as one of their home languages. Parents paid close attention to their children's education. In particular, they expected teachers to read the children's written work frequently and to evaluate it. The teacher therefore felt obliged to put a mark in every boy's exercise book at least once during every fifty-minute session as evidence that writing tasks had been given to the children and that the children's work had been evaluated. It was generally recognised that teachers' evaluations of their pupils' work in these circumstances were sometimes perfunctory; nevertheless, parental expectations were so strong that it was essential for teachers to go through the marking process at least once in every lesson.

The reason why more than fifty children were crammed into a relatively small classroom could be found in the school's reputation. It is perceived by its clientele as being a successful and relatively prestigious school. There is consequently high demand for places and the school responds by accepting as many children as can be fitted into the available space.[4]

And why was the teaching material far too easy and unchallenging for the pupils? Again, parental expectations played a significant role. The main purpose of the school, in the eyes of parents, was to prepare children for examinations so that in due course they would be able to progress smoothly to the next level of education. The book which I saw being used was the official national textbook and it followed the national outline syllabus for English in upper-primary classes. Indeed to all intents and purposes the book had become the national curriculum for English at this level. The examinations were also based on the textbook. The teacher's responsibility, then, was not so much to develop the children's competence in English. Instead, it was to ensure that the boys were prepared for the examinations by being taken very carefully and systematically through the textbook.

The conclusion to be drawn from this observation and from our understanding of the context in which it took place is that this classroom event constituted the best adaptation to local circumstances which could be achieved at that moment in that context. This was the way in which a resolution or compromise could be reached between competing pressures, demands and constraints. Movement around the classroom was impossible because of the number of children in the small space; but the teacher had to demonstrate to parents that pupils had been given writing tasks and that their written work had been duly marked. The teacher therefore had no alternative but to tolerate a degree of informal behaviour by pupils as they made their way under the desks to the front of the room and back again. At least, with the collusion of the pupils, this mildly anarchic behaviour took place beneath the desks, out of sight, and so it could be ignored. In this way, the teacher's face was saved for – if the same behaviour had been more visible, more public – it would probably have been necessary for the teacher to take action to impose discipline. But time pressure meant that the teacher could not afford to be distracted from the marking task and so the teacher was prepared to turn a blind eye to what was happening under the desks. At the same time, because the marking process was so time-consuming, progress through the textbook was very slow. And in any case, the need to prepare children for the end of year examination meant that nothing in the textbook could safely be skipped.

The solution to this conundrum is a local adaptation of the classroom event which successfully accommodates the pressures and constraints which characterise this context. However, development of language competence does not appear to have high priority in this species of classroom event; it is unlikely that the lesson was contributing much to the boys' ability to use English.

Case study 2

The second case study draws on an extensive audio-recording of an interview with a teacher who teaches English at the university level in a country in Africa.[5] The interviewer is asking the teacher a series of questions about the techniques which are used to evaluate students' written work.

In most of my papers, I usually underline, make some changes; and there are also some corrections that I make up unconsciously, unconsciously. While reading, I correct it. And sometimes, especially when it comes to the, to adding these commas or full stops, I do them unconsciously...

when I was a student we had a course in teaching, one of the courses. There, we were taught this technique and it says it helps you to achieve objectivity, and it did, of course. But there is this subjectivity which we cannot avoid also, along with that... I don't know any other technique. I mean, any other technique which should be considered better than this; this has been working good as far as I am, I mean, I am concerned, as long as I know, this has been effective with me. Maybe there is another technique which I do not know.

Especially these long phrases and clauses that I underline are things that I don't understand. What does the writer want to say? Or I sometimes find it, or even boring, time consuming to correct it, very long one...

the problem is I wish we had fewer students in class so that we know, and quite well, and follow their progress. I can give exercises on these writing activities, but since the number of students in one class is really big size, I couldn't make this marking after every assignment or I couldn't make this evaluation for every writing activity that I give; I couldn't do that...Since the number of the students in, in one class is really big in size, it's not interesting to collect students' writing and then to correct them, to collect them to correct them is really tiresome because the number in one class is most of the time above 50; especially in [course] 101, you don't find any class less than 50. So it's really killing job, I could say.

Some of the students, I think, might not be happy whenever they see lots of circles and underlined phrases with these, with red pens. They don't feel happy. In fact, you can read also some of the students' face that they are completely sad whenever they see such kind of, what you call, type of corrections. But for me, I think I have to show the mistakes or the errors that the learner is making. Whether it is a true or not true way of evaluating, of course, it's another question because...I haven't taken any training on evaluation.

From this very honest interview we learn that this teacher is teaching writing to several different classes, each of which has at least fifty students. The principal technique employed is to underline or circle inaccurate parts of students' written work with a red pen. In some cases incorrect punctuation is not only underlined but also corrected. Not every piece of student writing is evaluated in this way. Why does the teacher adopt this approach to evaluating students' work? From the interview extracts, we can identify the following influences:

- The teacher has been formally trained to use only one evaluation technique and so the repertoire on which s/he can draw is extremely limited
- Large numbers of learners are being taught at the same time. The implication is that techniques other than the one already employed might demand an even greater expenditure of effort
- Some of what the teacher does is intuitive ('unconscious'), and so the teacher is presumably drawing on his/her exposure to other

influences, possibly including his/her own language learning experience

- The teacher feels a strong duty to identify errors, probably without being able to identify consciously where that obligation derives from.

On the other hand, the teacher is conscious of a number of weaknesses in or negative consequences of the procedure which is being used:

- Students are often dismayed by the amount of red ink on their written work
- The evaluation procedure is not as 'objective' as it is claimed to be
- The procedure is exhausting and tedious for the teacher her/himself.

We see evidence here, therefore, of a teacher consciously making compromises between what s/he would like to be able to do, what s/he feels obliged to do and what is practically feasible in the circumstances. In other words, despite its weaknesses, this marking procedure constitutes the best local adaptation which is currently available in this context at this point in this teacher's professional development.

The achievement of local adaptation

It would be easy for us to criticise the teacher in Case study 1 for the way in which the classroom event was managed, for his/her failure to come up with more imaginative solutions to the problem which the classroom context presented, or for his/her apparent willingness to sacrifice real language learning for other matters. But we would not be justified in making such criticisms, since for that teacher at that point in time in that situation this was the most effective way to achieve a reconciliation between competing pressures and to ensure survival. This was this teacher's 'best fit' in this pedagogical niche.

Similarly, for the teacher in Case study 2, we might be tempted to condemn the teacher for not seeking more meaningful and less discouraging ways of providing feedback to learners. Yet here too we cannot reasonably make such criticisms since the uneasy compromise which has been achieved in this particular pedagogical environment is the most suitable local adaptation which is available.

Figure 6.1 characterises the way in which a reconciliation is achieved between competing pressures, demands and expectations. The diagram cannot be exhaustive and the particular constellation of pressures will in

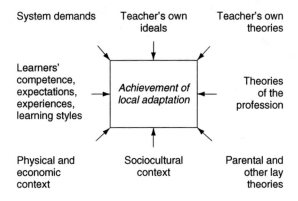

Figure 6.1　The achievement of local adaptation in classroom events

any case vary from context to context. Nevertheless, the eight categories of pressure identified here are likely to be significant in many teaching contexts, and especially those in which there are large numbers of learners:

- *System demands* include the requirements of the education *system* in which the classroom event occurs. These range from national regulations concerning the completion of set textbooks by certain points in time down to individual school rules about recording pupil attendance. The expectations of colleagues and the ethos of the school also fall into this category.
- The *teacher's own ideals* refer to what the individual teacher, in an ideal world, would like to be doing in the classroom. The teacher's *ideals* may be related to or influenced by his or her *theories* (see the next category) but they may also be distinct from these theories. *Not* making learners 'completely sad' (Case study 2) is an example of a teacher's ideal which, nevertheless, may need to be compromised in certain circumstances.
- The *teacher's own theories* are derived from multiple sources, including the teacher's experiences as a learner, their initial and in-service training, and their experiences as a teacher. This area is the focus of research into *teacher cognition* (for example, Borg, 2003; Woods, 1996).
- *Theories of the profession* include both currently and formerly dominant theories which may be manifest in national curriculum documents, textbooks, examinations and so on. The teacher may not be aware of

the formal status of these theories; nevertheless, he or she may be required to work with textbooks which have been influenced by them. It is important to recognize that the various 'theories of the profession' lurking under the surface in a particular context are unlikely to be coherent and consistent with one another. Textbooks, curriculum and examinations may reflect incompatible philosophies, but it remains the responsibility of the teacher to achieve a reconciliation between their competing demands.

- *Parental and other lay theories* include popular ideas about education, parents' demands of the education system and their expectations as to what is appropriate in classrooms.
- The *sociocultural context* includes a broad range of issues including patterns of behaviour in society at large which may be mirrored in educational institutions, the tendency in many societies for different social groups (for example, religious groups) to organise their own education systems, and so on. This category of pressures upon the classroom event is of particular concern to what we might refer to broadly as 'appropriate methodology' research (see, for example, Coleman, 1996; Holliday, 1994).
- The *physical and economic context* is a category of environmental features which is often ignored by writers working in relatively privileged contexts. As the physical and economic context becomes more extreme, though, greater pressure falls upon the teacher and the learners. How are the demands of other parts of Figure 6.1 to be satisfied if, for instance, only two or three children in a class can afford to buy the set textbook or if the teacher has to invest large amounts of time marking written work? Class-size studies address just one aspect of the physical context (for example, Coleman, 1989b).
- The final category is concerned with the *learners* in the classroom, including their language competence, their expectations, their previous experiences as learners and as users of the language and their learning styles. Research in the field of 'cultures of learning' investigates several of these issues (see Cortazzi and Jin, 1996, for instance).

Conclusion

The argument presented here is not a new one, though the linking with the theory of natural selection probably is. Pennycook (1989: 606), following Stern (1983), noted that there is a problem with the idea that 'methods' possess 'conceptual unity':

teachers make a whole series of decisions about teaching based on their own educational experiences, their personalities, their particular institutional, social, cultural and political circumstances, their understanding of their particular students' collective and individual needs, and so on. Any relationship [*sic*] between these decisions and theories about pedagogy and language learning are highly complex and need to be studied without the use of a priori categories, especially when those categories are as clumsy and unspecific as methods... there is a remarkable disparity between, on the one hand, the dictates of 'experts' and teaching textbooks, and on the other, actual classroom practice.

One value of the Darwinian metaphor, then, is that it permits us to reject the deficit model of teaching which – explicitly or otherwise – appears to underlie much teacher development activity. The deficit model assumes the existence of an *ideal or prototype lesson* against which all classroom events in the real world can be judged. Frequently, real-world classroom events are judged to be inadequate or mutant variants of this prototype.

The Darwinian approach enables us to understand that each classroom event represents the current 'best fit' available in that context for the teacher and other participants who may be endeavouring to balance their needs, to get through the event, to maintain face (their own and others'), to make a living, to achieve a reasonable degree of order, to implement their own individual and communal understandings of what 'teaching' and 'learning' involve, to prepare for examinations, to be seen to be getting through the set textbook, to cope with institutional pressures and external social demands, to implement their own professional ideals and so on. The space that is left for actually learning the language once an equilibrium has been achieved between all of these other competing pressures may be extremely limited.

The Darwinian metaphor should encourage us to understand that the achievement of local adaptation to pedagogical niches is a *dynamic process*. A particular instance of a classroom event may exhibit a number of 'mutations', some of which will prove to be useful and will be accommodated into future events in the same context, others of which will prove to be disadvantageous and will be rejected on future occasions. In this way, we can see teachers (and other participants in classroom events) *working* at achieving a reconciliation between competing demands. The Darwinian analysis allows every lesson to be an original and individual achievement.

Notes

* An early version of this chapter was presented at the Fourth Language and Development Conference in Hanoi, Vietnam, 13–15 October 1999. I am grateful to Tony Crocker, Simon Gieve, Inés Miller and Amol Padwad for comments on other versions. Tony Crocker, independently, has been using concepts from Darwinian theory in his own work on project sustainability.

1. Somewhat similar observations can be made of 'small' classes. For example, for some Japanese teachers a class of twenty is problematically small (LoCastro, 1989: 5), whilst in other contexts a class is considered to be too small only when it has just one learner. What distinguishes teachers' thinking about 'large' classes from their conceptualizing of 'small' classes, however, is that many teachers never actually experience classes as small as those which they imagine to be problematically small, whereas the numbers which teachers claim to be problematically large are always within their experience.
2. Another major theme in the literature has been the investigation of relationships between class size and quantity of learning. Despite a century of research the findings continue to be contradictory and inconclusive.
3. All the original names have been replaced with Welsh names.
4. This is a common (though not universal) phenomenon in contexts where available educational resources do not match demand. Schools perceived as being successful may have much larger classes then those institutions which are thought of by the local community as having lower quality. In such situations, small classes are not attractive to parents but rather they are taken as evidence of the school's failure to recruit.
5. I am very grateful to Kiflemariam Zerom for permitting me to make use of this unpublished data.

References

Allwright, D. 2006. Six promising directions in Applied Linguistics. In: *Understanding the language classroom*, eds S. Gieve and I.K. Miller. London: Palgrave Macmillan, Chapter 1 in this volume.

Borg, S. 2003. Teacher cognition in language teaching: a review of research on what language teachers think, know, believe, and do. *Language Teaching* 36, 2:81–109.

Bullock, A. and S. Trombley 1999. *The new Fontana dictionary of modern thought.* 3rd edition, London: HarperCollins.

Carver, D. 1988. *Teachers' perceptions of trends and problems in ELT methodology.* Research Report 3. Edinburgh: Scottish Centre for Education Overseas, Moray House College.

Coleman, H. 1987. Teaching spectacles and learning festivals. *English Language Teaching Journal* 41, 2:97–103.

Coleman, H. 1989a. *Large classes in Nigeria.* Project Report 6. Leeds: Lancaster–Leeds Language Learning in Large Classes Research Project.

Coleman, H. 1989b. *The study of large classes.* Project Report 2. Leeds: Lancaster–Leeds Language Learning in Large Classes Research Project.

Coleman, H. 1995. Appropriate methodology in large classes. In: *Appropriate methodology: from classroom methods to classroom processes*, ed. R. Budd, 113–26. (Special Issue of *The Journal of TESOL France* 2, 1.) Paris: TESOL France.

Coleman, H. 1996. Shadow puppets and language lessons: interpreting classroom behaviour in its cultural context. In: *Society and the language classroom*, ed. H. Coleman, 64–85. Cambridge: Cambridge University Press.

Coleman, H. 1997. Large classes and training for sustainability. In: *The development of ELT*, eds G. Abbott and M. Beaumont, 149–59. Hemel Hempstead: Prentice Hall Phoenix ELT.

Cortazzi, M. and L. Jin 1996. Cultures of learning: language classrooms in China. In: *Society and the language classroom*, ed. H. Coleman, 169–206. Cambridge: Cambridge University Press.

Darwin, C.R. 1859. *On the origin of species by means of natural selection*. London: John Murray.

Darwin, C.R. 1871. *The descent of man, and selection in relation to sex*. London: John Murray.

Darwin, C. Robert and A.R. Wallace 1858. On the tendency of species to form varieties; and on the perpetuation of varieties and species by natural means of selection. *Journal of the Proceedings of the Linnean Society: Zoology* 3, 9:53–62 (20 August 1858).

de Beer, G., ed. 1960. *Darwin's notebooks on the transmutation of species*. London: British Museum of Natural History.

Embi, Mohamed Amin 1997. Classroom learning behaviours in classes of different size. *Jurnal Pendidikan* 22:115–30.

Frank, R.H. 2000. *Luxury fever: money and happiness in an era of excess*. Princeton, NJ: Princeton University Press.

Gayon, J. 2003. From Darwin to today in evolutionary biology. In: *The Cambridge companion to Darwin*, eds J. Hodge and G. Radick, 240–64. Cambridge: Cambridge University Press.

Gould, S.J. 1978. *Ever since Darwin: reflections in natural history*. London: Burnett Books with André Deutsch.

Hashim, Nor Hashimah 1997. Teachers' responses to class size and educational media at the primary level in Malaysia. Unpublished PhD thesis, University of Leeds, UK.

Holliday, A. 1994. *Appropriate methodology and social context*. Cambridge: Cambridge University Press.

Holliday, A. 1996. Large- and small-class cultures in Egyptian university classrooms. In: *Society and the language classroom*, ed. H. Coleman, 86–104. Cambridge: Cambridge University Press.

Howard, J. 1982. *Darwin*. Oxford: Oxford University Press.

Itzen, R.J. 1986. Teaching at an open university. *TESOL Newsletter* 20, 6:27.

Jones, G. 1999. English by numbers. *The Sunday Telegraph Magazine*, 24–27, 9 May 1999.

LoCastro, V. 1989. *Large size classes: the situation in Japan*. Project Report 5. Leeds: Lancaster–Leeds Language Learning in Large Classes Research Project.

McLeod, N. 1989. *What teachers cannot do in large classes*. Project Report 7. Leeds: Lancaster–Leeds Language Learning in Large Classes Research Project.

Mebo, P. 1995. Class size and student behaviour: a comparison of the strategies employed in different size classes by students studying communication skills in the Kenyan state universities. Unpublished PhD thesis, University of Leeds, UK.

Naidu, B. 1992. Coming to terms with the problems of large classes by reflecting on classroom practice. In: *Teaching and learning English in challenging situations*, eds B. Wijasuriya and H. Gaudart, 258–65. Selangor Darul Ehsan (Malaysia): Malaysian English Language Teachers' Association.

Pennycook, A. 1989. The concept of method, interested knowledge, and the politics of language teaching. *TESOL Quarterly* 23, 4:589–618.

Sarangi, U. 1989. A consideration of methodological issues in analysing the problems of language teachers in large classes. Project Report 10. Leeds: Lancaster–Leeds Language Learning in Large Classes Research Project.

Shamim, F. 1993. Teacher–learner behaviour and classroom processes in large ESL Classes in Pakistan. Unpublished PhD thesis, University of Leeds, UK.

Shamim, F. 1996. In or out of the action zone: location as a feature of interaction in large ESL classes in Pakistan. In: *Voices from the language classroom: qualitative research in second language education*, eds K.M. Bailey and D. Nunan, 123–44. Cambridge: Cambridge University Press.

Stern, H.H. 1983. *Fundamental concepts of language teaching*. Oxford: Oxford University Press.

Veenhoven, R., J. Ehrhardt, M.S.D. Ho and A. de Vries 1993. *Happiness in nations: subjective appreciation of life in 56 nations 1946–1992*. Rotterdam: Centre for Socio-Cultural Transformation, Erasmus University of Rotterdam.

Wallace, A.R. 1864. The origin of human races and the antiquity of man deduced from the theory of 'Natural Selection'. *Journal of the Anthropological Society of London* 2:158–70.

Wallace, A.R. 1871. *Contributions to the theory of natural selection*. London: MacMillan and Co.

Woods, D. 1996. *Teacher cognition in language teaching: beliefs, decision making and classroom practice*. Cambridge: Cambridge University Press.

Wu Hsiao Li 1993. Is teaching in large classes really an insoluble problem? *Wen Tzao Junior College* (Taiwan), 87–114, November.

7
Recognizing Complexity in Adult Literacy Research and Practice*

Ming-i Lydia Tseng and Roz Ivanič

Introduction

The main aim of this chapter is to show the usefulness of taking the 'six promising directions in Applied Linguistics' which Allwright (2006, Chapter 1 in this volume) has identified as an interpretative lens for examining the learning–teaching relationship in adult literacy education. In keeping with his first 'direction', we propose that the intellectual project of adult literacy practitioners and researchers should not be to *prescribe* nor merely to *describe*, but rather to *understand* what is happening in adult literacy educational settings (direction 1). The pursuit of the understanding of learning should be a continuous process, as advocated by Allwright (2001a), Allwright and Bailey (1991), Breen (1985, 2001), Pinto (2001) and others, because learning is not always predictable as a product of input, but occurs through constant negotiations between individuals, social environments and ideologies. This leads us to recognize the move *From simplicity* to *complexity* (Allwright, 2006, direction 2) as a particularly fruitful direction for understanding the nature of learning and of learning–teaching events in the adult literacy field, incorporating and integrating the many understandings which we owe to Allwright. To be more specific, in this chapter, we discuss both the learning–teaching *relationship* and the learning–teaching *process*, and both are found to be complex. In the main part of this chapter, we develop a comprehensive model of factors which should be taken into account in recognising complexity as a key characteristic of adult literacy learning in pedagogic settings. First, however, we suggest links between what we see as the overarching concept of *complexity* and the other directions Allwright identifies.

Awareness of complexity shifts researchers' goals from *prescription* as to how to teach to *understanding* of learning (Allwright, 2006, direction 1). The complexity of the learning–teaching process derives from the inter-relation and integration of different factors. A consequence of complexity is that learning is not the total sum of what has been 'taught' in class. Recognising complexity implies understanding learners and learners' contributions not in terms of *commonality* but in terms of *idiosyncrasy* (Allwright, 2006, direction 3), a move which is extremely relevant to any form of adult education. Allwright summarizes the implications for pedagogy of understanding learning–teaching events in terms of complexity, and of understanding learners in terms of idiosyncracy, as a move *From precision* to *scattergun* (Allwright, 2006, direction 4), and a move from treating teaching and learning as work to teaching and learning as life (Allwright, 2006, direction 5): implications which, in our view, have great relevance for adult literacy education. These perspectives on learning–teaching events have implications not only for pedagogy but also for how research is undertaken, with *practitioners* working for 'locally helpful understandings', and hence being recognized as *knowledge-makers* (Allwright, 2006, direction 6). In this chapter, we examine the dimensions of complexity which need to be taken into account in seeking to understand learning in adult literacy education, but we will make links to these other, interrelated 'directions' for applied linguistics as we proceed.

Adult literacy education takes place in a wide variety of educational settings, and in this respect differs from the English language teaching field (hereafter ELT) in which learning and teaching are primarily studied in classrooms. Thus, the model of the complexity of the learning–teaching relationship which we develop in this chapter applies not only to classrooms, but also to a wide range of forms of provision. The defining characteristic is not that the event is happening in a class-room, but that there is a teacher or some other professional whose aim is, among other things, to *facilitate literacy learning for adults*. This could include such forms of provision as support in a workplace, community projects with an educational dimension, jobcentre provision to support job-searching. When we use the terms 'classroom', 'educational setting' and 'learning–teaching event' we are referring to all such types of provision.

Research specifically on the topic of learning in relation to teaching is scarce in adult literacy education (Beder and Medina, 2001). The first study since 1975, centred on this topic, was undertaken by Beder and Medina (2001), who analysed the delivery of instruction and its underlying processes in adult basic education (ABE) in the USA. Whereas Beder and Medina (2001) focused on classroom behaviour and classroom dynamics, the aim of the present chapter is not only to describe features of classroom interaction but to identify the full range of factors which affect how adult literacy learning can be accomplished in educational settings. Throughout the chapter, we evaluate insights about the learning–teaching relationship obtained from the ELT field (Allwright, 1984a, 1984b, 2001a, 2001b, 2003a, 2006; Breen, 1985, 2001; Nunan, 1992, 1999; Pienemann, 1984, 1989; and others) to seek their applicability to adult literacy education and thereby to indicate fruitful areas for future research and practice.

We begin by identifying factors which enter into learning–teaching events: what participants bring with them, and the contextual factors which enable them and constrain them. We then consider the features which characterize a learning–teaching event and add to the complexity of what happens within it, and discuss how the relationship between learning and teaching might be conceptualized, and the range of types of learning accomplished in learning–teaching events. We end by proposing a conceptual framework which integrates all the elements discussed and indicating how the framework might be of use for adult literacy research and practice.

Factors affecting learning–teaching events

In the applied linguistics literature, we have identified six major sets of factors affecting learning–teaching events: *participants' beliefs, participants' intentions, participants' resources, learning and teaching resources, the political and institutional context, sociocultural factors and issues of inequality.* These factors exist outside and beyond the learning–teaching event, and may appear in different forms in different contexts, but they are of crucial significance when attempting to understand what is going on in the learning–teaching event itself, and we propose that all merit investigation in adult literacy educational settings.

Participants' beliefs

Researchers in applied linguistics claim that it is crucial to understand teachers' and learners' beliefs about the nature of language, the nature of learning and about the role of teaching in relation to learning. Pinto (2001) reminds us that unpacking ideologies interwoven in the learning–teaching process is not likely to be straightforward. Not all beliefs are articulated through verbal interactions: beliefs about learning and teaching, and about the nature of literacy, may be reified by the curriculum, and/or embedded in educational materials, and/or instantiated in approaches to teaching; these, in turn, may reconfigure the beliefs of learners and teachers who encounter them. In this section, we discuss the significance and nature of such beliefs. In the section on *The nature of learning–teaching events*, we discuss how these beliefs and their discourses are enacted in pedagogic practices.

Teachers' beliefs are shaped by historical, social, political, cultural beliefs and practices through their biographical histories, pre-service training, teaching activities and professional experience. Teachers' beliefs permeate teachers' knowledge, and affect teachers' behaviour in the classroom (Gertzman, 2001; Woods, 1991: 3–4). Their beliefs may possibly be, or become, part of their *habitus* (that is, part of the embodied dispositions which shape their practices: Bourdieu, 1977). For example, if a teacher believes that learning is not pre-determined by the curriculum, s/he is likely to structure learners' learning following a 'scattergun approach' (as described in Allwright, 2006, direction 4, and by Crabbe, 2003). Learners also bring beliefs of their own to learning–teaching events, and these have a stronger influence on their actions than those of their teachers or colleagues (Block, 1994, 1996; Long, 1989; Pinto, 2001).

Learning and teaching in adult literacy are underpinned not only by participants' beliefs about learning and teaching but also by participants' particular ways of conceptualising *literacy*. What counts as 'literacy' is highly contested, and should be discussed explicitly in any research project on adult literacy provision. Researchers in literacy studies have identified distinctions among views of literacy that sustain practitioners' endeavours in teaching, learning, researching and devising policies (for detailed discussion of different views of literacy, see, for example, Barton, 1994; Barton, Hamilton and Ivanič, 2000; Baynham, 1995; Beder and Medina, 2001; Cope and Kalantzis, 2000; Hamilton, 1996; Prentiss, 1998; Purcell-Gates, Degener and Jacobson, 1998; Purcell-Gates et al., 2000; Street, 1995; for an analysis of beliefs about the nature of writing, see Ivanič, 2004).

The revisiting of beliefs of participants in other sections of this chapter indicates the impossibility of isolating any one factor from others or from the *cyclic* nature of learning and teaching. As Allwright argues (2000, 2001a, 2001b), differences among participants' beliefs should not be seen as a problem. They are instead a fundamental characteristic of learning and can be seen a starting point for pursuing better understandings of the complexity of learning.

Participants' intentions

As applied linguists and educational researchers (for example, Block, 1994; Ramani, 1991; Woods, 1991) argue, teachers' intentions are considered to include both *prior planning* and *minute-to-minute decision-making*. Both are complex processes, which may often be implicit and unreflective, having contributed to teachers' behaviour in learning–teaching events. *Learners' intentions* are also important in shaping what happens in learning–teaching events (Allwright, 1984a, 1984b; Breen and Littlejohn, 2000; Pinto, 2001); their intentions are attributed more to personal long-term convictions about learning (Long, 1989; Block 1994) or views of self, not to the learning tasks assigned to them.

In adult literacy educational settings, it has been shown that intentions for learning may be related to participants' perceptions of their social status: not only learners' low self-image but also teachers' sense of powerlessness. Hart (1998) studied adult literacy programmes in the USA which aimed to involve teachers and learners in civic movement activities. Hart showed how despite being ambivalent and dubious at the outset, all participants became less sceptical of their own power, more aware of purpose and more convinced of their right to learn. The influence of such work may not be seen within a short period but such intentions for learning make participants feel that they are engaged in meaningful work for both learning of literacy and for their personal lives (Hart, 1998: 5).

Participants' intentions for learning are an important part of the complexity of adult literacy classrooms. Explicit discussion of their intentions will be beneficial to both teachers and learners, and taking them into account contributes to a fully rounded picture of the learning–teaching event. Those intentions appear to be fluid, diverse and socioculturally or historically constitutive, which is of direct relevance to Allwright's insight regarding the importance of uncovering *idiosyncrasy* rather than seeking for universal patterns in the characteristics and outcomes of learning (Allwright, 2006, direction 3).

Participants' resources

Learners as social beings come to the classroom with a range of attributes, as researchers have noted (for example, Larsen-Freeman, 2001), including age, gender, aptitude, personality traits, motivation, cognitive styles, learning disabilities, social identity, life experience, interests, attitudes and values. Each of these tends to be seen and researched alone, but ought to be investigated with the others since all are integrated in their *impact upon learners* (Allwright, 2006, direction 2). Lumby (2002: 51), responding to a recent national survey of colleges for further education (hereafter FE) colleges in the UK, points out that, while curriculum managers offer different provisions according to students' age, previous educational experience and ethnicity, such decisions may interfere with rather than enable learning, since individual profiles are so diverse.

Work on multilingualism has identified the rich repertoire of languages, literacies, learning and discursive social practices (see, for example, Martin-Jones and Jones, 2000) which constitute learners' linguistic resources. Practitioners and researchers in adult literacy need to understand learners' and teachers' multilingual linguistic resources as potential contributions to learning, and to trace how these resources are, or might be, drawn upon in pedagogic settings. The focus on the development of practitioners' understandings in recent adult literacy projects (for example, National Research and Development Centre for Adult Literary and Numeracy projects) echoes Allwright's call for integrating research with learning and teaching. The key implication is that teachers and learners are no longer the researched, but are *knowledge-makers* who research their own practices (Allwright, 2006, directions 5, 6), and this is of particular relevance for adult learners who are bringing multilingual resources into their learning.

Learning and teaching resources: curriculum documents, textbooks, syllabi and other teaching materials

Beliefs about learning, teaching and the nature of literacy, as described earlier, can be brought into pedagogic settings indirectly by being inscribed in the learning–teaching resources which are used there (see Littlejohn, 1992). Such beliefs provide the theoretical and empirical bases for policy-makers, commercial publishers and practitioners devising syllabuses, curriculum documents and teaching materials in adult literacy. Different beliefs are reflected in different resources in different contexts. These resources will interact with classroom participants' beliefs about learning – sometimes reinforcing them, sometimes conflicting with them. The use of such resources will to a greater or lesser extent be affected by the *educational objectives of dominant stakeholders*, which we now turn to discuss.

The political and institutional context

Participants' individual histories, beliefs, intentions, personal attributes, expectations, expertises and capacities to formulate plans for what should be taught or learned are subject to political imperatives. Institutional constraints and (lack of) resources primarily result from control by government education authorities, funding regimes, assessments, prescribed curricula, institutional infrastructures – and, in particular, refinements and changes of policies (see Allwright 2001a, 2001b; Carrington and Luke, 1997). Learning and teaching are *political acts* operating in a context largely determined by particular policies, inscribed in policy documents. Learners and teachers are not allocated power to evaluate different outcomes of learning – desirable, additional or unexpected; rather, these are judged and acknowledged by the institutions which produce and administrate policies and curricula. Learners' and teachers' intentions for learning and teaching (see the section on *Participants' intentions*, p. 140), are renegotiated and shaped by such external forces, and teachers' autonomy over their pedagogic practices is thereby reduced. In our view, this is an important, and often neglected, factor to take into account in the study of literacy learning in pedagogic settings. The interconnection between beliefs, resources, the policy context and other factors contributing to learning confirms Allwright's appeal to eschew the pursuit of simple statements of causality about learning and teaching, and seek instead to understand the *complexity* of this relationship (Allwright, 2006, direction 2) These issues are particularly significant in adult literacy education, in view of its low status, as mentioned in the section on *Participants' intentions* (p. 140).

Sociocultural factors and issues of inequality

There have been productive attempts to remind teachers, researchers and curriculum designers of the value of the culturally diverse literacy practices and resources individuals bring with them as they embark on adult literacy courses (Carrington and Luke, 1997). Referring to Bourdieu's (1977) notion of 'cultural capital', Carrington and Luke suggest that for adult literacy practice and research, learners' *sociocultural capitals* should be identified and analysed as a factor which will affect their learning.

A critical perspective on sociocultural context (Carrington and Luke, 1997; Holliday, 1994) suggests that participants in sites of learning should not merely celebrate difference and provide differential treatment, but search for means to incorporate the instability and diversity of the sociocultural context into the fabric of classroom culture. Understanding how sociocultural context works in relation to one's learning and life may be more effective than generalized solutions which promise equal opportunities for learning (Allwright, 2006, direction 5).

Researchers might productively identify the *structuring* of different contexts: an individual classroom at a school, local context, regional context, national context, within the all-encompassing context of globalisation. Adult literacy research should pay attention to constraints, regulations and tensions alongside choice, coherence and freedom within the broader sociocultural context of the learning–teaching events which are being studied. An important implication is that emphasis should increasingly be placed on practitioners' understandings of their own learning or teaching practices in the adult literacy field. The value of such *practitioner understandings* is evident in empirical work on classroom learning based on the principles of Exploratory Practice (see Allwright, 2006, direction 6).

In this section on *Factors affecting learning–teaching events* (p. 138), we have explained that participants in classrooms do not go in 'empty-minded' but that they bring with them their beliefs, intentions, resources and sociocultural capital, and are subject to institutionally and politically shaped constraints. Recognising these factors leads not to the devising of solutions to improve the effectiveness of practice, but to the gaining of understandings of quality of classroom life for learning, personal and professional development (Allwright, 2006, directions 1, 5). Allwright's six interweaving directions help to redefine the concepts of 'sociocultural context' and of 'research' (Allwright, 2006, direction 6) in relation to learning and teaching, and provide avenues for researching learning and teaching which are extremely productive for the field of adult literacy education.

The sequence in our discussion of these factors does not suggest relative importance among them and they are, in fact, hard to investigate in isolation because they interrelate with one another and contribute to learning in a variety of ways. Although learning does not only or necessarily happen in pedagogic settings, there are particular contexts that mark the learning process explicitly with the presence of a teacher. In the next section, we shall discuss the elements which constitute such contexts, and add further dimensions to their complexity.

The nature of learning–teaching events

Understanding the complexity of the learning–teaching relationship requires researchers to get into the classroom as 'crucible' (Allwright and Bailey, 1991: 18). Applied linguistics and adult literacy researchers have identified several key factors that comprise the complexity and fluidity of classroom life – such as structure of instruction, participation structures, participants' perceptions and interpretations, change in literacy culture within and out of class and others (Beder and Medina,

2001; Purcell-Gates, Degener and Jacobson, 1998; Purcell-Gates et al., 2000; Santa Barbara Classroom Discourse Group, 1992).

Our intent in this chapter is not to look at classroom processes for their own sake, but to pinpoint factors to take into account in studying learning in terms of the *creation of learning opportunities* and how learning is accomplished as these opportunities are exploited. This emphasis reinforces the goal of working for *local understandings* in classroom research proposed by Allwright (2006). Rather than pinning down patterns of classroom processes, we discuss what happens in the classroom, including the *context of the learning-teaching event, approaches to teaching in adult education, social interactions* and the *construction of social identities*.

The context of the learning–teaching event

The learning–teaching event itself occurs in a specific physical context (see, for example, Breen, 1985) A number of aspects of context are worth bearing in mind for understanding the nature of learning–teaching events, including space, layout, arrangement, timing, social relations and use of resources and technology. *Context* is a key term in the literature on teaching and learning, differentially used and explicated in different research settings. Researchers in adult literacy (for example, Barton, Hamilton and Ivanič, 2000; Beder and Medina, 2001) talk not only about the immediate context of interaction, but more about actions mediated by *discourses*. 'Context' thus includes not only the physical aspects of the classroom environment but also the values, beliefs and intentions of participants, the political–institutional context and sociocultural factors and issues of inequality, as described in previous sections. These are brought into the event through the words and actions of the learners and teachers, by being inscribed in teaching materials and other resources and often more indirectly.

The context also includes the *social relations* among participants, as theorized by researchers in the Santa Barbara Classroom Discourse Group (for example, Green and Dixon, 1993; Prentiss, 1998). Their studies conceptualize each classroom as a *local event*, intertextually shaped by past events within the participants' experience. In their theoretical approach, prior discursive and social practices create common knowledge which guides learners as to how to participate in class. Learners experience institutional and classroom positioning, and negotiate social roles, relationships among members and situated understandings of text, context, meaning and content.

These studies indicate that research on adult literacy teaching and learning should document the characteristics of the immediate context in which they take place, and that this may be a useful starting point for identifying the effects of the broader sociocultural and political context, as discussed in the previous section.

Approaches to teaching

The approach taken by the teacher is related to her/his beliefs about *learning* and the role of the teacher in it, and her/his beliefs about the nature of *literacy*. These may either be in harmony with or at variance with the beliefs underpinning the curriculum documents or resources available to the class. The teacher may be depicted as a technician tutoring or assessing literacy skills, a manager of the classroom, or a facilitator to guide students exploring their literacy practices. We do not aim to provide a detailed explanation of each approach here, but to show the range of considerations which shape approaches to teaching and contribute to the complexity of classroom life in adult literacy pedagogy.

In adult education in general, teachers, curriculum specialists and researchers have experimented with alternative ways of organising teaching and learning which take account of the maturity of the learners. Recent investigations in adult learning have supported theoretically motivated arguments in favour of individualized instruction, self-directed learning and personal autonomy (Brookfield, 1984; Hok, 1980; Rogers, 1992, 2002). The intent is to put the learner in an *active role*, selectively exploiting learning opportunities and sharing decision-making for lesson planning. This accords with the *scattergun approach* (see Allwright, 2006, direction 4), and with Allwright's proposal for the modification of teachers' and learners' roles (2006, direction 6). The teacher needs to adjust him/herself from taking a privileged position in relation to received wisdom, to one of working alongside learners to make knowledge.

Many approaches to adult literacy teaching emphasize *authentic and purposeful communication* as the context for literacy learning. Seen from this perspective, literacy education is not simply about the mastery of techniques for communicating fluently and appropriately, but is concerned with the *construction and shifting of identities* (Norton, 2000, 2001; Tusting and Barton, 2003). In this paradigm, learning is accomplished by *apprenticeship*: by identification with a community and participation in its social practices. Learners may belong to more than one community and move across different communities. Learning conceived of in this way is to do with understanding how to grasp opportunities to acquire knowledge, to get things done and to assert identities in the community. Such a view of learning is in accordance with Allwright's proposition that the aim of teachers and researchers should be to achieve *understanding* rather than prescribe specific approaches to teaching (2006, direction 1).

Social interaction in pedagogic settings

The research conducted by Beder and Medina (2001) is a rare investigation of classroom dynamics in adult basic education (ABE) in the USA. They chose classroom processes as the focus for their research, and learning is examined largely in terms of successful classroom strategies, such as teachers sharing information about their personal lives in order to develop and maintain a sense of community. Tardiness, dropping out and 'tuning out' were observed as part of the reality of ABE classrooms, highly tolerated and seldom negatively sanctioned compared to other educational sectors. Applied linguistic research on social interaction adds to our understanding by studying not only classroom processes but also the characteristics within them. In the following, we focus on the nature of talk, and then on its role in learning, with a view to identifying factors worthy of attention in research on adult literacy pedagogy.

Classroom discourse and classroom interaction as factors contributing to the complexity of learning have been of interest to researchers in education, linguistics, literacy studies and other disciplines. The importance of classroom interaction comes from its characteristic of having a multitude of forces interact in complex ways to trigger *learning outcomes*. Participation in classroom processes is important for 'talking knowledge and understanding into being' (Green and Dixon, 1993), for engagement, motivation and confidence-building, whatever the subject-matter (for example, Cazden, 2001; Mercer, 1995, 2000; Santa Barbara Classroom Discourse Group, 1992). Detailed study of classroom interaction can reveal the nature of the *learning opportunities* which are made available discursively to each learner, and the ways in which they are taken up. Social interactions can then be related to other factors identified in this chapter to build an understanding of the relationships between learning and teaching in the adult literacy field (for further discussion of learning opportunities, see the section on *The creation of learning opportunities*, p. 148).

In some studies of classroom interaction, learners are represented as *recipients* of 'teacher talk'. Classroom interaction might be better characterized as a *co-production* between participants, especially in adult literacy pedagogy. Learners are not passive recipients of teacher talk under the sway of institutional authority but are social individuals with agency, who shape and are shaped by divergent discourses of learning. To facilitate learner control over their learning processes, teachers need to share classroom power with learners, allowing them to select what they come across in interaction and to organize their learning through interaction. This redefinition of teachers as equals of adult literacy learners and learners as researchers of their learning processes is relevant to Allwright's view of learners and teachers as *knowledge-makers* in the learning-teaching event (2006, direction 6).

The construction of social identities within pedagogic practices

An important aspect of learning–teaching events which should be considered in research on adult literacy pedagogy is the way in which they are shaped by and shape the *social identities* of the participants. Researchers in the fields of applied linguistics and education (Piaget, 1976; van Lier, 1996; Vygotsky, 1993; Wood Bruner and Ross, 1976) have pointed out that the cognitive aspects of classroom interaction are inextricably intertwined with social aspects. Participation in learning–teaching events is a *social process* which in itself positions participants and affects their learning opportunities. Learners and teachers are positioned in relation to their ethnicity, gender occupational or social status, age, sexuality, physical and intellectual capacities. Participants continually and mutually influence each others' construction of identities as there are many complex ways to play and interpret teacher, student or other roles, as well as to establish relationships with others. Studies in writing and literacy classrooms by Rex (1994) and Prentiss (1998) show how roles as readers, writers, teachers and students are created and shift through classroom interaction and written discourse.

The *positioning* of learners is an important dimension to take into account in researching adult learners' experiences of literacy learning–teaching events. Hybrid subjectivities, issues of power and contested definitions of the construct 'student' have all been identified as factors which deserve more attention in the study of adult education (Brookfield, 1984; Rogers, 2002). The multilayered and changing nature of social identity indicated in recent studies, such as those of Sunderland (1998), Rex (1994), and Rogers (2002), suggests that we need to look beyond the surface of differential treatments in terms of social identity such as ethnicity, gender and others. The rigid distinction between two groups according to the clear-cut features of their identities rests on a superficial view of identity as constituted by permanent labels, denying its hybridity and potential socioaffective value. Such a view unwisely rationalizes learning and teaching as de-contextualized processes with simplicity as the norm – and, as Allwright argues, reveals the necessity of addressing the complexity of learning and teaching events: what learners learn from classrooms should be explained with reference to *discursive and social context* and a *mutually informing process of identity construction and negotiation* (2005a, direction 2).

In this section on *The nature of learning–teaching events* (p. 143), we have identified four aspects of learning–teaching events which contribute to their complexity as they unfold. These combine with factors which enter into learning–teaching events to create the dynamic set of interactions which invite exploration by learners, teachers and researchers in adult literacy educational settings. The focus of the next section is the point of intersection between these sets of factors: the *learning opportunities* which may or may not be made available in a learning–teaching event. We explain what is meant by this concept and discuss the factors which influence the extent to which pedagogic practices actually become opportunities for learning.

The creation of learning opportunities

Since the 1980s, it has been recognized that there is likely to be only a partial relationship between interactions in pedagogic settings and learning. That is, it is not possible to guarantee that learners learn what teachers teach (Allwright, 1980, 1984a, 1984b, 2003b; Breen, 1985; van Lier, 1988, 1996). In this section we discuss the interplay between factors which affect learning–teaching events and the pedagogic practices within them. We focus on the *concept of learning opportunities*, the *management of learning, participation and engagement in learning, learnability and teachability* and consider their relevance to adult literacy education.

The concept of learning opportunities

The value of the concept of 'learning opportunities' is that it does not imply that what a teacher plans to convey is the same as what a learner gains from a lesson. Teaching is thought of as sowing seeds: only some, not all, of which will turn into fruits (Allwright, 2006, direction 4), Crabbe (2003: 10) points out that the concept of learning opportunities should be inscribed in the curriculum, which should be considered as 'an organization of learning opportunities' made by teachers into public, easily identified things. However, the take-up of opportunities by learners is rather private and less frequently reported. Research and practice in literacy studies (for example, the Santa Barbara Classroom Discourse Group in the USA, the Research and Practice in Adult Literacy group in the UK; see RaPAL Bulletin 1985–2004; see also Hamilton, Ivanič and Barton, 1992) reveal that opportunities may be exploited by learners to negotiate their roles, relations to others and understandings of content and meaning in class practices.

In literacy education, meaningful interaction with texts and with literacy activities can provide learners with opportunities to learn literacy by engagement in them: to learn by doing, as well as by talking about them. It is important to emphasize that learning opportunities created by participation in literacy events are neither quantifiable nor universal, as they may differ from one learner to another. Teaching can be no more than the scattering of seeds, only some of which will turn into fruits (Allwright, 2006, direction 4). The emphasis on Individual Learning Plans and one-to-one teaching in adult literacy education suggests a commitment to differential take-up of learning opportunities. However, these procedures are not in themselves enough to ensure the take-up of learning opportunities.

The 'management of learning'

The concept of 'learning opportunities' allows for the teacher's role to be redefined. Rather than taking full responsibility for determining what is to be learned, teachers are responsible for the altogether more flexible and creative task of 'managing' the creation of learning opportunities: for what Allwright and Bailey (1991) call 'the management of learning'. Allwright (2006) suggests that, rather than hoping to identify the most effective method of teaching, teachers and researchers should seek to understand *how learning is achieved*, and hence be in a better position to manage the provision of learning opportunities. 'Learning opportunities' can, in principle, arise anywhere, not only in classrooms; when teachers are present, however, they can use their professional knowledge to facilitate, increase and enhance such opportunities.

Any moment in interaction where learners participate, overtly or covertly, may provide a possible learning opportunity. This opportunity is more to do with the quality of classroom life than with the quality of learners' work (Allwright, 2006, direction 5). Learners do not simply do the classroom task technically. As Allwright (2006) points out, the emphasis on managing the 'quality of life' might avoid the danger of learners being merely attentive students who work hard for good classroom performance, and instead may promote an interest in lifelong learning.

We take 'learning opportunities', 'management of learning' and 'quality of classroom life' as valuable concepts in research on learning in adult literacy education, particularly in view of the emphasis in that sector on learning in a wide range of settings including, but not restricted to, classrooms. However, these concepts should be opened up for scrutiny: should 'work' and 'life' be viewed as a dichotomy – and, if not, what is their relationship? And how should 'quality of classroom life' be defined? These are questions for learners, educators and researchers to bear in mind when studying learning and teaching in any field.

Participation and engagement in learning

Another factor in the interplay between the factors affecting a learning–teaching event and the characteristics of the event itself is the nature of learners' *participation and engagement* (see, for example, Allwright, 1980 for a study of the relevance of participation in turn-taking to learning). Since not all forms of participation are observable (Allwright and Bailey, 1991), it still remains a thorny issue for both researchers and teachers to identify what counts as evidence of *participation*. While the term 'participation' focuses on the social aspects of learning–teaching events, 'engagement' covers also the cognitive aspects. The concept of 'engagement' foregrounds learners' perspectives on learning: visible and invisible evidence of participation and engagement construct learners as active agents of learning. As a follow-up to their classroom dynamics study in ABE, Beder and Medina (2001: 114–15) are undertaking a study of *engagement*. They identify 'engagement' as a key factor in students' relative persistence in learning. They are interested in what types of classroom teaching lead to engagement and how to minimize disengagement in order to ameliorate student drop-out.

Widening our lens, we may refer to Allwright's insights to examine the concept of 'engagement' and to consider possible applications in adult literacy education. A simplistic delivery model of teaching and learning associated with the aims of precision and commonality would lead to a reductive definition of engagement in learning, as reproducing conventions or behaving according to routine. An alternative perspective on 'engagement', however, is that it requires learners to invest their own efforts in interpreting input encountered in the learning process, identifying the purpose, understanding context and balancing social and pedagogical pressures in communication.

Such a view of engagement brings learners and teachers to work on understanding what is going on in their classroom, through the integration of learning, teaching and research.

Learnability and teachability

An interesting way of interpreting the relationship between teaching and learning is the suggestion by Pienemann (1984, also in Allwright and Bailey, 1991: 104) that learners will not learn new things until they are ready. Proposing the concept of 'learnability', he argues the things at just the next stage to the 'natural' development of each individual learner are the only 'learnable' things that s/he will learn. Pienemann further claims that the developmental process does not have rigid sequential stages, and that learning and teaching proceed not in a linear fashion, but in a *continuous tension* between the two. We interpret this to mean that there are not universal 'stages', but that what will constitute 'the next stage' varies from learner to learner.

This hypothesis, although proposed specifically in relation to language learning, is more generally applicable to the whole field of adult education, including adult literacy. It neatly indicates that different learners are able to learn different things, that not everything teachers teach will be learnable to all learners. This hypothesis is particularly relevant to adult literacy education in the UK at this time, where a hierarchical curriculum has been proposed with standards, targets and tests at five stages. On the other hand, it has been recognized that adults have 'spiky profiles' (DfEE, 1999) of capabilities, and cannot be fitted into neat stages or levels. Pienemann's hypothesis implies that teaching which is geared to 'levels' is not appropriate for adult literacy education, and that a scatter-the-seed approach would be preferable, in which each learner consciously or subconsciously selects what is learnable next for them. Despite no detailed explanation of how his stages of acquisition might be accessible to learners' awareness, Pienemann's hypothesis supports Allwright's observation that learning is characterized less by *commonality* and more by *idiosyncrasy* (2006, direction 3).

In his later work Pienemann (1989) relates the learning processes outside the classroom to the teaching in English as a second language (ESL) classrooms and suggests that systematic integration of these two is the basis of a successful course. This seems to be much in line with views held by many literacy researchers that learners can act as *ethnographers of the literacies in their own lives* (Barton, 1994; Barton, Hamilton and Ivanič, 2000; Yeager, Floriani and Green, 1998), and with the idea of merging what some call 'acquisition learning' into formal learning in adult education[1] (Rogers, 1986, 1992, 2002).

However, this hypothesis poses several challenges to teachers and researchers when putting it into practice, for example:

- Is there any way to sharpen teachers' skills in identifying learnable things and learnability moments?
- Are things which are teachable also those which are learnable, and vice versa?

From interaction to learning? Different types of learning

Taking into account all the factors mentioned so far, it seems unlikely that learners will learn a predictable body of knowledge and skills which can be turned into some sort of performance measures. A further consideration in the complexity of the learning–teaching relationship is the different types of 'uptake' which can constitute learning in relation to teaching. We use the term *uptake* in order to focus on what people actually learn, which may be very different from what they are taught. The nature of possible learning, in particular in adult literacy, can be identified within the following five categories, and types of learning may be accomplished singly or in combination. Due to our focus in this chapter being on the complexity of the relationships between learning and teaching and the limited space we have here, we can only name these categories, indicating the main relevant references. We have discussed different types of learning in detail elsewhere (Ivanič and Tseng, 2005). However, we want to stress that in research and practice in adult literacy educational settings, it is important to pay attention not only to the first, but to all of these outcomes.

Learning about content

In adult literacy education, content translates into *knowledge about* literacy and *ability to use* literacy in practice.

Learning about learning

Allwright (2001a, 2001b); Burns (1999); Culham (2001); Pinto (2001).

Learning about language

Allwright (2000, 2001a); Cazden (2001); Mercer (1995, 2000); van Lier (1988, 1996).

Learning about social relations and reconstructing identities

Allwright (1984a); Bartlett and Holland (2002); Breen (1985); Cazden (2001); Green and Dixon (1993); Ivanič (1998); Litosseliti and Sunderland (2002); Norton (2000, 2001); Prentiss (1998); Rex (1994); Sunderland (1994); Sunderland et al. (2002); Wenger (1998).

Wider benefits of learning

These include 'increased confidence and positive attitude to [learners] themselves, enhanced social skills, assertion, self-respect and motivation' (Overton, 2001: 49); see also Appleby (2003); Garner (1998); Gleeson (2001); Hammond and Preston (2002); Vorhaus (2001); Webber (1998).

Recognising complexity: a conceptual framework

In this chapter we have argued in favour of Allwright's (2006) proposal that learners, teachers and researchers should replace simplicity with complexity in their conceptualization of the relationship between learning and teaching. 'Complexity' as identified by Allwright is an inspiring orientation to research, and has generated substantial understandings of learning and teaching. In particular, we have focused on the relevance of complexity for thinking about learning and teaching in the field of adult literacy. By way of summary, we propose a framework (Figure 7.1) which represents the complexity of the learning–teaching relationship in terms of the concepts and insights we have presented in this chapter.

We note that the word 'learning' is often used to refer to 'learning-as-product' – something to be evaluated by gatekeepers or assessors. However, the further we widen our lens from seeing the accomplishment of learning as the accumulative effects of the interplay between contributing factors and classroom practice, the more we find ourselves focusing on 'learning-as-process'. This is in accord with the shift in emphasis recommended by Allwright from what he calls the quality of work (associated with 'learning-as-product'), to the quality of classroom life (associated with 'learning-as-process') (2006, directions 5, 6). Learning is best seen as *social interaction* in which transformation emerges over time and among people, stored or revealed in their bodies, minds and behaviours. It is situated in specific communities of practice at particular sites and may have different meanings from one participant to another.

Figure 7.1 represents the complexity of what is happening in a learning–teaching event. It shows the relationship between 'teaching' (top right), 'learning-as-process' (bottom right), and 'learning-as-product' (centre right), with double-headed arrows linking them, to represent the insight that there is not a simple one-way relationship between teaching and learning. Rather, the two activities shape each other moment by moment: as learners are changed by teaching, so

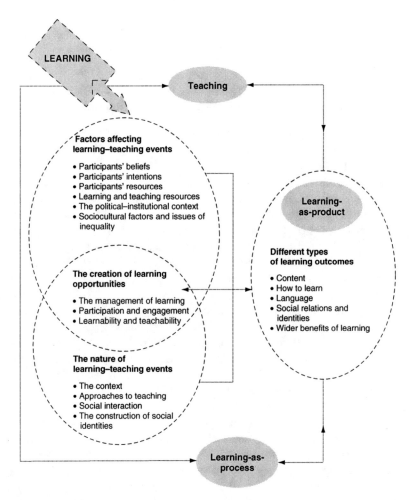

Figure 7.1 The relationships between teaching and learning: a conceptual framework

teachers may adjust their teaching to improve the chance of it leading to more learning. The outer frame also represents the interplay between teaching and learning more broadly conceived: teaching may lead to learning not only by those designated by the pedagogic setting as 'learners' but also by 'teachers-as-learners', and this type of learning, too, has the potential to feed back into teaching.

We have identified the factors which are brought into learning–teaching events (Factors affecting learning–teaching events in Figure 7.1), how they interact with one another and construct classroom interaction in ongoing ways (The nature of learning–teaching events) to shape learning opportunities (The creation of learning opportunities) that have the potential to result in various types of learning outcome (Different types of learning outcomes). In Figure 7.1, what happens in the classroom (or other site of learning) is represented by the overlapping circles, and by the line bracketing these together as inseparable elements in the learning–teaching relationship. 'The creation of learning opportunities' occupies the space at the intersection of the two circles to represent the way in which learning opportunities are constructed in the *interplay among factors* contributing to learning and pedagogic practices. The reverberative effect of one factor on others is indicated by the dotted outlines of all three circles. These dotted lines also imply that researchers should remain open-minded as to what may happen in classroom practice, and as to what can be named.

The arrow between 'The creation of learning opportunities' and 'Different types of learning outcomes' is drawn with a dotted line to indicate that not all learning opportunities will automatically be translated into learning outcomes: the different types of learning are *potential*, not predictable, products of learning opportunities. Learning outcomes may be identified as evidence of learning, but are insufficient representations of learning-as-process. The arrow is double-headed to represent the way in which immediate accomplishments of learning may feed back into the creation of learning opportunities moment by moment during the course of a learning–teaching event. This represents the fact that some learning outcomes further contribute to the creation of learning outcomes moment by moment in pedagogic sites. The section of Figure 7.1 representing 'Learning-as-product' is drawn across the frame of the diagram, to represent the way in which the outcomes of learning opportunities are not likely to be evident until some time after the event.

The final element in Figure 7.1 is LEARNING, in the sense of a lifelong process, represented in capital letters in the box (top left). The double-headed arrow linking this box to the learning–teaching events indicates that this process infuses the whole teaching–learning relationship in educational settings, which may, in turn, later feed back to the cyclic process of lifelong learning. Allwright (2006) highlights the importance of 'life' in classrooms, but the link between this and everyday life is elaborated and researched in the adult literacy field. Adult educators and literacy researchers (for example, Barton, Hamilton and Ivanič, 2000; Rogers, 2002) argue that everyday life may be suffused with learning opportunities and that planned learning events are only small episodes in lifelong and lifewide learning. LEARNING brings resources into learning–teaching events, and learning–teaching events have the potential to help people become more aware of learning opportunities in everyday life. This interplay between 'LEARNING' as discussed here, and 'learning' within successive learning–teaching events is dynamic and open to change and reconstruction as life continuously provides new learning opportunities.

We believe that this conceptual framework provides a useful working understanding of the complexity of learning in pedagogic settings, indicating relationships among the factors that contribute to this complexity. Our analysis of the relevant factors affecting learning and in adult literacy educational provisions leads to leads us to endorse Allwright's (2006) conceptualization of the teaching–learning relationship in terms of *managing learning opportunities*, rather than identifying specific learning moments or outcomes. Along with Allwright, however, we emphasize that more needs to be done to throw light on murkier issues, and to allow more puzzles about learning to be unravelled.

Conclusion

Our underlying purpose for this chapter, as stated in the opening paragraph, has been to elaborate on Allwright's six promising directions for research on language learning: from *simplicity* to *complexity* (2006, direction 2). We believe this conceptualization of the learning–teaching relationship offers research perspectives that have been missing from many published studies in adult literacy education. However, these perspectives are in harmony with the current research emphasis on *socially situated understandings* of learning in adult language, literacy and numeracy and on the interplay between learners' everyday lives, literacy practices and their experience of literacy education.

This research orientation implies that researchers should be wary of making casual links between teaching interventions and learning accomplishments and of looking for universalistic types of learning outcome. The recognition of the complexity of learning and teaching in adult literacy education foregrounds the value of exploring idiosyncratic features of particular classrooms, seeing participants as social beings and looking for ways to make sense of puzzles preoccupying learners. Within the research on adult literacy, the emphasis on the socially situated nature of literacy leads to teachers and learners researching the literacy and learning practices which are integral to their lives both inside the classroom and beyond.

The pursuit of understanding implies that research should be integrated into learning–teaching events, in particular as promoted in 'Exploratory Practice' (Allwright 2001a, 2001b, 2003a, 2006). Research in this paradigm is conceived of as something which should not be done *on* learners but *with* and *for* learners, with learners themselves as researchers. Allwright's claim about the worth of local understanding is in harmony with the principles of the New Literacy Studies (Barton, 1994; Barton and Hamilton, 1998; Barton, Hamilton and Ivanič, 2000) which underpin much current research and practice in adult literacy education.

'Understanding' as a key motivation for pedagogic practice may be radical but is, in our opinion, very attractive. It opens up a new arena for teachers and learners to envisage the interplay between teaching, learning and research and to recognize the roles one may simultaneously play in the classroom and life: a teacher, a learner and also a researcher. The collaborative search for understanding can reduce the possibility of teachers controlling how learning should be perceived and accomplished. In adult literacy research, prioritizing 'understanding' in learning–teaching events may lead educators, policy-makers and administrators to reconsider the requirement to adhere to a centralized curriculum, and to question the need to present concrete outcomes for assessment. (We should add, however, that it is nevertheless necessary for researchers to take the sociopolitical imperatives of contexts into account when making their recommendations.)

We acknowledge that the picture of learning in relation to teaching presented here remains incomplete and disconcertingly complex, as more unsettling factors are brought into the picture. However, we believe that it can be inspiring and challenging to perceive pedagogy from the perspective that the learning process should be considered prior to teaching, putting learners in the central position in learning–teaching events – an insight which, although not new, is often submerged in research inquiries which focus on teaching interventions. We hope to have explored territories that have been rarely trodden but will be fertile for future researchers, teachers and learners in adult literacy to work on together, to complement and extend existing theories and findings and to shed more light on the complexity of the learning–teaching process.

Notes

* The research on which this chapter is based was part of the National Research and Development Centre for Adult Literacy and Numeracy (NRDC) project 'Adult Learners' Lives' (PG1.2), directed by David Barton and Roz Ivanič.

1. Rogers (1986, 2002) and Schön (1983) identified two kinds of learning in adult education: *acquisition learning* (as a subconscious learning process which takes place while people are undertaking tasks relevant to their lives) and *formalised learning* (as a socially constructed activity in which people master structured pieces of knowledge in specific settings for desirable purposes). These two terms should not be portrayed as a dichotomy, as learning is dynamic and both may be present at various times and at different points along the continuum of learning, as Rogers (2002) points out.

References

Allwright, R.L. 1980. Turns, topics and tasks: patterns of participation in language learning and teaching. In: *Discourse analysis in second language research*, ed. D. Larsen-Freeman, 165–87. Rowley, MA: Newbury House.

Allwright, R.L. 1984a. Why don't learners learn what teachers teach? – The interaction hypothesis. In: *Language learning in formal and informal contexts*, eds D.M. Singleton and D.G. Little, 3–18. Dublin: IRAL.

Allwright, R.L. 1984b. The importance of interaction in classroom language learning. *Applied Linguistics* 5, 2:156–71.

Allwright, D. 2000. Exploratory Practice: an 'appropriate methodology' for language teacher development? Paper presented in 8th IALS Symposium for Language Teacher Educators, Edinburgh, Scotland.

Allwright, D. 2001a. Three major processes of teacher development and the appropriate design criteria for developing and using them. In: *Research and practice in language teacher education: voices from the field*, eds B. Johnston and S. Irujo, CARLA Working Paper, 19:115–33. Minneapolis: Minnesota.

Allwright, D. 2001b. Learning (and teaching) as well as you know how: why is it so very difficult? In *Pædagogik og læring I fremmed- og andetsprog* (Odense Working Papers in Language and Communication), ed. J. Wagner, 22:1–41. Denmark: Odense Univeristets Trykkeri.

Allwright, D., ed. 2003a. *Language Teaching Research* 7, 2. Special Issue: Exploratory Practice.

Allwright, D. 2003b. Exploratory Practice: re-thinking practitioner research in language teaching. *Language Teaching Research* 7, 2:113–41.

Allwright, D. 2005. From teaching points to learning opportunities and beyond. *TESOL Quarterly* 39:9–31.
Allwright, D. 2006. Six promising directions in Applied Linguistics. In: *Understanding the language classroom*, eds S. Gieve and I.K. Miller. Palgrave Macmillan, Chapter 1 in this volume.
Allwright, D. and K.M. Bailey 1991. *Focus on the language classroom.* Cambridge: Cambridge University Press.
Appleby, Y. 2003. Retention and achievement: a focused review. Lancaster Literacy Research Centre Working Paper 1. Lancaster: Literacy Research Centre.
Bartlett, L. and D. Holland 2002. Theorizing the pace of literacy practices. *Ways of Knowing Journal* 2, 1:10–22.
Barton, D. 1994. *Literacy – an introduction to the ecology of written language.* London: Blackwell.
Barton, D. and M. Hamilton 1998. *Local Literacies: Reading and Writing in One Community.* New York: Routledge.
Barton, D., M. Hamilton and R. Ivanič, eds 2000. *Situated literacies: reading and writing in context.* London: Routledge.
Baynham, M. 1995. *Literacy practices.* London and New York: Longman.
Beder, H. and P. Medina 2001. *Classroom dynamics in adult literacy education.* NCSALL Reports 18, National Center for the Study of Adult Learning and Literacy, Harvard University Graduate School of Education. Cambridge: MA, Harvard University.
Block, D. 1994. A day in the life of a class: teacher/learner perceptions of task purpose in conflict. *System* 22, 2:153–75.
Block, D. 1996. A window on the classroom: classroom events viewed from different angles. In: *Voices from the language classroom*, eds K. Bailey and D. Nunan, 168–94. Cambridge: Cambridge University Press.
Bourdieu, P. 1977. *Outline of a theory of practice.* Cambridge: Cambridge University Press.
Breen, M. 1985. The social context for language learning – a neglected situation? *Studies in Second Language Acquisition* 7, 2:135–58.
Breen, M. 2001. Overt participation and covert acquisition in the language classroom. In: *Learner contributions to language learning: new directions in research*, ed. M. Breen, 112–40. Harlow: Pearson Education.
Breen, M. and A. Littlejohn, eds 2000. *Classroom decision-making – negotiation and process syllabus in practice.* Cambridge: Cambridge University Press.
Brookfield, S. 1984. *Adult learners, adult education and the community.* Milton Keynes, UK: Open University Press.
Burns, A. 1999. *Collaborative action research for English language teachers.* Cambridge: Cambridge University Press.
Carrington, V. and A. Luke 1997. Literacy and Bourdieu's sociological theory: a reframing. *Language and Education* 11, 2:96–112.
Cazden, C.B. 2001. *Classroom discourse: The language of teaching and learning.* 2nd edition, Portsmouth, NH: Heinemann Educational.
Cope, B. and M. Kalantzis, eds for the New London Group 2000. *Multi-literacies: literacy learning and the design of social futures.* London: Routledge.
Crabbe, D. 2003 The quality of language learning opportunities. *TESOL Quarterly* 37, 1:9–35.

Culham, A. 2001. Practitioner-based research in FE: realities and problems. *College Research Journal* 4, 3:27–8.

DfEE 1999. *A Fresh Start – improving literacy and numeracy*. The report of the working group chaired by Sir Claus Moser. London: Department for Education and Employment.

Garner, B. 1998. Build motivation by building learner participation. *Focus on Basics* 2, A:11–12.

Gertzman, A.D. 2001. 'Who will teach the children?': a critical ethnographic case study of teacher beliefs and practices in an all-male, African American third-grade classroom. PhD thesis, Lancaster University, UK.

Gleeson, D. 2001. Transforming learning cultures in further education. *College Research Journal* 4, 3:30–2.

Green, J. and C. Dixon 1993. Introduction to talking knowledge into being: discursive and social practices in classrooms. *Linguistics and Education* 5, 3:231–9.

Hamilton, M. 1996. Adult literacy and basic education. In: *A history of modern British adult education*, ed. R. Fieldhouse, 142–65. Leicester: National Institute of Adult Continuing Education [NIACE].

Hamilton, M., R. Ivanič and D. Barton 1992. Knowing where we are: participatory research in adult literacy. In: *ALPHA92: Literacy strategies in community-based organizations*, ed. J.P Hautecoeur, 105–18. Hamburg: UNESCO.

Hammond, C. and J. Preston 2002 *The wider benefits of further education: practitioner views*. Centre for Research on the Wider Benefits of Learning, Institute of Education University of London, UK.

Hart, G. 1998. Power, literacy and motivation. *Focus on Basics* 2, A:1–5.

Hok, R. 1980. Some thoughts on study circles and their potentials for language teaching. *TESOL Quarterly* 14, 1:117–19.

Holliday, A. 1994. *Appropriate methodology and social context*. Cambridge University Press: Cambridge.

Ivanič, R. 1998. *Writing and identity: the discoursal construction of identity in academic writing*. Amsterdam: John Benjamins.

Ivanič, R. 2004. Discourses of writing and learning to write. *Language and Education* 18, 3:220–45.

Ivanič, R. and M.L. Tseng 2005. Understanding the relationships between learning and teaching: an analysis of the contribution of applied linguistics. *NRDC Research Review*. London: NRDC Publications.

Larsen-Freeman, D. 2001. Individual cognitive/affective learner contributions and differential success in second language acquisition. In: *Learner contributions to language learning: new directions in research*, ed. M. Breen, 12–24. Harlow: Pearson Education.

Littlejohn, A. 1992. Why are English language teaching materials the way they are? PhD thesis. Lancaster University, UK.

Litosseliti, L. and J. Sunderland, eds 2002. *Gender identity and discourse analysis*. Amsterdam: John Benjamins.

Long, M. 1989. Task, group and task-group intentions. University of Hawai'i Working Papers in ESL 8, 2:1–26.

Lumby, J. 2002. Managing teaching and learning: diversity and innovation. *College Research Journal* Summer: 50–2.

Martin-Jones, M. and K. Jones 2000. *Multilingual literacies: reading and writing different worlds*. Amsterdam and Philadelphia: John Benjamins.

Mercer, N. 1995. *The guided construction of knowledge.* Clevedon: Multilingual Matters.

Mercer, N. 2000. *Words and minds.* London: Routledge.

Norton, B. 2000. *Identity and language learning: gender, ethnicity, and educational change.* Harlow: Longman/Pearson Education.

Norton, B. 2001. Non-participation, imagined communities, and the language classroom. In: *Learner contributions to language learning: new directions in research,* ed. M. Breen, 159–71. Harlow: Pearson Education.

Nunan, D. 1992. *Collaborative language learning and teaching.* Cambridge: Cambridge University Press.

Nunan, D. 1999. *Second language teaching and learning.* Boston, MA: Heinle & Heinle.

Overton, C. 2001. The Wales research project on retention. *College Research Journal* 3, 4:46–9.

Piaget, J. 1976. *The grasp of consciousness: action and concept in the young child.* Cambridge, MA: Harvard University Press.

Pienemann, M. 1984. Psychological constraints on the teachability of languages. *Studies in Second Language Acquisition* 6, 2:186–214.

Pienemann, M. 1989. Is language teachable? Psycholinguistic experiments and hypotheses. *Applied Linguistics* 10, 1:52–79.

Pinto, C. 2001. Intentions and interpretations in the language classroom case study of ELT in a Portuguese polytechnic. PhD thesis, Lancaster University, UK.

Prentiss, T.M. 1998. Teachers and students mutually influencing each other's literacy practices: a focus on the student's role. In: *Reconceptualizing the literacies in adolescents' lives,* eds D.E. Alvermann, K.A. Hinchman, D.W. Moore, S.F. Phelps and D. Woff, 103–28. Mahwah, NJ.: Lawrence Erlbaum.

Purcell-Gates, V., S. Degener and E. Jacobson 1998. *US adult literacy program practice: A typology across dimensions of life-contextualized/decontextualized and dialogic/monologic.* Cambridge, MA: National Center for the Study of Adult Learning and Literacy.

Purcell-Gates, V., S. Degener, E. Jacobson and M. Soler 2000. *Affecting change in literacy practice of adult learners: impacts of two dimensions of instruction.* Cambridge, MA: National Center for the Study of Adult Learning and Literacy.

Ramani, E. 1991. Theorizing from the classroom. In: *Currents of change in English language teaching,* eds R. Rossner and R. Bolitho, 3–11. Oxford: Oxford University Press.

RaPAL Bulletin 1985–2004.

Rex, L. 1994. A social view of composing from insiders' perspectives: the roles and relationships of teacher and students. In: *Multidimensional aspects of literacy research, theory and practice,* eds C.K. Kinzer and D.J. Leu, 560–71. 43rd Yearbook, National Reading Conference: Selected Papers: Charleston SC, USA.

Rogers, A. 1986. *Teaching adults.* Milton Keynes: Open University Press.

Rogers, A. 1992. *Adult learning for development.* Cassell: Education for Development, UK.

Rogers, A. 2002. Constructing adult learning and teaching. Unpublished paper.

Santa Barbara Classroom Discourse Group (J. Green, C. Dixon, L. Lin, A. Floriani and D. Bradley) 1992. Constructing literacy in classrooms: literate action as social accomplishment. In: *Redefining student learning: roots of educational change*, ed. H. Marshall, 119–50. Norwood, NJ: Ablex.

Schön, D.A. 1983. *The reflective practitioner: how professionals think in action.* New York: Basic Books.

Street, B.V. 1995. *Social literacies: critical approaches to literacy in development, ethnography and education.* Longman: London.

Sunderland, J., ed. 1994. *Exploring gender: questions and implications for English language education.* London: Prentice Hall.

Sunderland, J. 1998. New dimensions in the study of language education and learner gender. CRILE Working Paper 43. Centre for Research in Language Education: Lancaster University, UK.

Sunderland, J., F.A. Rahim, M. Cowley, C. Leontzakou and J. Shattuck 2002. From representation towards discursive practices: gender in the foreign language textbook revisited. In: *Exploring gender: questions and implications for English language education*, eds L. Litosseliti and J. Sunderland, 223–55. London: Prentice Hall.

Tusting, K. and D. Barton 2003. *Models of adult learning: a literature review of models applicable to skills for life.* NRDC Research Review. London: NRDC Publications.

van Lier, L. 1988. *The classroom and the language learner: ethnography and second language classroom research.* London: Longman.

van Lier, L. 1996. *Interaction in the language curriculum: awareness, autonomy and authenticity.* London: Longman.

Vorhaus, J. 2001. Lifelong learning and personal autonomy: a response to John Field. *College Research Journal* 4, 3:11–13.

Vygotsky, L.S. 1993. Extracts from *Thought and language* and *Mind in society*. In: *Language, literacy and learning in educational practice*, eds B. Stierer and J. Maybin, 45–58. Clevedon: Multilingual Matters.

Webber, V. 1998. Dismantling the altar to mathematics: a case study of the change from victim to actor in mathematics learning. *Literacy and Numeracy Studies* 8, 1:9–22.

Wenger, E. 1998. *Communities of practice: learning, meaning and identity.* Cambridge: Cambridge University Press.

Wood, D., J.S. Bruner and G. Ross 1976. The role of tutoring in problem solving. *Journal of Child Psychology and Psychiatry* 17, 2:89–100.

Woods, D. 1991. Teachers' interpretations of second language teaching curricula. *RELC Journal* 22, 2:1–18.

Yeager, B., A. Floriani and J. Green 1998. Learning to see learning in the classroom: developing an ethnographic perspective. In: *Students as inquirers of language and culture in their classrooms*, eds D. Bloome and E. Egan-Robertson, 115–39. Cresskill, NJ: Hampton Press.

8
Language Lessons: A Complex, Local Co-Production of All Participants

Elaine E. Tarone

Introduction

Dick Allwright (2006, Chapter 1 in this volume) identifies six directions in Applied Linguistics, directions that have strengthened over the last fifty years. Several of those trends are related: for example, classroom language learning and teaching are now seen both as irreducibly complex, and as essentially local and idiosyncratic, so that centralized prescriptions on 'how to teach foreign languages' are unlikely to be universally successful. In this view, applied linguists should not prescribe simplistic solutions that are supposed to apply to all language learning and teaching situations and classrooms. Rather, each classroom should be seen as both *complex* and *unique*. A more productive approach than centralized prescription is the development of local, detailed descriptions of classroom learners, teachers and their activities; such descriptions are more likely to lead to the individual teacher's under-standing, which in turn can support a more effective classroom practice by that teacher in his or her local, specific context.

This recent formulation is related to an earlier insight (Allwright, 1980): that language lessons are best seen as 'a co-production of all participants'. In this view, language lessons are not just created centrally and unilaterally by teachers, but are *locally negotiated* – in some sense, created by all the members of the classroom together. In other words, all the participants in the classroom have an impact on what goes on there, and all the participants may benefit from that interaction, whether or not they are personally involved. Participants influence one another's speech production, they influence the way they perceive one another and they influence one another's second language acquisition processes. Allwright's (1980) study provided a detailed analysis of one Russian student's (Igor's) domination of class discussion with apparently off-topic contributions. At the end of his paper, Allwright made the interesting observation that, although Igor was ranked first by his teacher for 'frequency of contributions' throughout the course, Igor was NOT ranked first for 'progress' in acquiring English over the course of the class; rather, it was a relatively quiet Iranian woman who the teacher felt had made the most progress in class. Allwright memorably suggests that others in the class, like this relatively quiet student, may have benefited the most from the teacher's interactions with Igor; this may have occurred, he speculates, because 'communicative attempts like Igor's are more productive for the "audience" than for those who make them' (1980: 185). This early study provides a useful example of the sort of local, detailed description of complex classroom interaction that Allwright (2006) advocates in Chapter 1 in this volume.

In this chapter, I shall review more recent developments in second language acquisition research and theory that also support Allwright's view that each second language classroom should be thought of as a unique and complex speech community, one worth describing locally, in its own right, in its development of its own internal dynamics and norms. While the dynamics and norms of such classroom speech communities do follow certain complex patterns, they also result in unique local conditions that can strongly affect students' second language learning processes in ways that are not always easily predictable by either the teacher or the researcher.

The language classroom as speech community

Preston (1989, 1996, 2002), a prominent sociolinguist, has proposed that the language classroom should be viewed as a specialized kind of *speech community*. In sociolinguistics, a 'speech community' is defined as a group of people who share the same language norms, although different members and groups within that community may orient differently to those norms in their speech production. A speech community is complex and diverse in its structure. So, for example, New York City is a speech community that shares such phonological language norms as that the glide /r/ should be pronounced when it occurs post-vocalically. Although all members of this speech community believe it is 'correct' to produce /r/ after vowels, not all of them produce it themselves. Indeed, Labov's early work showed that different socioeconomic classes within New York City produce and delete the post-vocalic /r/ in highly predictable but different ways: higher SEC members supply it more and lower SEC members supply it less. The complex patterning of /r/ variation in the speech produced by different sub-groups of this speech community shows both specialization to those sub-groups and a common acceptance of language norms within New York City.

Preston's (1989) proposal that language classrooms are types of socio-linguistic speech communities emphasizes the fact that a language class, like any other group of people, is fundamentally *social*. It is a group of people who have relationships with one another, and who form sub-groups with alliances and animosities. If this is the case, then we should expect that students' patterns of language use with one another in deskwork and in structured teacher-initiated activities will be affected by their social roles within the classroom, and their relationships with the teacher and one another. Some social groups may produce target language sounds and grammatical forms more correctly than others. It is in this way that the social structure of the language classroom may influence students' acquisition of the second language in complex and unexpected ways. We shall now consider research evidence documenting the impact of this complexity of relationships within the language classroom on language learning.

Language immersion and diglossia

One of the most innovative experiments in the language education of the twentieth century originated in Canada with Wallace Lambert and other applied linguists (for example, Lambert et al., 1993), who sought to find a better way to make English-speaking children truly bilingual in French. Traditional foreign language classrooms were not producing good results. Lambert and his colleagues observed that when children moved with their families to places such as France, they appeared to be able to acquire French 'through immersion', without instruction and with great success. By analogy, Lambert and his colleagues reasoned, it ought to be possible to use a 'language immersion' approach in the public schools; simply surrounding children with French through the entire school day ought to provide the same immersion conditions and result in the same resounding success in the acquisition of French. Accordingly, French immersion schools were developed in Canada to produce graduates who were to be completely bilingual in French and English. Children attended schools in which all school interactions occurred in French; while their teachers understood them when they spoke their native language, English, their teachers always spoke to them in French. And so the children learned all the normal school content in French, learned to read in French in the first grade, and (though they began to get some English language instruction in the second grade) continued to study academic studies through French.

The language immersion experiment was phenomenally successful in producing excellent speakers of French, far superior to the traditional foreign language classrooms they replaced. In the lower grade levels, immersion children spoke French to do all school business, and even pronounced French like native speakers. However, in the upper grade levels, their willingness to speak in French all day dissipated; they began using English with one another, and even at times with the teacher. While third graders (age eight) were happy to use the immersion language almost all the time, and had very native-like L2 pronunciation patterns, fourth and fifth graders (aged nine and ten) increasingly preferred to use their native language in the classroom, and when they spoke the L2, increasingly spoke it using non-native pronunciation patterns. This pattern was characteristic of older immersion students both in Canada and the USA, and occurred in spite of every effort of their teachers to reward their L2 use and penalize their native language use. Teacher strategies of reward and penalty that worked in the third grade no longer worked in the fifth grade. So in the end, language immersion graduates did not perform exactly as originally predicted by Lambert and his colleagues: they did not sound like native speakers of French. They did not speak native-like French like children who had moved overseas. Educators began to use the term 'immersion French' to describe the new variety of French spoken by language immersion graduates.

What causes the increasing inability of language immersion students and teacher to agree on the simple principle that one should use the second language in the classroom? What happened to the simple, top-down solution embodied in the language immersion experiment? Why can't we make the school a French immersion culture that produces the same results as travel to a French-speaking country? The simple principle proposed by Lambert and his colleagues encountered the concrete reality of pre-adolescent children with social roles and social needs, interacting in complex classroom speech communities that differed in important ways from society outside the classroom.

Tarone and Swain (1995) explore the reasons for the increasing unwillingness of older immersion students to speak the school language. They invite Suzannah, a high school graduate of a French immersion program in Canada, to talk about her views and experiences in an early French immersion programme. They remind her of the way in which older immersion children speak in English rather than French (the second language) in immersion classrooms:

(1) Researcher: *...immersion teachers tell us that...kindergarten to grade three, they can keep the kids speaking in French in class, but then there's sort of the shift as...[children] get older, that they start moving into using English in class, and that...[teachers] find it practically impossible to encourage them to use French.*

The researchers ask Suzannah why she thinks immersion children behave in this way. Suzannah responds that the social needs of older children, specifically, their need to talk to each other in French 'the way kids speak', is the cause of the problem:

(2) Suzannah: *Maybe that's because when...[we] get older...we start speaking in a way that they don't teach us, in French, how to speak. So I don't know if it's slang or just the way kids speak...I speak differently to my friends than I do to my parents. It's almost a whole different language, and...they don't teach us how to speak [French] that way...*

So I'd like to be able to sit in a classroom and have someone teach me how to say, 'Well, come on guys, let's go get some burgers' and stuff like that.

Tarone and Swain (1995) propose that one of the main factors causing older learners to turn away from the second language (L2) is sociopsychological. They hypothesize that the learners in immersion school communities, as they grow older, have an increasing need to use language for in-group social interaction among themselves. But what language can they use for this purpose? The only variety of the L2 that teachers model is academic talk. But these pre-adolescents require a vernacular – a casual, in-group variety that will allow them to project an adolescent in-group identity. The academic variety of the L2 spoken by immersion teachers cannot be used by immersion students for this purpose – it can never 'sound cool'. And their adult immersion teachers cannot ever, by definition, talk like that: provide them with linguistic input appropriate for adolescent vernacular French language use. They cannot provide this input precisely because they are adults and not teenagers: any attempt by adult French immersion teachers to talk like French teenagers would simply make them seem ridiculous, because of their age and their role in the classroom.

Thus, immersion students don't have a way of learning French 'teen talk', or the L2 adolescent vernacular, inside the classroom speech community. Tarone and Swain (1995) hypothesize that their need for an in-group vernacular leads them to turn to their native language vernacular, which they know through the media and their interactions outside the school. Increasingly, the immersion language, French, comes to be used only for academic purposes, and the native language, English, comes to be used for off-task social interactions between students – in spite of the best efforts of the teacher to enforce the use of French. In the end, therefore, language immersion classrooms in the upper grades become increasingly diglossic (Ferguson, 1959) speech communities (Tarone and Swain 1995).[1] The early ability of teachers and students to co-construct a relatively homogeneous language classroom community with a shared orientation to the French norm is undermined because this speech community, like all speech communities, contains sub-groups who have their own specialized needs for speech varieties to serve their social and psychosocial purposes. What we see is that the language immersion school, its classrooms and its students are far more complex and idiosyncratic than the founders of the immersion approach imagined, and that this complexity has made the immersion experiment turn out rather differently than its founders originally imagined it would. (I am not saying that language immersion education is a failure; far from it! But the founders of this approach did not anticipate the impact of the complex social structure of schools, classrooms and the social needs of growing children on language learning outcomes.)

Complexity of social factors influencing language use in the classroom

Broner (2000; under review) provides fascinating detail, with the aid of a powerful sociolinguistic statistical model called VARBRUL,[2] on the sociolinguistic dynamics that exist in a fifth grade Spanish immersion classroom. Her study shows that, while this classroom does indeed adhere to the general pattern of diglossia described above, the factors that influenced individual fifth graders' willingness to use Spanish L2 were, in keeping with Allwright's (2006) 'recognition of the essential and irreducible complexity of the phenomenon of classroom language learning and teaching', even more complex than Tarone and Swain (1995) suggested (of course). Pre-adolescent immersion children did switch to English when they made reference to teen culture, but their overall willingness to use Spanish L2 was also significantly influenced, not just by whether they were focused on academic tasks or not (an on-task vs. off-task dichotomy), but by such factors as who they were speaking to (teacher vs. different children in the class) and the particular subject matter, or content of the lesson (creative writing vs. mathematics).

Broner tape-recorded the language produced by three fifth grade immersion students in their classroom over a six-month period, describes their overall language use and analyses the factors affecting their second language use in that classroom with VARBRUL. There were strong individual differences in the language use of her three subjects: Leonard, Caroline and Marvin, all very good students in the class. Leonard and Caroline, who were relatively popular and well situated in the classroom social network, used Spanish and English roughly equally in the class. But Marvin, who was not as popular, and existed at the periphery of his class's social network, used Spanish almost all the time. In spite of these differences, Broner's results support the position that this language classroom is indeed a speech community with shared language norms. Broner's statistical analysis shows that although the three students had their own idiosyncrasies in language usage, their overall willingness to use Spanish L2 was significantly affected by exactly the same three factors: (1) whether they were on-task or off-task (Spanish when they were on-task, and English when they were off-task); (2) who they were addressing (they always spoke Spanish to the teacher, and with more English for peers, though with rather idiosyncratic preferences for language use with particular peers); and (3) the subject-matter they were studying (all three used more Spanish in creative writing than in arts and crafts, for example). While Marvin tended to use proportionally more Spanish than the other two students in all situations, the factors that caused Marvin to increase the amount of his Spanish or English language use were exactly the same factors that caused Leonard and Caroline to increase theirs. Thus, the same language norms applied to all three of them – they simply oriented to those norms in different ways – just as Preston (1989) suggests they would, as members of a class-room speech community.

There were, of course, very idiosyncratic patterns: for example, Marvin's normally high percentage of Spanish language use dropped dramatically when he was talking to Caroline, but rose even higher than normal, to 100 per cent, whenever he addressed Leonard. The overall picture provided to us by Broner's VARBRUL model of this fifth grade Spanish immersion classroom is a picture of a complex, dynamic community of learners who share basic norms of language behaviour, but whose use of the second language they are learning is affected in complex, systematically predictable ways as they interact with one another and adults, in engaging in academic tasks, pre-adolescent socializing, creative language play and in meeting the demands of academic subject-matter.

The teacher in the fifth grade immersion class studied by Broner was unaware of the complexity of these patterns of language use, since the children always spoke Spanish with her. She had set up a clear system of rewards for Spanish use and punishment for English use. However, she had no way of actually consistently tracking each child's language use in deskwork over the course of the entire day because she could not be at ten different desks at once. Indeed, only a careful coding of each utterance produced by the children, and analysis of all utterances by means of a complex multiple regression procedure, was able to reveal the system in these children's verbal behaviour. While the teacher sometimes overheard their use of English when she quietly approached their table, and consistently warned the students when she heard it, the students' general pattern of language use, described above, was unaffected by her direct interventions. These were clearly dynamics over which the immersion teacher had little or no real control (cf. Allwright, 1980). Nevertheless, it is very likely that her ability to understand the forces that are at work in their language use in her classroom may be able to lead her to make better pedagogical and human decisions in working with such classes in the future.

Impact of interlocutors and role relationships on acquisition

One factor that seems to hold across all second language learning contexts is the impact of different *interlocutors* on the speech production of second language learners. Learners speak differently with their teachers than they do with various of their peers in the classroom, or with interlocutors outside the classroom. One study that highlights this essential characteristic of second language learners and the interlanguage they produce is Guo-qiang Liu's study of 'Bob'. Bob was a six-year old English-language learner in Australian mainstream classes (Liu, 1991; also reported in Tarone and Liu, 1995). Because he was learning his second language in a country where that language was used outside the classroom, Bob used his second language more than the immersion children did; in fact, in school, none of his classmates or his teacher even understood his native language. However, like the immersion children,

Bob used his second language in systematically different ways with different interlocutors: his teacher, his classmates and a family friend at home. Liu tape-recorded Bob's interactions in these three contexts, defined (in Liu's terms) by Bob's role relationships with these different interlocutors. In a longitudinal study, Liu was able to show not only that Bob's language use differed with these different interlocutors, but that his acquisition of second language syntactic structures was affected by his interactions with them. He seemed to learn faster with some interlocutors than with others. Bob tried out his newest language forms in the safety of his home with the researcher, who was a family friend. In his interactions with the researcher, Bob was very comfortable. He played with him, insulted and bullied him and competed with him. He took risks with his new language, trying out new forms in his efforts to communicate with his adult friend. In tracking Bob's acquisition of five stages of question formation, each new stage appeared first in interactions at home with the researcher. Days or weeks later, Bob would use these same forms in conversations with his classmates at deskwork; in this context, Bob was a member of a group of bright, competitive, talkative little boys who were constantly competing for the floor and for status in such matters as their drawing ability. Bob's friends modelled all manner of insults and phrases useful for making invidious comparisons, and Bob picked up on those models immediately. In this social context, Bob used his new stages of question next. The third role relationship was the one Bob had with his teacher. Bob, as a good student, wanted to impress his teacher. He treated his teacher with respect, speaking only when spoken to, and being very very careful to be accurate with his English. Only when he was sure of the new stage of question formation, weeks after he'd been using it with his friends, would he use it with his teacher. Thus, in a very real sense, Bob's teacher was always the last to know when Bob had moved to a new stage of acquisition of English question forms. (Indeed, the teacher probably never knew about Bob's mastery of English insults and other vernacular English expressions he addressed to his friends at deskwork – unlike the immersion students, Bob *was* exposed to an L2 vernacular through his conversations with his peers, and even in the first grade, seemed to know it was inappropriate to use the vernacular with his teacher.) What we see in Liu's study of Bob is, again, that second language learners are highly social beings, in influential role relationships with a wide range of different interlocutors, and that their second language acquisition is affected in important ways by these complex interactions. Significantly, we also see that Bob's progress as a second language learner is best understood when it is described, in detail, at the local level, as Bob interacted with specific interlocutors for different purposes.

Social groupings and language use in college language classrooms

The studies I have described thus far have focused on child classroom language learners. However, there are similar findings in studies of the second language learning processes of young adults in college-level language classrooms. Such classrooms are also highly social, with complex and idiosyncratic sub-groupings, and this fact has a clear impact on language usage patterns within those classes. Bailey (1983) documented the way in which her willingness to use the second language in the classroom was conditioned by her own assessment of her hierarchical social relationships with other students in the classroom. Bailey described the way in which she competitively estimated her place in the hierarchy of the classroom on the basis of how 'good' she felt she was in the language, as compared with others in the class, and adjusted her class contributions accordingly. Her place in the social hierarchy of the classroom and her language use were related. Lynch, Klee and Tedick (2001) interviewed students in a Spanish Foreign Language Immersion Program (FLIP) at the University of Minnesota. In this programme, students learning Spanish as a second language can spend half a year taking all their content courses in the medium of the Spanish language: readings, lectures, discussions are all delivered through Spanish. Typical content courses may include a sociology course, a history course and a literature course. Lynch, Klee and Tedick (2001) found that two major social groupings emerged early in the school term. In these college immersion classroom 'societies', students with higher levels of L2 proficiency had higher status, and those with lower levels of L2 proficiency were often excluded from interaction with students of the first type. Learners' membership in these social groupings was related to their use of the second language. The first group of students used the L2 extensively both inside and outside the class, for both academic and social purposes; the other student group used the L2 only for very restricted academic purposes and hardly ever for social interactions inside or outside the class. The members of these two social groups reported having negative feelings about one another, and interacted minimally with one another in and outside of[3] class, in spite of the best efforts of their teachers to encourage such interaction. Here again, even with adult language learners, we see that language classrooms have social structures that are mutually constructed, with hierarchical sub-groups, and student–student interactions, over which the teacher may have minimal control.

Conclusion

As stated at the beginning of this chapter, centralized prescriptions on 'how to teach foreign languages' are unlikely to be universally successful. Prescriptive, simplistic solutions that are supposed to apply to all language learning and teaching situations and classrooms cannot in fact be universally applied; they can easily founder on the realities of actual language classrooms, with their various sub-groups, language needs and language varieties and role relationships. A host of complex factors may interact to counteract the efficacy of the prescription being given. The research studies I have described in this chapter, focusing on the way in which 2L learners interact in real language classrooms, support Allwright's (2006) contention, laid out at the beginning, that language lessons are not created centrally and unilaterally by teachers, but are *locally negotiated*. All the participants in the classroom have an impact on what goes on there, and influence one another's speech production, the way they perceive one another and one another's second language acquisition processes. Descriptive case studies such as those described here, situated in intact language classrooms, focused in detail on the way in which learners interact with one another and their teacher, can provide us with insight and understanding, because they show how those interactions affect the language use of those learners. More such studies should be done not to develop universalistic prescriptions for 'the best way to teach a foreign language', but rather to help *practitioners* – researchers and teachers – better to understand the complex nature of language classrooms, and some of the ways in which they may function

Notes

1. Ferguson used the term 'diglossia' to characterize societies in which one language is used for 'high' functions such as academic or religious purposes, and another language is used for 'low' functions, as in the home or the marketplace.
2. VARBRUL is a form of multiple regression analysis that was developed specifically to handle the unique characteristics of sociolinguistic data. It calculates the relative influence different social and linguistic factors have had, independently

of one another, on given speakers' linguistic choices – in this case, immersion students' choices to speak in English (L1) or Spanish (L2).
3. In this programme, students took several of the same classes, and could socialize together during lunch breaks outside of class. The more advanced students would speak Spanish with each other in these outside of class interactions.

References

Allwright, R. 1980. Turns, topics and tasks: patterns of participation in language teaching and learning. In: *Discourse analysis in second language research*, ed. D. Larsen-Freeman, 165–87. Rowley, MA: Newbury House Publishers.

Allwright, D. 2006. Six promising directions in Applied Linguistics. In: *Understanding the language classroom*, eds S. Gieve and I.K. Miller. London: Palgrave Macmillan, Chapter 1 in this volume.

Bailey, K. 1983. Competitiveness and anxiety in adult second language learning: looking at and through the diary studies. In: *Classroom-oriented research in second language acquisition*, eds H. Seliger and M. Long, 67–103. Rowley, MA: Newbury House Publishers.

Broner, M. 2000. Impact of interlocutor and task on first and second language use in a Spanish immersion program. Unpublished PhD thesis, University of Minnesota, Minneapolis, USA.

Broner, M. (under review). 'Talking in the fifth grade full immersion classroom: context and language choice'.

Ferguson, C. 1959. Diglossia. *Word* 15: 325–40.

Lambert, W., F. Genesee, N. Holobow and L. Chartrand 1993. Bilingual education for majority English-speaking children. *European Journal of Psychology of Education* 8, 1: 3–22.

Liu, G. 1991. Interaction and second language acquisition: a case study of a Chinese child's acquisition of English as a Second Language. Unpublished PhD thesis, La Trobe University, Melbourne, Australia.

Lynch, A., C. Klee and D. Tedick 2001. Social factors and language proficiency in postsecondary Spanish immersion: issues and implications. *Hispania* 84: 510–24.

Preston, D. 1989. *Sociolinguistics and second language acquisition*. Oxford: Basil Blackwell.

Preston, D. 1996. Variationist perspectives on second language acquisition. In: *Second language acquisition and linguistic variation*, eds R. Bailey and D. Preston, 1–46. Amsterdam: John Benjamins.

Preston, D. 2002. A variationist perspective on SLA: psycholinguistic concerns. In: *Oxford handbook of applied linguistics*, ed. R. Kaplan, 141–59. Oxford: Oxford University Press.

Tarone, E. and G. Liu 1995. Situational context, variation and second-language acquisition theory. In: *Principles and practice in the study of language and learning: a Festschrift for H.G. Widdowson*, eds G. Cook and B. Seidlhofer, 107–24. Oxford: Oxford University Press.

Tarone, E. and M. Swain 1995. A sociolinguistic perspective on second-language use in immersion classrooms. *Modern Language Journal* 79: 166–78.

9
Take 1, Take 2, Take 3: A Suggested Three-Stage Approach to Exploratory Practice*

John F. Fanselow and Roger Barnard

Introduction

Dick Allwright's reflections (2006, Chapter 1 in this volume) on the history of Applied Linguistics ties in with the work of many through the years who have tried to understand language learning and teaching from the perspective of the participants. In order to obtain student perspectives on classroom interaction, much recent research has been carried out using diary and journal studies (Gebhard and Oprandy, 1999; Jarvis, 1992; Numrich, 1996; Richards and Ho, 1998; Wiener and Rosenwald, 1993); peer observation (Crookes, 2003; Richards, 1998; Tsui, 2003); stimulated recall (Burns, 1996; Calderhead et al., 1981; Gass and Mackey, 2000); and private speech (Barnard, 2003; Broner and Tarone, 2001; De Guerrero, 1994, 1999; Lantolf, 1997; Saville-Troike, 1988).

Important as gaining a rich understanding of student perspectives is, part of our approach is to do some analysis when the perspectives of all the actual participants are not possible. Of course students can use our approach just as well as teachers, teacher trainers or researchers. In fact, a central goal of our approach is to support Allwright's decades-long attempt to show that all of these roles are *overlapping* (1983, 1988; Allwright and Bailey, 1991). Students who explore classroom interaction are researchers just as are teachers or researchers or teacher trainers who investigate classrooms. And as researchers share their results with others they are of course teachers, and those who use exploratory practice as part of their regular planning of classes are teacher trainers – for they are training themselves. We hope that as we illustrate a three-stage approach to Exploratory Practice, many who identify themselves with one label will see that all of us can use multiple labels to describe our roles.

In this chapter, in addition to our primary goal of speaking to Allwright's (2006, direction 6, *From academics to practitioners as the knowledge-makers in the field*, we deal with a second goal: moving from the one-dimensional interpretations of teaching practice that are so prevalent in the field. To reach this goal, we address two of Allwright's (2006) other direction: 1, *From prescription to description to understanding* and 2, *From simplicity to complexity*. We address direction 1, 2 and 6 by introducing a three-stage approach to exploratory practice.

In the first stage of our approach, *Take 1, recreating interaction*, we select and prepare transcripts from our own or published sources which are intended to highlight a particular problem or issue that has arisen in the classroom. *Take 2, reflection on action*, comprises three steps. In step 1, we interpret the transcript from an '-emic' perspective – that is, with an insider's knowledge of significant contextual features such as the background of the students, the teacher's aim, the actual setting and so on. In steps 2 and 3, we make alternative interpretations with no knowledge of the contextual features (that is, an '-etic' perspective), and by applying different theoretical perspectives from that taken by the original interpreter. In *Take 3, reconstructing for action*, we compare the three perspectives in Take 2 in order to generate an alternative classroom plan, with a view to dealing with the issue more effectively in our own professional practice.

The idea is that we might then repeat the three stages – Take 1, 2 and 3 – on this reconstructed classroom plan after it has been put into practice. We have two ultimate goals: first to understand our teaching and our students' learning more deeply, in Allwright's words moving '*From prescription to description to understanding*' (2006, direction 1) and moving '*From simplicity to complexity*' (2006, direction 2) and, second, to realize the overlapping roles we play as teachers, students, researchers and teacher trainers – Allwright's (2006) direction 6: '*From academics to practitioners as the knowledge-makers in the field.*'

We will demonstrate the three-stage approach – our three 'takes' – with two published transcripts: 'Painting and a box' from Richard-Amato (1988) and 'Carlos' trousers' from Long (1980). We will invite you to apply the three-stage approach with 'Hats and ties', an excerpt from Fanselow (1977b).

Painting and a box

Transcript 1, Take 1, recreating interaction

We have selected the following extract, published in a methodology book (Richard-Amato, 1988, 2nd edition, 1996), which seeks to illustrate the issue of the negotiation of meaning between teacher and learner.

Although this is not made explicit, it may be assumed that Richard-Amato was aware of the specific features of the context in order to make her interpretation (S = student, T = teacher):

1. S: I throw it – box. (Points to a box on the floor.)
2. T: You threw the box?
3. S: No, I threw in the box.
4. T: What did you throw in the box?
5. S: My...I paint...
6. T: Your painting?
7. S: Painting?
8. T: You know...painting. (Makes painting movements on an imaginary paper.)
9. S: Yes, painting.
10. T: You threw your painting in the box.
11. S: Yes, I threw my painting in box.

(Richard-Amato, 1988: 40)

Transcript 1, Take 2, recreating interaction: step 1 – an emic perspective

Based on her understanding of Krashen's (1982, 1985) notion of $i + 1$ (see p. 183), Richard-Amato (1988: 40) suggests that the transcribed episode illustrates the negotiation of meaning because it has the following characteristics of comprehensible input:

 (i) The words refer to the immediate environment
 (ii) The vocabulary and structures are simple
 (iii) There is a lot of repetition
 (iv) Acting or gestures – pointing to objects, for example – are used to illustrate meanings
 (v) Attention is given to the meaning of what is said and not to the form – there is no explicit comment about the incorrect tense in line 1, for example.

Also, if we listened to a recording of the teacher's speech, we would probably find that it was delivered at a slower than usual pace, with some exaggeration and pauses, features of 'motherese' and 'foreigner talk', to which Richard-Amato had earlier referred (1988: 36, 39).

According to the author (Richard-Amato, 1988: 40), these characteristics are sufficient to enable meaning to be negotiated by collaboration between a teacher and a learner, although she notes that it would take a lot more comprehensible input containing the grammatical features before they could be firmly acquired.

Transcript 1, Take 2, reflection on action: step 2 – a first etic perspective

An experienced teacher was asked to comment on the 'Painting' transcript in terms of the setting and participants, the intentions of the participants and the extent to which, and how, mutual understanding is achieved.

I can think of two possible contexts: one in a school classroom in which a teacher was interacting with a young learner, and the other a home setting where an adult (perhaps a mother) was talking to a small child. I infer the age of the child by fact that s/he was talking about a painting in a box, a typical activity for young children, and – more significantly – by the limited language being used or expressed by the child. I think the former scenario is more probable, but in either case an adult was probably scaffolding the child in a wider zone of proximal development – so as to enable the latter to move from her/his present developmental level to a higher one.

It is difficult to be certain about the participants' intentions as there are no clues about the discourse which immediately preceded the child's first utterance. It could be, for example, that the adult asked a question such as 'What did you do?' or 'Where did you put the painting?' Alternatively, the child could have initiated the interaction by simply informing the adult of what s/he had done. I think the latter is more likely, as the following exchanges indicate that the adult seemed to want to find out what the child wanted to say – and also to provide a grammatically correct model, to which the child eventually approximated. I think the child's intention was to tell the adult what s/he had done (with the limited linguistic resources at her/his command).

It seems to me that mutual understanding did occur but was limited by the child's speech or vocabulary knowledge. To compensate for this, both the child and the teacher used gestures to support or convey the 'missing' meaning of words that the child did not know or understand. The child, I noticed, did not immediately know how to say the word 'painting', and when corrected, did not initially understand the word until some additional information about the meaning of the word 'painting' was supplied. In this case, the teacher made painting movements on imaginary paper to support the meaning of the word 'painting'. This can also be said for the child's first sentence in discussing what was thrown into the box. The child omitted the words *in the*, but supported her/his lack of speech with action to help convey her/his meaning. S/he pointed at the box. The teacher responded by asking if it was thrown in the box. So – a limited amount of meaning was shared, but was restricted by the child's speech or vocabulary knowledge.

Transcript 1, Take 2, reflection on action: step 3 – a second etic interpretation

One way to remind ourselves of Allwright's (2006) direction 1, *'From prescription to description to understanding'*, direction 2 *'From simplicity to complexity'*, and direction 6 *'From academics to practitioners as the knowledge-makers in the field'* is to turn each characteristic into a null hypothesis. Thus, since Richard-Amato's first characteristic is 'the words refer to the immediate environment' (1988: 40), we need to find examples of words in the lines that do not refer to the immediate environment. Some of the words that seem not to refer to the immediate environment are *it* (line 1) and *the* (line 2, 3, 4, 10), *no* (line 3), *what* (line 4), *did* (line 4), and *yes* (line 9).

The word *it*, in line 1, by its nature, can refer to anything – including places close to us in the immediate environment, or far away in a different environment. Although the student seems to be using *it* in the first line to refer to something close at hand, the teacher seems not to notice the word *it* itself, much less what it might refer to in the immediate environment. Even at line 10, she (hereafter the teacher is always referred to as 'she' and the student as 'he') seems not to realize that *it* in line 1 in fact could be grouped with words that refer to the immediate environment. She seems not to realize that *it* might have been used to refer to the painting – close at hand – in the first line of the exchange.

Had she considered the painting to be close at hand, there would be no reason for making painting movements on an imaginary paper in line 8. Nor would there by any reason for her to say *Your painting?* in line 6. It is only in line 10 when she says *You threw your painting in the box* that she seems to realize that there has been a painting in the immediate environment from the beginning. Had she considered the painting to be in the immediate environment, she would have looked in the box and seen it, at line 6, when she asks, *Your painting?* Instead, she tries to illustrate the meaning of the action of painting in line 8. Moreover, the painting movements on an imaginary piece of paper seem not to take into account the fact that since the student introduced the word *paint* in line 5, he not only probably knows what *paint* means, but is trying to indicate that there is an actual painting in the immediate environment.

Ironically, even the word *box* which, when first mentioned in line 1, is pointed to by the student, and thus obviously and literally close at hand, is not treated by the teacher as if it is in the immediate environment. Her question in line 2 *You threw the box?* would be unnecessary if she considered the box to be in the immediate environment. She could have seen if it had been thrown, either by its size and weight or the way it was resting on the floor or table. Various questions might race through our mind if we considered the box in the environment where we could see it – for example: 'Is the box the student just mentioned upright? Is the box he just mentioned on its side with the contents spilled? Is anything in the box? Is the box he mentioned too large to be thrown or so small that if thrown it would be broken?'

Transcript 1, Take 3, reconstructing for action

In *Take 3, reconstructing for action*, having now compared the three perspectives, we can suggest a range of alternative courses for the teacher to take to more efficiently co-construct the intended meaning of the student's first utterance in line 1. Faced with the seemingly incomprehensible input of *I throw in – box*, there are a number of alternatives to the paraphrase in line 2. It seems that the teacher was not attending closely to the student: she apparently did not notice that the student was pointing to the box, nor did she listen to the word *it* in the student's utterance, and the significant pause that followed.

Rather than paraphrasing, the teacher might look in the box and then ask a close-ended question such as 'Did you throw your painting in the box?' It is of course, possible that the box contains other items as well, but in this case the teacher might select one of these for her question. Were she to do this, she would reduce the range of choices and, by simplifying the student's task, negotiate meaning perhaps more efficiently. If she wants to engage the student's mental and verbal processing more directly, she might write what the student said on the board; and then ask him to look at it and add some words; alternatively, the student could write what he has said on a piece of paper, or even draw what he wants to say, as a stimulus for a more protracted negotiation. Since the teacher does not understand the referent for *it*, she might say 'Touch it' or 'Give it to me', thereby directing the student to actually foreground the key element in the immediate environment.

It is often the case that when teachers do not understand something said by their students, they will say something like 'Again, please'. A similar recast here by the teacher, preceded by and indeed followed by a significant wait time, would clearly indicate to the student that a verbal reformulation would be helpful.

Assuming that the original dialogue had continued, at line 4 the teacher might have asked a close-ended question rather than the open-ended *What did you throw in the box?* As indicated above, this would have simplified the student's task, and also avoided the unnecessary diversion into the word 'painting', the meaning of which (despite the teacher's gesture in line 8) the student evidently understood. Rather than negotiating or co-constructing meaning, this exchange (lines 5–8) merely suggests that the teacher is confounding the issue, and creating a problem where none seems to exist.

It is clear that in the irreducible complex reality of any classroom, a teacher has to make many executive decisions very rapidly, and cannot be expected to call to mind a wide range of possible courses of action and then reflect *in* action on which of them might be most appropriate in the particular circumstances. This obvious point merely highlights the benefits of reflection *on* action – the *a posteriori* consideration of how alternative courses of action derived from general principles might enhance our understanding of classroom interaction. Then, by choosing from various alternatives, we may enhance our classroom practice in a subsequent similar interaction – reflection *for* action.

Carlos' trousers

Transcript 2, Take 1, recreating interaction

We have selected the following extract, which, according to Long (1980: 14) illustrates how, through interaction with students, a teacher re-asserts authority after it appears to be threatened.

1. T: ...OK? Chemical pollution. OK.
2. S4:   (yawning) O o o.
3. T: Trousers! Alright. Carlos [S4], do you wear trousers?
4. S4:   Alway...All my life.
5. Ss: (laughter)
6. T: Always. You've worn, I have...
7. S4:   Eh wear wear (inaudible).
8. T: I have...well do you wear trousers?
9. Ss: I wear.
10. Ss: I wear, I wear.
11. S4:   Yes, I I do.

12. T: Yes, you do. What's how do you say that word?
13. S4: Trousers.
14. T: Trou*se*rs.
15. S4: Trou*se*rs.
16. T: *Trou*sers.
17. S: Trou*se*rs.
18. S3: Trousers.
19. T: Mm hm. Have you got trousers on?
20. S3: Yes, I have.
21. T: What kind?
22. S3: Jeans.
23. T: Jeans…Say the word jeans. Jeans.
24. S3: Jeans.
25. T: Jeans.
26. S2: Jeans.
27. T: Jeans.
28. S1: Jeans.
29. T: OK OK. Huh! Does anyone need an ashtray?

(Long, 1980: 13–14)

Transcript 2, Take 2, reflection on action: step 1 – an emic perspective

Long (1980: 14) makes the assumption that the teacher takes Carlos' yawning to be a manifestation of boredom, rather than fatigue – and an indirect challenge to the value of the lesson. In reaction to the hilarity occasioned by Carlos' joking response to the teacher's odd question about his trousers in line 3, the teacher seeks to maintain control by drilling the pronunciation of a couple of items: *I wear* and *trousers*.

Long wonders why the teacher asked the students to repeat the form *I wear* (lines 9, 10), which is not a structurally accurate response to *Do you wear trousers?* And when Student 4 said *trousers* in 13, Long says that on the tape the word is correctly pronounced. Why then the teacher's repetition tasks? Long claims that the teacher was behaving 'not unlike a sergeant-major who, catching some unruly recruits in an act of disobedience, attempts to break their spirit with a dose of "square-bashing" on the barracks parade-ground' (1980: 14). Thus the purpose of the repetition tasks is not to practise language, but to re-establish order. And, again, what purpose is served by repeating incorrect responses to a question *I wear* (lines 9 and 10) in response to *Do you wear trousers?* (line 8) and repeating a word Student 4 had in fact said correctly in line 13? The only purpose, Long believes, is the establishment of control by the teacher.

Further evidence that the purpose in the exchange is control rather than practice or language learning comes from lines 19–20 when another student is able to respond correctly to a yes/no question: *Have you got trousers on? – Yes, I have.* Still further evidence that the purpose in the exchange is other than teaching language comes from lines 24–28 when the teacher is again asking students to repeat individual words out of context: there is no evidence to show they cannot say *jeans* correctly either individually or in meaningful phrases or sentences. Long (1980: 15) says a key reason that they are being docile is that the teacher has re-established order by insisting requesting that the students repeat words they in fact have no difficulty with.

The main reason for Long's claim that the purpose of the exchange is for the teacher to reestablish control rather than to practise language is to show that instruments designed for interaction analysis would miss this underlying purpose (1980: 15). Later, in Take 2, step 3, we shall suggest that there are ways in which at least one particular instrument could in fact produce the same, or even a richer interpretation.

Transcript 2, Take 2, reflection on action: step 2 – a first etic perspective

Long's extract can be viewed in the way that Richard-Amato explains the negotiation of meaning. The teacher's reaction to Carlos's yawning sets off a chain of events in which teacher and students collectively, though implicitly, reach an understanding. It is not at all clear why the teacher should begin this negotiation of meaning by a reference to the student's trousers, but in Richard-Amato's framework, the words do tie the medium of language to concrete objects in the immediate environment, thereby realising an important criterion of Krashen's (1985) notion of $i + 1$ – that is, input just above the learner's present knowledge. Similarly, both syntactical structures and the vocabulary are simple, with the key words very frequently repeated by both the teacher and the students. There is no verbal evidence of acting or gestures to clarify meanings, although it may be assumed that turn-taking and cueing are accompanied by appropriate eye contact and probably some form of gesture, such as pointing.

Very little attention is paid to syntactical form – for example, the teacher does not heed the awkward responses in lines 9 and 10; indeed, in this extract the students are expected to say no more than one or two words. However, the teacher does pay attention to the phonological form of the words – the pronunciation of the word *trousers* – but there is no explicit explanation of how the words should be pronounced.

The chain of repetition of this word and *jeans* concludes with the teacher's final acknowledgement *OK. OK*, which suggests that mutual understanding has been achieved, a topic boundary reached, and a new phase of the lesson is about to begin.

The identification of another object in the immediate environment (an ashtray) suggests that the tenets of comprehensible input are about to be activated. All of this would suggest that communication is successful because the input is comprehensible. But what has been understood? Surely not the meaning of trousers and jeans, nor the revelation that the students wear them, nor that the words are pronounced in certain ways. What appears to be the case is that the teacher has used a familiar language-teaching routine ('listen and repeat') implicitly to convey a meaningful message concerned with how classroom interaction should occur – by manifestly listening to the teacher. Since this message has never been made explicit, understanding must have been co-constructed by means other than that of direct, comprehensible input. In order to interpret this, we need another angle of vision.

Transcript 2, Take 2, reflection on action: step 3 – a second etic perspective

The extract can also be considered in the light of an interactional coding instrument. The fact that on one level the teacher in the transcript about trousers follows some of the features of negotiated meanings that Richard-Amato notes (1988) does not detract from Long's interpretation. But Long's claim that his 'understanding of the extract would not be captured by an instrument designed for interaction analysis' (1980: 15) is open to question. He notes that many instruments provide for multiple coding (1980: 6), but to support his claim that instruments could not capture the interpretation he makes, he fails to take note of the richness of instruments that provide for multiple coding. He says that an interaction instrument would simply be coded something like 'T asks question – S responds – T models – S responds, etc.' (1980: 15).

If we used the categories in FOCUS (Fanselow, 1977a, 1987), we could in fact show an interpretation of the transcript richer than Long's interpretation. FOCUS notes five characteristics of communication. In the 1980 article which contains the excerpt with Carlos, Long notes the first characteristic, source of the communication (1980: 15). And he mentions the second, whether a task is being set or performed. And he touches on the third characteristic when he refers to models (1980: 15). In FOCUS, modelling is a characteristic called 'use: ways mediums are used' (1977a: 25) and includes providing models. But the two characteristics of FOCUS that would clearly lead to the same interpretation Long has made are first, the medium of communication used and, secondly, the content of the communication.

The yawning in line 2 would be coded as a paralinguistic medium of communication that can be seen and heard. And the content of the yawning would have to be coded in three ways: either as the expression of personal feelings – part of the category of content called LIFE; or the expression of some form of classroom behaviour, part of the category of content called PROCEDURE; or the expression of some language point to be learned, part of the category called LANGUAGE. It seems clear that the student is not yawning to demonstrate the meaning of the word, as there is no mention of the word in the exchange. Thus, LANGUAGE is eliminated as a coding category that could fit. Moreover, since the teacher does not ask about the reason for the yawn with a question such as 'Did you go to a party last night?' the teacher does not treat the yawn personal experience, a sub-category of LIFE. So we are left with the category PROCEDURE. And one of the sub-categories of PROCEDURE is classroom social behaviour, which of course can be positive, negative or neutral. In this instance, it seems to be negative and would be so coded.

Once a coder determined that the initial exchange was dealing with inappropriate classroom behaviour, the coding of the content of the subsequent lines would be done with this interpretation in mind. When the teacher has the students repeat the words, the repetition would be double coded. It would perhaps be coded LANGUAGE, sub-category pronunciation. But it would also have to coded PROCEDURE, sub-category classroom social behaviour. Since the students tend to get the language right in their repetitions, another meaning has to be considered for the repetition of the words. And given the coding of the opening lines as PROCEDURE, classroom social behaviour, it seems reasonable to interpret the subsequent lines in the same way.

Once two or three independent coders finished their coding and came together to compare their coding, they could negotiate any disagreements. If of course the coders agreed on the coding, then no negotiation would be needed. But in coding systems with multiple categories, disagreements tend to happen. And one of the values of multiple-category systems, especially one like FOCUS with many sub-categories, is that one person tends to pick up something another misses.

So while Long argues that his 'understanding of the extract would not be captured by an instrument designed for interaction analysis' (1980: 15) we are claiming that by using existing characteristics of communications and categories and sub-categories to apply to data, those interpreting the data have both a framework and a set of options that can be used to richly interpret interaction. Though Long states that FOCUS has seventy-three categories – the highest of any he lists – in fact, each communication is coded with a minimum of five characteristics. Thus by using the categories in combination we can code thousands of distinct communications, not just a few score. By providing many lenses, FOCUS allows multiple facets with which to interpret data in a wide range of ways and is designed to stimulate exploratory talk – not merely to label or categorize communications.

Without any categories, people new to exploration of their own teaching, or that of others, would have little direction. But categories not only provide direction – where to look – but a way to focus discussion of the data and provide a taxonomy within which the interpretation can be made – a point emphasized by Allwright (1988: 56, 242). 'Is the teacher developing language, or controlling students, or having a personal conversation?' is the sort of question that the category CONTENT would stimulate. 'Is the yawn, or smile or raised finger being used to teach a gesture, words that name gestures, cultural content, or something having to do with classroom behaviour and procedures?' These types of questions which the categories in FOCUS are designed to stimulate have been used to produce many types of interpretations in addition to the one that Long has made of the Carlos' trousers transcript.

Transcript 2, Take 3, reconstructing for action

Whether we interpret this transcript using a systematic coding system, or theoretical perspectives, or insights from our experience or – which is usually the case – some combination of all three, we are unlikely to further our professional development unless we generate alternative practices – reconstructing *for* action.

So let us provide alternatives we can use in our classes to the 'sergeant-major approach' drilling to reassert our authority (Long, 1980: 14). If we were using FOCUS, we would have a range of options in front of us. Publications by Fanselow (for example, 1977a, 1987) are filled with coding of interactions and suggestions for generating alternative interactions simply by substituting communications from different categories. As we said above, the content of the student's yawn in line 2 would be coded PROCEDURE, classroom social behaviour. And the teacher/sergeant-major's call to Carlos to pay attention in line 3 (*Trousers!*) would be coded in the same way.

We can substitute either LIFE or STUDY OF LANGUAGE as the content of our communication after the student's yawn. An example of a communication in the category LIFE would be a personal comment or question, such as: 'Carlos, sorry, you seem tired. I feel tired too. Any others?' If in fact many students indicated that they were tired, the teacher could move from LIFE to PROCEDURE, classroom social behaviour, in a positive rather than negative way by saying, for example, 'Let's take a short break. Let's walk out in the hall to get our blood moving'.

Or, in line 3 we could substitute a different task. In FOCUS, there are five types of tasks: one to take in mediums by listening, reading silently, observing: *attend* (1) and four to produce mediums. In FOCUS, mediums can be produced to *characterize* (2) by commenting or categorizing, to *present* (3), by stating facts and answering questions the person asking knows the answer to, to *relate* (4), by making inferences, speculating or giving original explanation or to *re-present* (5) by imitating, copying, writing a dictation, or paraphrasing (Fanselow, 1977a: 25–6).

The task Carlos is asked to do is to answer what is commonly called a 'display question', *present* (3) in FOCUS. He is asked to respond to a question to which the teacher, and in this case probably everyone in the class, knows the answer, and might be wondering why a question with such an obvious answer was uttered. One alternative would be to move from the category *present* (3) to *re-present* (5): 'Those who are wearing new trousers raise your right hand; those who are wearing old trousers raise your left hand.' As the direction indicates, the students are meant to show whether they comprehend by performing one of two actions, changing spoken words, objects, the trousers they are wearing, into an action. In this way, the experience of appropriate kinesic activity facilitates or reinforces the meaning being processed mentally and verbally.

Another task in the category, *re-present* (5), would be to ask the students to draw a pair of cool trousers and a pair of not so cool trousers, or make a list of the students who they thought had the coolest trousers. Both the teacher and the students could look at the sketches or the lists to see the extent to which they could build on their familiarity with various types of trousers to extend their vocabulary – comparison of colour, styles, materials and so on. Sketching or raising hands or drawing would provide a few seconds for the teacher to consider options to engage the class.

Returning to the content of communications, LANGUAGE has a dozen or more sub-categories, one of which is pronunciation. With a list of sub-categories on a chart in a class, a teacher could take a quick glance and see whether there were other aspects of language that could be dealt with other than pronunciation: word order, for example. By using the whiteboard dynamically, the teacher could indicate that she wanted the students to generate questions, either orally or in writing – noting 'How many' and 'Who' in one column and in another column dollar signs to indicate cost, in another column a sketch of trousers, a skirt and jeans, or the first initial of these words, as in the substitution table below, and a question mark at the end, as below:

A substitution tale for manipulating language

How many			$$$$		
	is	w		t	
	are		$$	s	?
Who				j	
			–$		

'How many are wearing expensive/cheap/very expensive trousers/ skirts/jeans?' and 'Who is wearing cheap/expensive/very expensive trousers/ skirts/ jeans?' would be among the possibilities. Changing sketches into spoken or written words and forming the question pattern requires more concentration than repetition and at the same time would fulfill the teacher's wish to regain control. But the first letter of the words requires more thinking than the words themselves. Some combination of sketches, symbols like the dollar sign and first letters would require the most mental processing.

Hats and ties

Transcript 3, Take 1, recreating interaction

We have chosen the following extracts as they were discussed in an article on error correction (Fanselow, 1977b).

1. T: What are you holding? (Expects student to tell him.)
2. S: What are you holding?
3. T: The answer!
4. T: What material is this? (Holding a tie.)
5. S: Linen.
6. S: Wool.
7. S: Cotton.
8. T: It's linen.
9. S: He holding hat.

10. T: Again.
11. S: She holding hat.
12. T: She?
13. S: holding...
14. T: It's blue.
15. S1:   It blue.
16. T: It's blue.
17. S2:   It's blue.
18. T: It's blue.
19. S1:   It blue.
20. T: It's blue.
21. S1:   It blue.

Transcript 3, Take 2, reflection on action: step 1 – an emic perspective

We provide Take 2, step 1 in the Appendix (p. 193) and we suggest that before considering our insider's interpretation of this transcript, you, the reader, make your own, outsider's reflections based simply on what can be inferred from the transcript data. We hope that by your engagement with the data you will experience the multiple roles that we are suggesting we all play and also have an opportunity to actually do what we are advocating.

Transcript 3, Take 2, reflection on action: step 2 – a first etic perspective

Here, we invite you as a reader to actively engage in providing your own etic perspectives. Since one of our goals is to show how our roles as teacher, researcher, student and teacher trainer overlap, by inviting you as a reader to apply the three-stage approach to exploratory practice we hope we can demonstrate the importance of each of us seeing ourselves in multiple roles. In the Appendix we provide Take 2, step 2, a first etic perspective you can compare with your own.

Transcript 3, Take 2, reflection on action: step 3 – a second etic perspective

For step 3, we would like you to show the transcript (only) to a colleague and ask him/her to provide a second outsider's perspective. Again, we provide an alternative etic perspective in the Appendix.

Transcript 3, Take 3, reconstructing for action

We now invite you to attempt Take 3, reconstructing for action. To do this, you can compare the takes written above with the emic and etic interpretations in the Appendix. By doing so, you will help us reach our goal of showing the overlap in roles we all fill – Allwright's (2006) direction 6: *Moving from academics to practitioners as knowledge-makers in the field*. It will also help us more fully attain our second goal: shifting from the one-dimensional interpretations of teaching practice which are so prevalent in the field – thus addressing Allwright's (2006) directions 1 and 2: *From prescription to description to understanding* and *From simplicity to complexity*.

Conclusion

Our aim in this chapter has been twofold: to emphasize our overlapping roles and the need for multiple interpretations of teaching practice rather than one-dimensional interpretations. We have also tried to show that it is more useful to analyse *interactional data* in order to illuminate classroom activity than to prescribe effective ways of teaching – Allwright's (2006) direction 1: *From prescription to description to understanding*. We have also reminded ourselves that the one-dimensional interpretations that were part of some often-quoted books and articles failed to take heed of Allwright's (2006) direction 2: *From simplicity to complexity*. Finally, we hope we have demonstrated the overlap between the various roles we each fulfil. We are neither teacher nor researcher nor teacher trainer nor student. We are all learners. We are all knowledge-makers. The divide between so-called 'academics' and 'practitioners' has been breaking down for years. We hope our three-stage approach can contribute to this useful deconstruction, as has Allwright's writing and teaching through the years (1983, 1988; Allwright and Bailey, 1991).

Central to our position is the view that multiple perspectives are needed in order to both describe and understand what occurs in classrooms. Thus, we have selected (Take 1) three short published extracts of interactions in very different classroom contexts. The reason why we chose to present and discuss published accounts is so that readers may locate the original works and thereby appreciate both the teaching context and the theoretical assumptions current at the time of writing. (In itself, this historical perspective should prove a salutary lesson in avoiding pedagogical prescription!) In Take 2, reflection on action, each of the extracts has been examined from three different standpoints: those of the insider with an emic knowledge of the context, and two of outsiders informed by implicit or explicit theories of the nature of interaction and the negotiation of meaning. We have tried to show that none of these points of view is necessarily 'correct', and certainly not complete in itself, but each may provide a partial understanding of the interaction. In doing so, we provide a palimpsest of interpretation which may allow insights for the generation of ideas (Take 3, reconstructing for action) for subsequent lesson planning in relatable situations. In short, we believe that analysis of classroom events is enriched by multiple perspectives and attention to both Allwright's (2006) direction 1 – *From prescription to description to understanding*, and to his direction 2 – *From simplicity to complexity*. Our hope is that this approach illustrates how we might systematically reflect on, and for, action as part of our ongoing development as teachers, teacher trainers, classroom researchers – and learners.

We suggest that teachers periodically record some of their lessons. On occasion, it will appear that some of the classroom interactions are in some way significant. Why these particular events are salient may differ: an event may be selected because communication broke down and was then successfully repaired (or not!); it may be that – at least on the surface – the communication was entirely successful, and the teacher/researcher/teacher trainer wishes to know why this was so; perhaps the event was significant because it developed in unexpected and interesting ways. For whatever reason, the teacher/researcher/ teacher trainer (and students if the data is available for the students) thinks that the interaction could be worthy of closer investigation. Thus, the first step would be to listen to the recording and transcribe the particular interaction as accurately as possible (Take 1, recreating interaction). Then, the teacher would analyse the extract from his/her own perspective, adding as much 'thick' description of the contextual features as possible – reflection *on* action (Take 2, reflection on action: step 1 – an emic perspective).

It would then be appropriate to show the transcript – with no other details – to a colleague, and ask him/her to write a paragraph or two, for example about what s/he can infer from the data about the setting and the participants, the intentions of student and teacher and the extent to which, and how, mutual understanding is achieved (Take 2, reflection on action: step 2 – a first etic perspective). In itself, this will provide an external point of view and a richer interpretation. However, we would argue that while two heads are better than one, this is not sufficient. The reason is that two standpoints may be seen as contrastive and oppositional, rather than complementary, thought-provoking and heuristic (Fanselow, 1988, 1992). Therefore, it is extremely desirable to seek a third interpretation (Take 2, reflection on action: step 3 – a second etic perspective), which could be obtained in various ways. For example, if the teacher is undergoing a formal programme of professional development, the third standpoint could be obtained from the course leader. Alternatively, if the teacher is taking independent responsibility for development, s/he could seek an interpretation from one of the many published explanations of classroom interaction, and apply a framework such as those we have illustrated in this chapter. It may be that the teacher has to hand an experienced analyst who could be approached for an informed interpretation. Having compared these various points of view, and considered the validity of each, the teacher is ready to reconstruct *for* action (Take 3) by envisaging a similar scenario and planning an appropriate course of action.

The ultimate step would be to repeat the three stages after recording the part of the lesson in which the refined plan was implemented. And for the teacher to invite interested parties (colleagues, teacher trainers, researchers and students) to engage in the three stages with the transcribed data.

Clearly, our proposed approach is not one recommended for everyday teaching! It is a painstaking, even laborious, process that requires detailed attention and a readiness to critique one's own position as well as those of others. Thus we suggest that it is a tool that can be used sparingly – but, we believe, effectively – to illuminate certain aspects of professional activity that the individual teacher/researcher/ teacher trainer wishes to explore in some depth. As implied above, this approach would be a very useful component of a mentoring scheme – or, indeed, any formal programme of reflective professional development. In such an environment, teachers could be inducted into the process by an experienced analyst, and co-construct understanding and share interpretations with other participants, thereby preparing themselves for autonomous investigation of their own particular teaching contexts. And at the same time, researchers and teacher trainers would be engaged in the exploration of actual classroom interaction, which can be understood only by engagement in the exploration of day-to-day practices with the teachers involved. Our roles overlap, as do the directions we all need to explore, no matter what our official/assigned roles. In short, taking our cue from Dick Allwright (2006), we need to move *From prescription to description to understanding* (direction 1), *From simplicity to complexity* (direction 2) and *From academics to practitioners* as the *knowledge-makers in the field* (direction 6). And, equally importantly, we have to move from what we consider to be our primary role to other, complementary roles.

Appendix

Transcript 3, Take 2, reflection on action: step 1 – an emic perspective

The transcripts above were from a series of videotapes of lessons designed to teach adjective word order before a noun – colour, material, object – in the pattern 'I'm/he's/she's/we're holding/wearing...'. A dozen of us used the same bag of materials: a yellow polyester tie, a blue felt fez, a black woollen beret, a white woollen hat, a blue woollen ski cap and a red paper bag. We each had a copy of the same lesson plan. A key part of the lesson plan was the suggestion that each teacher draw vertical lines on the blackboard to show the slots or columns that were to be the focus of the lesson. The suggestion was also made that in the subject slots stick figures be drawn rather than written pronouns to represent male and female.

The students in the classes were adults, aged from around eighteen to sixty. The classes were held in the evening two or three times a week for two hours per session. The adults paid a small fee to cover the cost of materials. The teachers had some experience and were in the process of completing their post-graduate degree in TESOL.

Although the purpose of the lesson was to enable the students to use the correct subject verb agreement in contractions and learn adjective word order before a noun, the intention of video-taping the lessons and transcribing them was to describe how a dozen teachers treated errors during oral lessons. In the event, as the small sample of transcripts suggest, the teachers tended to focus on either colour or material or object rather than adjective before a noun. And rather than practise the agreement between personal pronouns and *to be* in contractions, there was a lot of attention to the contraction *it's*.

Though the lesson plan was not followed, meaning that some classes focused on colours, others on materials used to make hats, ties and bags and others repeated the names of objects, there was an amazing similarity in how the teachers treated errors. This was in spite of the fact that there was nothing in the lesson plan or in the discussions before the lessons were taught about the treatment of error.

This result is similar to one Bellack et al. (1966) found in a study of social studies classes, in which secondary teachers were given a reading passage on free trade to discuss with their classes. A number of key points were highlighted in the plan that accompanied the reading passage. Like us, after transcribing his lessons, Bellack and his team found that each teacher focused on different parts of the reading passage. But the bulk of the questions all the teachers asked were restatement of facts from the reading.

Transcript 3, Take 2, reflection on action: step 2 – a first etic perspective

The following analysis makes use of the Initiation – Response – Feedback (IRF) structure suggested by Coulthard (1986), and will comment on the frequency of implicit, rather than explicit feedback by the teacher. Before discussing what emerges, a few preliminary observations are necessary. In the first place, nothing was known (at the start of this analysis) of the context in which the interactions occur, except that they took place some thirty years ago. Nothing about the teacher, students or setting has been revealed, although the internal evidence strongly points to it being an English language lesson, and it may be inferred that the teacher's goal is for the students to be able to orally produce key items correctly. Secondly, it is assumed that the episode is not a continuous dialogue between teacher and students, but it is not known how many, or which, of the students are verbally interacting with the teacher. Indeed, internal evidence in these excerpts suggests that they are not from one lesson, but from a number of lessons where a teacher (the same? or different? in each case) applies alternative techniques to elicit the target language.

Lines 1–3 clearly follow an IRF format, where the teacher initiates an exchange by an elicitation. Her intention (according to the side note at line 1) is for the students to answer the question. The student's response echoes what she has said in a conventional 'listen and repeat' mode, thus misinterpreting the cue. The teacher's feedback (line 3) implicitly contradicts this interpretation because she starts another exchange with an instruction to answer her question, not to repeat it. The next exchange follows the IRRRF format: the teacher's elicitation is followed by different responses from three students before she (again, implicitly) confirms the first response as correct. It may be assumed that her intonation, and perhaps other non-verbal signals, would be sufficient indication to the students that she is satisfied with their responses. In the exchange that follows in lines 9–13, the teacher's feedback (*Again* in line 10) serves as both feedback and initiation intended to imply that what the student said needed to be reformulated. The student understands the implied illocutionary intent, but has apparently not understood exactly what adjustment needs to be made, assuming that the pronoun is the target. When he uses another pronoun instead of the missing *Is* (line 11), the teacher's feedback is in the form of a recast – she echoes the student's utterance with a questioning intonation. Again, the student understands the teacher's intent, but again fails to produce the desired form, and merely repeats a single word, *holding*. It may be inferred that the teacher's attempt to negotiate meaning implicitly was unsuccessful. The final exchange here (lines 14–21) again shows an absence of explicit feedback. The teacher's initiation (line 14) receives an incorrect response from the first student. In spite of the implicit feedback (and initiations) in lines 16, 18 and 20 – and the correct response from another student (line 17) – the first student fails to produce the desired, correct form. Considering these four exchanges as a whole, it may be considered that implicit cues alone are ineffective: the teacher's feedback should be both more explicit and the student's attention focused more precisely on what the teacher wants; otherwise, the students are left to guess 'what's in the teacher's head?'

Transcript 3, Take 2, reflection on action: step 3 – a second etic perspective

On reflection, a number of issues arise that seem obvious looking at the transcripts. First, asking a person what they are holding or wearing when we can see what they are holding or wearing seems curious if not absurd (Carlos would have felt very much at home in this classroom!). Had we included blindfolds with the materials, we could have avoided the type of error in the first transcript in which the student repeats the question the teacher asks rather than answering the question. The student might have had the same insight we had – why would a person ask another person what was being held if the person asking the question could clearly see the object? Wearing a blindfold might seem absurd also. But if the students were aware that the goal was to practise a pattern and the game-like atmosphere was a way to make the practice a bit more acceptable, the result might have been positive.

The adjective word order of colour and material before a noun could have been practised with a command such as 'Put the yellow silk tie on Juan's desk and the blue felt fez on Ali's desk.' Though this task is also contrived, it would provide practice in understanding how we distinguish objects and draw students' attention away from the adjective word order pattern to meaning. This task would have got students out of their seats and also provided student-to-student interaction. Though we had the students asking each other what they were wearing or holding in pair work, since they could see what the answers were supposed to be, trying to figure out how to say the pattern was not engaging.

At the time that these exchanges were originally reported by Fanselow (1977b), there was an emphasis on the teaching and testing of discrete linguistic forms in a structural syllabus. Long (1988) referred to this approach as 'focus on forms' and argued that it was both outmoded and ineffective. He has also rejected a 'strong' form (Howatt, 1984) of communicative language teaching, in which any explicit attention to grammar is discouraged. Taking the view that a communicative approach to language learning is reasonable, he has subsequently elaborated an alternative approach to the explicit teaching of grammar which he has termed focus on *form* (Long, 1991), which he defines as 'overtly draw[ing] students' attention to linguistic elements as they arise incidentally in lessons whose overriding focus is on meaning or communication' (Long, 1991: 45–6). Similarly, Doughty and Williams (1998: 3) and Ellis, Loewen and Basturkmen (1999) suggest that a focus on form (in contrast to a focus on *forms*) always entails 'isolation or extraction of linguistic features from context or from communicative activity'.

Transcript 3, Take 3, reflection on action

If these suggestions were followed in current practice, the Take 3 emphasis would not be, as it was in Fanselow (1977b) on the deliberate presentation and practice of pre-determined linguistic forms – which Krashen (1982) referred to as 'the structure of the day approach'. Rather, there would be incidental and transitory attention to grammatical issues (Ellis, Loewen and Basturkmen, 1999) as they arise in a lesson, possibly because they impede communication, or because either the teacher or the learners wish to draw attention to a formal issue. Therefore, the misunderstanding in the first exchange above (line 1, *What are you holding?*) would unlikely to arise because in a communicative activity students would not expect to repeat a question asked by the teacher. There would, of course, have to be a (communicatively) valid reason for the teacher to ask this particular question if she wised to avoid a sarcastic response such as 'Can't you see?' The second exchange, about a tie (line 4–8), would be mutually understood as relevant – but only if the activity the students were engaged in required the material to be specified, but would not in itself constitute a form-focused episode but one about meaning. The third example (lines 9–13), where the teacher attempts to draw attention to the student's formal mistake, would be regarded by Ellis, Loewen and Basturkmen (1999) as a good example of a form-focused episode – assuming that the error occurred in the course of a communicative activity, and the teacher considered intervention useful. As it is, the exchange would not be regarded as a complete form-focused episode, as – despite the two cues by the teacher – there is no indication of understanding (which Ellis, Loewen and Basturkmen (1999) refer to as 'uptake') on the part of the student. It would be a matter of rapid executive decision-making by the teacher as to whether she should complete the episode, or to leave well alone and allow the communicative intention of the student to proceed. The final exchange (lines 14–21), beginning with the teacher's prompt (*It's blue*) would not usually be regarded as form-focused unless the teacher's move were stimulated by something (wrong) that the student had said. Moreover, merely reiterating the target form would not be considered a sufficient technique to arouse the student's awareness that an error had been made, let alone how it should be corrected.

Note

* We should like to thank Margaret Franken and Steven Donald for their useful input in the development our thinking for this chapter.

References

Allwright, R.L. 1983. Classroom-centred research in language teaching and learning: a brief historical overview. *TESOL Quarterly* 17, 2:191–204.
Allwright, D. 1988. *Observation in the language classroom.* London: Longman.
Allwright, D. 2006. Six promising directions in Applied Linguistics. In: *Understanding the language classroom*, eds S. Gieve and I.K. Miller. Palgrave Macmillan, Chapter 1 in this volume.
Allwright, D. and K.M. Bailey 1991. *Focus on the language classroom.* New York: Cambridge University Press.
Barnard, R. 2003. Private speech in the primary classroom: Jack, a Korean learner. In: *Bilingual children's language and literacy development*, eds R. Barnard and T. Glynn, 166–93. Clevedon: Multilingual Matters.
Bellack, A. et al. 1966. *The language of the classroom.* New York: Teachers College Press, Teachers College, Columbia University.
Broner, M.A. and E. Tarone 2001. Is it fun? Language play in a fifth-grade Spanish immersion class. *The Modern Language Journal* 85, iii:363–79.
Burns, A. 1996. Starting all over again: from teaching adults to teaching beginners. In: *Teacher learning in language teaching*, eds D. Freeman and J.C. Richards, 154–77. Cambridge: Cambridge University Press.
Calderhead, J. et al. 1981. Stimulated recall: a method for research on teaching. *British Journal of Educational Psychology* 51:211–17.
Coulthard, M. 1986. *An introduction to discourse analysis.* London: Longman.

Crookes, G. 2003. *A practicum in TESOL: professional development through teaching practice*. Cambridge: Cambridge University Press.

De Guerrerro, M.C.M. 1994. Form and function of inner speech in adult second language learning. In: *Vygotskian approaches to second language learning*, eds J.P. Lantolf and G. Appel, 83–116. Norwood, NJ: Ablex.

De Guerrerro, M.C.M. 1999. Inner speech as mental rehearsal: the case of advanced ESL learners. *Issues in Applied Linguistics* 10:27–55.

Doughty, C. and J. Williams, eds 1998. *Focus on form in classroom second language acquisition*. Cambridge: Cambridge University Press.

Ellis, R., S. Loewen and H. Basturkmen 1999. Focusing on form in the classroom. *Occasional Papers* 13. Auckland: Institute of Language Teaching and Learning, University of Auckland.

Fanselow, J.F. 1977a. Beyond *Rashomon*: conceptualizing and describing the teaching act. *TESOL Quarterly* 11, 1:17–32, reprinted in Allwright (1988).

Fanselow, J.F. 1977b. The treatment of error in oral work. *Foreign Language Annals*, X, 4:583–93.

Fanselow, J.F. 1987. *Breaking rules: generating and exploring alternatives in language teaching*. White Plains, NY: Longman.

Fanselow, J.F. 1988. Let's see: contrasting conversations about teaching. *TESOL Quarterly* 22, 1:113–130, reprinted in eds Richards, J.C. and D. Nunan (1990).

Fanselow, J.F. 1992. *Contrasting conversations: activities for exploring our beliefs and teaching practices*. White Plains, NY: Longman.

Gass, S.M. and A. Mackey 2000. *Stimulated recall methodology in second language research*. Mahwah, NJ: Erlbaum Associates.

Gebhard, J.G. and R. Oprandy 1999. *Language teaching awareness: a guide to exploring beliefs and practices*. Cambridge: Cambridge University Press.

Howatt, A.P.R. 1984. *A history of English language teaching*. Oxford: Oxford University Press.

Jarvis, J. 1992. Using diaries for teacher reflection on in-service courses. *ELT Journal* 46, 2:133–43.

Krashen, S.D. 1982. *Principles and practices in second language acquisition*. Oxford: Pergamon.

Krashen, S.D. 1985. *The input hypothesis: issues and implications*. London: Longman.

Lantolf, J.P. 1997. The function of L2 play in the acquisition of Spanish. In: *Contemporary perspectives on the acquisition of Spanish*, eds W.R. Glass and A.T. Perez-Leroux, 3–24. Somerville, MA.: Cascadilla Press.

Long, M.H. 1980. Inside the 'Black Box': methodological issues in classroom research. *Language Learning* 30:3–36.

Long, M.H. 1988. Focus on form: a design feature in language teaching methodology. Presentation given at the National Foreign Language Center European Council Foundation Conference on Empirical Research on Second Language Learning in Institutional Settings. Bellagio, Italy, June 20–24, mimeo.

Long, M.H. 1991. Focus on form: a design feature in language teaching methodology. In: *Foreign language research in cross-cultural perspective*, eds K. de Bot, D. Coste, R. Ginsberg and C. Kramsch. Amsterdam: John Benjamins.

Numrich, C. 1996. On becoming a language teacher: insights from diary studies. *TESOL Quarterly* 30, 1:131–54.

Richard-Amato, P.A. 1988. *Making it happen – interaction in the second language classroom, from theory to practice.* White Plains, NY: Longman, 2nd edition, 1996.

Richards, J.C. 1998. Through other eyes: revisiting classroom observation. In: *Beyond training,* 141–52. Cambridge: Cambridge University Press.

Richards, J.C. and B. Ho 1998. Reflective thinking through journal writing. In: *Beyond Training,* ed. J.C. Richards, 153–70. Cambridge: Cambridge University Press.

Richards, J.C. and D. Nunan, eds 1990. *Second language teacher education.* Cambridge: Cambridge University Press.

Saville-Troike, M. 1988. Private speech: evidence for second language learning strategies during the 'silent period'. *Journal of Child Language* 15:567–90.

Tsui, A.B.M. 2003. *Understanding expertise in language teaching: case studies of ESL teachers.* Cambridge: Cambridge University Press.

Wiener, W.J. and G.C. Rosenwald 1993. A moment's monument: the psychology of keeping a diary. In: *The narrative study of lives,* eds R. Josselson and A. Lieblich, 30–58. Newbury Park, CA: Sage.

10
Collegial Development in ELT: The Interface between Global Processes and Local Understandings*

Michael P. Breen

Introduction

In focusing upon ELT practitioners, this chapter identifies the wider influences upon teachers' work at the present time that may be undermining their personal professional identities. It explores current approaches to teacher development that can be seen as symptomatic of such changes. An initial purpose is to consider aspects of teacher development that may be contributing to this appropriation of the self as a professional. The second aim of the chapter is to identify alternative approaches in which teachers may confront present uncertainties through strategies that enable them to create positive opportunities for change on their own terms and to realize what Dick Allwright identifies as teachers' capacities as knowledge-makers in the dialogue between research and practice (2006, Chapter 1 in this volume). The chapter begins with a brief review of some of the pressures that teachers presently face. It then evaluates currently influential approaches to teacher development as responses to these pressures. Finally, it proposes possible future directions in teacher development that may overcome the present constraints upon professionalism and the limitations inherent in current approaches. The terms 'teacher development' and 'professional development' are treated as synonymous throughout the chapter. They are used to refer to any in-service programme or course for experienced English language teachers, be they planned and provided by teacher educators or others or generated locally by and for teachers themselves in planned or spontaneous ways.

The new millennium: a critical moment for teacher development?

It is widely recognized by those who closely study contemporary society, and it is directly experienced by teachers as members of society, that we live within a global culture that confronts us with unanticipated risks to our sense of equilibrium and with recurrent demands upon our adaptability that seem to sever our links with the conventional wisdom of previous generations. Traditional values and community ties that formerly sustained our sense of stability have been replaced by multiple sources of authority wherein increasingly intrusive media articulate on our behalf what we should regard as 'common sense', economically desirable and politically advantageous. While such global processes unify the human community, paradoxically, they may disrupt local and individual ways of living. Local communities, formerly sustainable through familial and other means of collaborative support, are experiencing fragmentation due to rapid changes in work opportunities, demography and the demands upon public services to the extent that many become sites of deep social tension (Bourdieu et al., 1999).

Individual identity, unavoidably framed in our participation in the global economy and, more directly, by our membership of local communities – including those in which we work – is being challenged and reconstructed by rapidly shifting values and by changes in the ways we conduct our lives that are beyond the imaginings of our grandparents (Beck, Giddens and Lash, 1994; Giddens, 1991). For most of us, we are obliged to take on a recurringly adaptable identity while, for increasing numbers of people, it becomes necessary to sever their community and cultural roots and move elsewhere. In parts of Asia, for example, the workforce at present includes many hundreds of thousands of migrant families and, in Europe, one-third of all people under the age of thirty now work in a country in which they were not born. Temporary or permanent, voluntary or forced, *migration* is a defining characteristic of our global community.

This embracing culture of change and the ways in which change is happening permeate the discourses in which we participate (Chouliaraki and Fairclough, 1999). In education, it is not surprising that such transitions in community and identity reverberate in the discourse of pedagogy which articulates our relationships with knowledge, with those in authority, with colleagues and with students (Bernstein, 1996; Gee, 1996; Giroux, 1997; Popkewitz and Brennan, 1998). Although on a smaller scale, perhaps, and located within a particular community of professionals, we can not expect that the working lives – and, therefore, the development of English language teachers – will be immune from all these wider influences. On the contrary, the teacher of English is confronted by a stark choice. Either we perceive ourselves as a teacher of language unconnected to wider social, cultural and political issues and, thereby, participate in the marginalization of our profession, or we accept the formative role we play in these processes and confront the contradictions and possibilities for beneficial change in the intercultural work that we do. Many teachers of English language working, for example, in many EFL situations or with recent migrants, struggle with such issues to varying extents in their daily work in classrooms. If we see professional development as simultaneously providing benefit to the individual practitioner and, thereby, to the wider community of ELT practitioners, we can also see it as beneficial local action for the classroom community, the school or institutional community and, indeed, the wider community from which our students come. And such local action is contextualized within the global processes briefly identified so far. Perhaps more than ever before, strategies for coping with such processes may be seen to be essential to any programme of professional development. Perhaps more than previously, we now recognize that a teacher's development is not merely an individual matter. Teacher development is professional action that, while unavoidably permeable to the impact of social, cultural and political forces, also provides the opportunity for positive change emanating outwards to the communities within which a classroom is located. This dual process of 'external' global influences upon contemporary approaches to teacher development and how approaches to teacher development may initiate creative responses and opportunities in such a context are the focus of this chapter. We need to begin by identifying some of the key challenges that confront teachers at the present time.

The uncertain practitioner

Towards the end of the twentieth century, an increasing body of research, mainly undertaken in countries where English is the dominant language, identified a crisis in the professionalism of teachers (Bottery, 1998; Furlong et al., 2001; Hargreaves, 1994; Whitty, 1996). While the crisis clearly reflects emergent external pressures upon teachers, teachers and teacher educators are contributing to the undermining of their own professionalism. In essence, many are resisting seemingly inevitable changes on the basis of former stances and values that are no longer sustainable. Furlong et al. (2001) identifies teachers' knowledge, responsibility and autonomy as three related aspects of professionalism that are being undermined by explicit governmental intervention in teachers' working lives in the same period when each of them is being redefined through the interaction between current global processes and local and individual responses to them. Focusing upon the work of English language teachers, I suggest that there are four key aspects of our work that are being challenged in the present context:

(i) The knowledge we may apply
(ii) The ways we may teach
(iii) Our accountability
(iv) Working conditions.

Each of these is related, of course, so that change is palpable because it touches most aspects of our work in an aggregative way. In considering each in turn and within the constraints of brevity, what I have to say may not apply equally across all teaching situations and for all teachers. However, many English language teachers will be experientially aware of the processes that are referred to here.

Transient knowledge

Teacher knowledge has been the focus of very close analysis over the last twenty years (Clark and Peterson, 1986; Day, Hope and Denicolo, 1990; Day, Calderhead and Denicolo, 1993; Elbaz, 1983; Shulman, 1987; *inter alia*). A major development in language teaching research since the early 1990s, strongly influenced by research investigations of teacher knowledge in Western countries, has been the study of how language teachers think about their work: the beliefs, theories and principles that guide their practices (Breen, 1991; Breen et al., 2001; Burns, 1993; Freeman, 1991; Freeman and Richards, 1996; Gimenez, 1995; Johnson, 1989; Woods, 1996; Borg, 2003 provides a comprehensive review). This sudden growth of interest is not merely coincidental. Echoing the extensive research interest in teacher thinking in the last two decades of the twentieth century, it is a particular investigative response to what constitutes language teachers' knowledge, responsibility and autonomy at a time when significant change is impacting upon each of these. As teachers' knowledge and principles are at the heart of curriculum change, then they need to be revealed, not least to discover their potential for adaptation. Giddens, in his influential work on late modernity and self-identity, identifies reflexivity as a key attribute of the self and of the wider society (Giddens, 1991). For Giddens, reflexivity is the process of incorporation – in the self and in society – of changes in beliefs and knowledge and changes that, in our present context, entail almost constant revision.

Simplifying somewhat, we may distinguish between language teachers' knowledge of the subject and their largely experientially informed knowledge of how to teach the subject – their pedagogic knowledge – or, in Schön's terms, their 'knowledge in action' (Schön, 1983). These two realms of knowledge are in constant relation. What a teacher knows about the English language is likely to influence significantly how that teacher works with it and how the teacher expects students to work upon it. If we focus only upon knowledge of the English language, it is becoming more explicitly recognized within professional development that the teacher whose first language is not English is highly sensitive to the real or assumed limitations of their subject knowledge and this, in turn, genuinely constrains the adaptations they are urged to undertake in their practice, most typically by academic researchers or curriculum planners beyond their classrooms. However, their subject knowledge and that of their peers whose first language *is* English has also been the target of relatively constant revision in recent years due to developments in applied linguistics. If we are to teach grammar, which model of grammar should it be? If we are to teach language as communication, which aspects of communicative competence should we focus upon? Perhaps we should adopt a lexical syllabus, so recently enriched by the reservoir of authentic computer corpora? And how can we disregard current studies of discourse, genres and literacies when they appear to offer our learners more comprehensive and revealing frameworks for uncovering how English is actually used? And diverse subject knowledge conveyed through the language is a more complex and dynamic matter, perhaps, for those engaged in content-based or special-purpose programmes. Of course, language teachers recognize the value of recent refinements in how subject-matter may be defined and presented. But these refinements have entailed a shift in professional identity in terms of a readiness to mistrust prior knowledge and replace this with sustained reflexive alertness.

Meantime, a number of applied linguists have not merely challenged *how* English should be described and taught, but *what* English? And, more significantly, *whose* English (see in particular Graddol, Obondo, Pennycook, Phillipson and Tollefson, in *The Kluwer handbook on English language teaching, I,* 2006). Patterns of globalization are revealingly articulated in current discussions of linguistic imperialism, particularly with reference to English. The issue directly confronts teachers' professional responsibility – and, most particularly, the dilemma between seeking to provide learners with potentially emancipatory access to other cultures while simultaneously complying within a process that may be exclusive or repressive in relation to other languages and cultures.

Role reconstructions

Teachers' practical pedagogic knowledge regarding how language may be best taught has been subject to two major interventions in recent years and what may presently constitute 'best practice' is characterized by contradictions within the interventions themselves. The interventions spring from academic theory and research and from innovations in technology. The contributory disciplines to ELT have been marked by rapid changes in recent years thereby providing teachers with shifting pedagogic imperatives on the nature of language use and language learning. One of the key roles of professional development is to mediate between academic exploration and classroom practice. Much of this mediation has sometimes contributed to teachers' perplexity rather than enlightenment, and a major cause of this has been vested interest. State and regional governments, in the context of global competitiveness, have sought to implement curricula that are as at least as 'good' as those of their nearest competitors. While this is understandable, such curricula are inevitably reinterpretations of innovations in theory and research adapted to perceived local conditions. And, as English language teaching is a global business, publishing corporations are keen participants in this process so that their textbooks may be adopted on a large scale. Much professional development made available to teachers at present directly serves these two interests. And such development positions the teacher as the recipient of 'new' knowledge rather than as a contributor to it; as novice rather than expert. The resulting tension between the inherent conservatism of governments and publishers and innovations driven by theory and research has resulted in contradictory messages to teachers to mistrust 'new ideas' coming from 'outsiders' while being obliged to interpret and express what they do in classrooms through the discourse of contemporary applied linguistics. A salient example of this is the widely held assumption that communicative language teaching (CLT) entailed replacing grammar work with speaking and listening activities and that more recent research identifying focus on form during negotiation as facilitative of language acquisition implies a rejection of CLT and a return to the explicit teaching of grammar. While both beliefs are misinterpretations of the original theory and research, the fragmentation of CLT at the present time – into task-based, collaborative or autonomous language learning – illustrates how pedagogic knowledge within the profession is being reflexively adjusted to deal with current uncertainties about the locus of control in classroom work.

Computer applications for language learning also exemplify the tension between genuine opportunities for innovation and apparent shifts in the locus of control in teaching that directly challenges teachers' former professional identities. Current changes are aggregative in their impact upon teachers and a major contributive factor in the construction of teachers as merely 'delivery systems' of externally designed curricula is the assumption – indirectly perpetuated by some CALL enthusiasts and more directly perpetuated by private companies selling the software – that computers will do as good a job as they can. Whilst there is little doubt that computers will continue to revolutionize networked learning, the shift towards machines as both the sources of knowledge of a language and how that knowledge may be accessed by a learner unavoidably contributes to a 'de-skilling' of the experientially honed pedagogy of the teacher and, thereby, the teacher's sense of worth.

Performativity

The concept of 'performativity' has been proposed by Lyotard in his analysis of significant changes in contemporary society (Lyotard, 1984). He argues that the 'meta-narratives' guiding education and informative research until recently have been issues of truth and justice. Lyotard's analysis reveals that both have been replaced by a preoccupation with action; with *how we do things*. This displacement has had a number of effects upon how we perceive our world – so that truth, for instance, is eroded into 'regimes of truth' that legitimize the actions of powerful groupings in society and thereby disempower the 'unknowing' (Foucault, 1980). The replacement of such values with performativity entails that individual worth is reduced to what a person or a community does and how well they do it.

The implications for the teaching profession have been palpable in recent years, especially in the 'developed' world. In the context of the wider performativity of nations and communities in a competition for economic survival and dominance, governments have mobilized standards of achievement and competencies in education, the account-ability of educators and the new rationalism of 'evidence-based' practices. Such measures have been put in place on the basis of two unproven assumptions: that whatever teachers achieved before is no longer adequate and that systems of bureaucratic surveillance of teachers' work will improve their students' performance. Such measures are permeating provision from pre-school to higher education and other forms of adult education. The more overt results have been the 're-skilling' of highly experienced senior teachers into managers of people and resources and an escalating exodus from the profession, particularly in Western countries. The reason most often given by teachers for their decision to leave is 'burn-out' due to the intensification of workloads entailed in regular testing of students and related accounting and reporting processes. More covert effects of the judgement of a teacher's worth, primarily in relation to nationally or internationally determined benchmarks of the outcomes of teaching, include the displacement of the teacher's broader and more interpersonally sensitive educational aims and the day-to-day process of enabling learning to occur within the complexities of a particular situation.

Insecurity

The final challenge to the individual and professional community identity of English teachers that warrants consideration here is not especially recent, although its combination with the changes to which I have so far referred contributes significantly to current uncertainty. I focus here upon the working conditions – or, more precisely, the contractual employment of the language teacher. There are important differences between the circumstances of the conventionally itinerant native speaker of English and teachers of EFL in their own countries whose first language is not English. A major difference, perhaps, is the relative opportunity for choice. However, the need to be 'on the move' either literally or intellectually impinges upon both. Being a global language, native speakers of English enjoy a measure of internationally transferable 'intellectual capital' and those who choose to work in other countries largely accept the transience of any teaching position and the temporary contracts that it will entail. Not least in reaction to the erroneous assumption that anyone who spoke the language could teach it, the latter years of the 20th century witnessed a professionalisation of English language teachers through the provision of initial qualifications by institutions such as the Royal Society of Arts (RSA) and International House while, with the support of organisations such as the British Council or through self-funding, large numbers of teachers sought access to the growing number of postgraduate or post-experience courses in ELT or Applied Linguistics at Diploma or Masters level offered by universities. In essence, increasing professionalisation occurred in the context of mobility and transitory local contractual arrangements and, indeed, facilitated both of these conditions.

Large numbers of teachers whose first language was not English also obtained access to these kinds of professional training and there was an equally significant increase of in-country training and development funded by governments or organisations such as the British Council and more usually staffed by English-speaking teacher educators. A contributory factor influencing the seemingly inevitable contractual insecurity of English teachers, perhaps especially in post-school education, has been the internal status accorded to language teaching. Languages are often located in, and perceived to be, a 'service' provision wherein teachers' knowledge of the language is regarded as having been obtained without the disciplinary demands and, subsequently, deserving of less recognition than that of specialists in conventional subject departments. Many of the most qualified teachers of EFL in their own countries are all too familiar with different contractual arrangements being applied to them and of the necessity of having to undertake more than one job in order to make ends meet. To achieve career mobility, these teachers confront the lower status attributed to their subject knowledge, wherein conventional disciplinary knowledge displaces practical pedagogic knowledge through the obligation to obtain higher academic qualifications.

In sum, I have so far suggested that four interrelated processes of change and destabilisation directly impact upon the work of the English language teacher at a time when societal challenges to self and community identity are also occurring. Recent reflexive revisions of how language knowledge may be defined, the tensions between research-based innovations in pedagogy and imperatives driven by governmental, publishers' and technological interpretations of what constitutes appropriate 'delivery', the 'new rationalist' emphasis upon the performativity of both teachers and students and the requirement to keep moving, in either work location or in academic qualifications, all contribute to a state of uncertainty in relation to the teacher's professional self. The key question, therefore, is how processes for professional development may enable teachers to adopt and engage strategies to deal with such circumstances in a personally developmental way. To approach this question, we need to consider whether current influential modes of in-service provision have the potential either to appropriate the uncertainty of teachers in order to maintain compliance with processes that can undermine their professionalism or whether such provision has the potential to enable teachers to appropriate *for themselves* a resilient professional identity. The following two sections address this ambiguity in current approaches to teacher development. The first focuses upon the prevailing stance of much in-service provision and a particular reaction to it, while the subsequent section evaluates three current alternatives that appear to point in positive directions.

Trainability or vernacular pedagogies?

It is not surprising that the majority of professional development opportunities available to teachers at present are short training courses largely serving central policy imperatives or teaching resources industry 'up-dating'. Follow-up development is rare. There is increasing evidence that this kind of training that focuses piecemeal upon aspects of teachers' 'skills' is transient in its benefit because it is inevitably superficial (Hargreaves, 1995; Little, 1993). In a climate in which professional identity and the related relationships with colleagues and students are being redefined in the ways we have seen by institutional and cultural forces, Bernstein identified the resultant recontextualisation of pedagogic knowledge as a pivotal process (Bernstein, 1996). He described how teachers' knowledge is most often positioned by the kinds of in-service provision that serve agendas other than those of teachers' themselves:

> The concept of trainability places emphasis upon 'something' the actor must possess in order for that actor to be appropriately formed and re-formed according to technological, organisational and market contingencies. This 'something', which is crucial to the survival of the actor, the economy and presumably the society, is the ability to be taught, the ability to respond effectively to concurrent, subsequent, intermittent pedagogics. Cognitive and social processes are to be specifically developed for such a pedagogized future. However, the ability to respond depends upon a capacity, not an ability. The capacity for the actor to project him/herself *meaningfully* rather than relevantly, into this future, and recover a coherent past. (Bernstein, 1996: 73, emphasis in the original)

Meaningful adaptation therefore rests upon an identity which, according to Bernstein, can readily integrate what may be required in the future with what has been achieved in the past. Bernstein (1996: 73) goes on to suggest that this identity:

> cannot be constructed by lifting oneself up by one's shoelaces. It is not a purely psychological construction by a solitary worker as he/she

undergoes the transitions which he/she is expected to perform on the basis of trainability. This identity arises out of a particular social order, through relations which the identity enters into with other identities of reciprocal recognition, support, mutual legitimization and finally through a negotiated collective purpose.

Therefore, the capacity to deal meaningfully with the challenges of recontextualisation of knowledge in an era of significant change depends upon the on-going interaction between the individual's career and its related social relationships in a collective context such as that of the school or community – including the community of colleagues in ELT.

Being positioned as someone to be trained in the latest innovations generated by Applied Linguistics theory and second language acquisition research has been the target of recent arguments against what might be described as 'pedagogic imperialism'. An alternative perspective asserts the authenticity of local pedagogic principles and various frameworks for classroom practice that are generated by teachers in real and diverse situations. Such vernacular pedagogies, it is argued, are more culturally and situationally sensitive than 'imported' innovations and, thereby, typically and justifiably resistant to them (Canagarajah, 1999; Ellis, 1996; Holliday, 1994; Kramsch and Sullivan, 1996; Kumaravadivelu, 1994). Although indicative of fertile ground for the seeds of future teacher development, local resistance to the potentials for interaction between vernacular pedagogies, research-informed innovation and alternative pedagogic innovations generated in other parts of the world may be non-developmental for the profession as a whole. While the assertion of the authenticity of local knowledge and practices is an understandable response to uncertainty, there is the risk of complacent inertia and the privileging of conventional ways of thinking and acting in language education that fail to confront unavoidable global and local changes – or, more positively, grasp the opportunities that they present. Such appeals to local authenticity, though symptomatic of the stresses upon established ways of thinking and acting, may paradoxically contribute to the marginalisation of ELT practitioners in the wider society.

However, in addition to reminding us that the profession of language teaching in the future will thrive if it is integrated with what has given meaning to our work in the past and is grounded in experienced situations of practice, this recent assertion of the integrity of vernacular pedagogies suggests that professionalism across ELT is unavoidably hybrid. And one of the positive opportunities of the current global unification of human society is a process of interchange that generates hybrid solutions in a context that supports the right and inclination of working people – including ELT practitioners – to cross former boundaries between ways of thinking and acting professionally. I suggest that much in-service training fails in this regard because it positions teachers as deficient before it commences and that the current romanticisation of vernacular wisdom that resists outside influence may be similarly retrograde because it positions teachers as guardians of pedagogies that somehow lack the capacity for evolution. I believe we need to turn to alternative perspectives on teacher development that appear to challenge both tendencies.

Reflective practice, action research and the critical stance

Although distinctive in their own ways, the three approaches to teacher development briefly evaluated here share the late-modern scepticism regarding the primacy of rationalism in our dealings with our environment and our formal and informal relationships with each other. Again, it needs to be emphasized, such disillusionment is a characteristic of post-industrial societies and the debates on how professional people may think and act in a 'postmodern' culture may be regarded as symptomatic of a more compliant participation in global economic, technological and institutional processes that simultaneously destabilize former personal and community identity. Focusing upon teacher professionalism, this questioning of rationalism coupled with the emphasis upon performativity encourages us to place greater faith in the wisdom of experientially based practice rather than the traditional knowledge systems that formerly gave it meaning. Contemporary language teacher development programmes that give primacy to modes of teacher reflection and action research locate practice as the source of understanding and, thereby, the crucible wherein problems may be solved, innovations accommodated and uncertainties reduced.

Schön, perhaps the most influential founder of the reflective practice movement, rejected the belief that professional people undertake their work by relying upon the systematic application of scientifically grounded theory and technique (Schön, 1983, 1987). For Schön, the complexities of day-to-day professional work render such reliance as inappropriate:

> [T]he problems of real-world practice do not present themselves to practitioners as well-formed structures. Indeed they tend not to present themselves as problems at all but as messy indeterminate situations. (Schön, 1987: 4)

It is precisely such 'messy indeterminate situations' in language classrooms and the close consideration and, crucially, the articulation of the ways in which we act in them that exemplify the focus of reflective practice as a mode for professional development.

For Schön, reflection within action during, for instance, classroom work, is most often a response to the unexpected and has the potential for a 'reflective conversation' leading to on-the-spot experimentation (Schön, 1987: 28). Such reflective conversations may be facilitated and undertaken in various ways, just as the act of reflection itself may be variously defined (Calderhead and Gates, 1993). In the context of language teacher development, the 'making sense' of practical problems through their identification, reflection upon them, and their articulation have been identified as the processes towards alternative solutions and, primarily, alternative ways of acting (Edge and Richards, 1993; Flowerdew, Brock and Hsia, 1992; Richards and Lockhart, 1994; Wallace, 1991; Woodward, 1991).

Kemmis, in the same tradition as Schön, proposed action research as a methodical extension of reflective practice (Carr and Kemmis, 1986; Kemmis, 1985; Kemmis and McTaggart, 1988; Burns, 1999 provides a review relevant to language teaching). Action research entails the teacher's own investigative exploration of the implementation of alternative ways of acting in the face of identified practical problems. Having identified either an innovation to be implemented or a problematic aspect of practice, the teacher moves through a cycle from a particular plan of implementation or focus of investigation to the collection of feedback on outcomes or other appropriate data and, thence, to a revised plan for action. The cycle may be repeated until the problem or issue is better understood and resolved. Classroom data, obtained by various means, may serve both to identify a need or a problem and to provide feedback on different ways the teacher has chosen to act or required the students to act. As with forms of reflective practice, action research addresses the teaching–learning process in a classroom as *the* location for teachers' development of alternative ways of thinking about their work, of implementing alternative practices that may be seen to be more facilitative of teaching and learning and of refining pedagogic knowledge. Both approaches can be seen as responses to change in terms of providing a means for enabling adaptability.

There remains, however, an inherent paradox in reflective practice and its extension in action research. In engaging teachers in the articulation of their practices – a task that many teachers understandably find difficult – the approaches appear to replace the former rationalism of pedagogic theories with a rationalisation of immediate personal experiences which has the potential to displace *other forms of knowing* that permeate the teaching process. While it would be hard to find a teacher who was not reflexive during on-going decision-making in the classroom in the sense of imposing some coherence on 'messy indeterminate situations', much research on teacher thinking has deduced that teachers' decision-making is often not rational and, in contrast to Schön's perception of other professions (his research focused mainly upon architects, doctors and psychologists), teaching is too complex an activity to be identified as action *based* upon reflection (Carlgren and Lindblad, 1991; Olsen, 1991). Lortie's classic account of the culture of teaching revealed that generally teachers prefer not to be analytical in the sense of stepping back from the taken-for-granted, experiential process of teaching (Lortie, 1975). Teachers often regard themselves as engaged in communicative action with students that evolves out of experience but, as an on-going process, is more complex than what may appear on the surface of classroom life. Introducing more recent explorations of teacher knowledge, Atkinson and Claxton (2000) propose that teachers work on the basis of three ways of thinking, only one of which is grounded in action or practice. For them, *intuitive practice* typifies teachers' immediate classroom decision-making: their tacit knowledge that is evident in practice. This can be contrasted with the *rational or analytical thinking* that teachers may engage in when planning for classroom work and with the *reflective thinking* which entails learning from experiences that are inevitably contextualized within the teachers' local circumstances. In essence, it may be argued that teacher development based upon reflective practice and action research will access only ways of thinking that, on the one hand, can be more readily abstracted from actual practice while, on the other, tend to be oriented to the teachers' perceptions of the more immediate context in which they work. This paradox suggests a limitation of such approaches: they re-construct teaching as rational activity *alone* while constraining teachers' vision within their own immediate work. This is limiting professionally as it fails to encourage and develop a questioning of the wider circumstances within which they work and a reflexive consideration of the constraints and opportunities of such circumstances.

There are a number of potential consequences of these approaches, one of which may be the limitation of professionalism rather than its enhancement. The onus for change is upon the *individual* teacher in her own classroom. Taking on the stance of a researcher is not merely an additional time-demanding role. It may displace those aspects of teachers' engagement in the classroom process with a disproportionate concern with effectiveness of delivery; with a primary focus upon means at the cost of content or broader learning outcomes. And both reflective practice and action research entail the risk of legitimising and reproducing classroom practices and routines that, in the event, may be harmful to learning. In an uncritical application, they may insulate the teacher's perspective and sense of responsibility within a primary concern with performativity in a specific context while distracting from the teacher's engagement as a member of a profession with broader educational and social objectives. The question remains as to whether reflective practice and action research *as currently implemented* within teacher development are little more than additional imported technologies that systematically appropriate the ways in which teachers *ought* to think about their work rather than enabling teachers themselves to appropriate language education in the situations in which they work in order to develop it.

It is this latter concern that underlies proponents of 'critical reflection' or the adoption of a critical stance within teacher professionalism (Barnett, 1997; Furlong, 1992; Hargreaves, 1994). Zeichner, a leading interpreter of reflective practice in relation to teaching, identified the culture of schooling, in its broadest sense, as antipathetic to critical inquiry and, in such a context, insists that genuine critical reflection will *directly* address the historical, cultural and structural conditions within which teachers work (Zeichner, 1994). Because of the inevitable constraints upon the individual teacher, such an undertaking, Zeichner argues, will need to be a collaborative endeavour between teachers, researchers and teacher educators. To be fair to Carr and Kemmis (1986), their original formulation of action research also argued for the collaborative implementation of a systematic critical approach to the conditions of teachers' work, although the current emphasis within much professional development upon performativity in one's local situation has weakened this stance. Proposals for critical reflection echo the ideas of Habermas, a leading critical theorist, and his distinction between 'communicative action' and 'discourse' (Habermas, 1970, 1974). In order to facilitate communicative action – to share many taken-for-granted presuppositions in the flow of interaction – we uncritically assume the common sense 'truths', norms and social practices of everyday life. In genuine 'discourse', however, we may collaborate with each other in overtly questioning the validity of our beliefs, ideologies, norms and actions that are governed by them. Given critical characteristics such as the willing questioning of both personal taken-for-granteds and those constraints inherent in the broader context of one's work, and a questioning undertaken in open collaboration with fellow practitioners, reflective practice and action research have the *potential* to overcome the limitations I have identified.

Exploratory practice

Partly developed out of a reaction against what were seen as the disproportionate demands of action research as compared to its longer-term perceived benefits to the working lives of language teachers, Exploratory Practice was first proposed by Allwright and Bailey (1991) as a means for teachers to confront the kinds of unanticipated 'puzzles' in the language classroom that Schön had earlier identified as 'surprises' in practice that generated opportunities for reflectively driven experimentation. Although an alternative to action research, Exploratory Practice is similarly grounded in the classroom but evolves out of the shared experiences of teachers in different situations, thereby echoing earlier development programmes that have been teacher-generated (Breen et al., 1989). Allwright and his colleagues in the Exploratory Practice Centre define the approach as:

> [A]n indefinitely sustainable way for classroom language teachers and learners, while getting on with their learning and teaching, to develop their own understandings of life in the language classroom. It is essentially a way for teachers and learners to work together to understand aspects of their classroom practice that puzzle them, through the use of normal pedagogic procedures (standard monitoring, teaching, and learning activities) as investigative tools. (http://www.lehras.puc-rio.br/epcentre/epcentre.htm)

Allwright proposes that reflection on classroom work enables teachers, in collaboration with learners, to identify particular puzzles – such as issues in dealing with aspects of language, or adopted working procedures, or the challenges of heterogeneity or size of classes, etc. Subsequent to reflection and before proceeding to undertake action to resolve such puzzles, it is argued that a crucial stage in the process is to achieve a deeper understanding of them. And it is the attainment of a situated understanding of the life of the classroom, not through the time-consuming design and use of conventional research tools and procedures but through everyday classroom activities and practices, that exemplifies the approach. Allwright proposes six design features characterising the kind of on-going professional development that exploratory practice would serve (Allwright, 2000, 2001):

1. Joint teacher–learner work towards understanding must precede/be undertaken instead of action for change.
2. Such work must not hinder teaching and learning, but rather make a positive contribution to it.
3. Whatever is focused upon in exploratory work must be seen to be relevant to those involved – learners in addition to teachers.
4. It must be indefinitely sustainable (unlike action research projects) by being integrated into the normal work of teaching and learning.
5. It must bring people together – teachers, learners, researchers, etc. – in a productive collegial relationship.
6. It must promote the development of understanding among all concerned.

Therefore Exploratory Practice may be seen to go beyond earlier forms of reflective practice and action research in being process-oriented, integrated within everyday ways of working rather than something added to it and driven by the local concerns and needs of both teachers and learners. It is distinctive in explicitly resisting performativity and a preoccupation with effectiveness by replacing these with a focus upon teachers' quality of life or professional well-being through the cooperative understanding of everyday puzzles in practice.

However, Allwright and his colleagues do not dismiss teachers' responsibilities regarding wider accountability and they are alert to the risk earlier identified regarding the potential insularity of vernacular pedagogies. The approach, having been evolved itself through a collegial process among teachers, would entail the public sharing of achieved understandings of language classroom processes with other groupings of teachers – not least through the opportunities provided by e-mail, accounts in websites and web-based 'lists' of collaborators. Furthermore, extending its collegial reach, such exploratory work might involve academic researchers and teacher educators. However, it entails for such 'outsiders' a different relationship to local practice than that typified by previous teacher development programmes. It necessarily entails a problematic shift in power relations. As a minimum, it would involve the researcher as a resource within the process of exploratory work serving the 'insiders'' agenda, while teacher educators would be positioned as students of those understandings revealed through such work – as participating in the understanding of what teachers and their learners discover locally and as means for the wider dissemination of these discoveries and the principles of Exploratory Practice for the benefit of the wider community of language teachers. Such possibilities may reduce the risk of insularity and mere reproduction in local practices. What may be distinctive in exploratory practice is its concern with the quality of teachers' *lives* as the primary motive for teacher development. In this way, it may also provide the space for critical reflexivity in relation to the wider conditions of teachers' work.

Collegial development and future directions

Building upon the potentials of all three of the above approaches, while confronting some of the ambiguities within them, what may be the characteristics of future language teacher development that may be both grounded in localized communities of practice while also generating strategies for engaging with more global issues that impact upon teachers' work? From the foregoing analysis, I deduce seven desirable features of future teacher development programmes, be these programmes generated within situated practice or provided by or for groups of teachers. I suggest that the seven features are interrelated and exemplify what I would identify as collegial development within language teaching. Four features address how the teacher may be positioned as an active participant in development while a further three are requirements upon the developmental process.

The teachers' position

As integrated individuals

One of the paradoxes of forms of reflective practice is their requirement that teachers rationalize about experience-based knowledge that is itself beyond rationalisation. Language teacher development to date has largely failed to be holistic in the sense of approaching practitioners who engage imagination, values, alignments and intuitions when enacting different knowledge systems during the teaching–learning process. As Bernstein (1996) argued in his critique of training, for teachers to integrate alternative ways of working into current practice, they need to make their own links between what has been personally meaningful in their work to the present and what has the potential to be personally meaningful in future ways of acting. Teacher development needs to address that professional self-esteem which is rooted in on-going achievements rather than in the attainment of other people's imperatives; it must start where teachers have come to and assume that their experience is evolving rather than something to be displaced by fashion.

As members of communities

A teacher's professional identity is sustained by, and constituted of, relationships with others. A teacher is a major player in the community of the classroom and is, most often, highly sensitive to its evolution. Like the layers of an onion, the classroom community is contextualized by a teacher within the institution and its particular patterning of peer and authority relations. The institution, private or public, serves and reflects the wider community in which it is situated – locally, regionally and nationally. And teachers' lives contribute to, and are subject to, the conventions and changes that reverberate through these communal strata. Global changes have had a direct impact upon the identity of teachers, and teachers of a major international language are participants in potentially positive and negative aspects of globalisation. Teacher development to date has rarely addressed teachers as members of institutional, local and wider communities and the requirements, pressures and benefits that such membership entails. Both the assertion of vernacular pedagogies and reflective practice in its various realisations, because largely focused upon the community of the classroom alone, encourages a kind of narcissism. Future teacher development can address the dynamic of relationships at each of these layers of community membership and the requirements and opportunities that these entail for day-to-day professional work. The global phenomenon of increasing migration, for instance, impinges directly upon the English teacher because classrooms may be seen as 'border crossings' between communities for many learners (Giroux, 1997). While some teacher development programmes touch upon learners' communities of origin, the interface between learners', teachers' and wider community identities, and what this interface implies for the teaching–learning process, can be seen as an urgent issue.

As cultural workers

English language teachers can comply in their own marginalisation as service providers delivering technocratic solutions to learners' linguistic needs, or position themselves as people at the heart of an educational and social agenda for inter-ethnic and inter-cultural communication. Much current teacher development gravitates uncertainly between these alternatives. Future work, although relating to the immediate agendas of teachers and learners in their classrooms, can actively support teachers in strategies which assert languages as pivotal in all educational provision for the benefit of regional and international understanding and well-being. To date, much professional development has been premised upon economic agendas and instrumental objectives and this has displaced the educational, social and cultural motives of teachers. This current tension between external pressures upon cultures and the lived cultures of communities needs to be addressed directly from the perspective of the socially transformative potential of language teaching. The implication for teacher development is that it actively engages teachers' identification with broader social and cultural endeavours as generative of a diversity of appropriate curricula.

As responsible for their own development

For teachers to develop in the present context, they are obliged to define their professionalism in dynamic ways, not least by reclaiming the wider educational agenda of their work through direct engagement with that agenda. Teachers willingly articulate those things for which they are accountable beyond narrow learning outcomes. They can rise above insular protectionism as a reaction to increased external intervention in their work through their pivotal mediating role in the curriculum. And they can transcend external imperatives regarding 'efficient' delivery through their negotiative spaces within those interpersonal relationships that a curriculum generates. Accountability, autonomy and responsibility do need to be addressed in these terms by teachers themselves at the present time. And development programmes need to explore with teachers and support diverse strategies for enacting their creative expression within classrooms and as professionals within the wider community.

Requirements for teacher development

Collegiality

Professional identity is not only constituted through classroom, local and wider community membership. Teachers are also members of the community of fellow practitioners with a shared awareness of the common demands and pressures in their work that are shaped by globalisation. A major failing of much teacher development in the past has been its short-term benefit. Recognising and acting upon the network potential of the practitioner community within the school or institution, within the region and internationally are crucial under-takings within English language teaching at the present time, not least because these levels of professional community membership are sites for the questioning of external interventions that may be undermining and educationally inappropriate in the longer term. Teachers strongly value networking and the personal benefits of follow-up work that remains collaborative. As a defining feature of exploratory practice, sustainability implies local collaboration between teachers within their communities on locally relevant issues. However, there remains a tension to be confronted in the future. While teacher development thrives in the ground of local practice, to be relevant to the development of such practice and *all* the people involved, and to be locally sustainable by them, it has to be permeable to ideas and insights from elsewhere. Just as local action can be further sustained by it being made known across the profession, through strategies of interchange local explorations can avoid the risks of insularity and reproduction. Local action needs to be re-contextualized for the wider access of fellow professionals. While more formal regional and international associations to which English language teachers may belong provide the arenas for collegial participa-tion, one of the significant benefits of modern technology is the emergence of 'electronic communities' of practitioners which can interact more regularly in more open-ended ways.

However, collegial development for the future also entails challenging perceived boundaries between activities that constitute English language teaching in its broader sense. Teaching, learning and researching are being seen now – occasionally rather superficially – as overlapping processes. Nevertheless much current research is dismissed by teachers as irrelevant to their concerns while some researchers assert immunity from practical matters. Given the current centralisation of language policies, the gap between these three activities and curriculum and materials planning appears to be greater than previously. Clearly, future teacher development should address both the interaction between *all* such activities and the necessary and unnecessary spaces between them. While recognising that each of the activities has its own integrity of purposes and action, collegial development can facilitate openness through the restoration of genuine interchange between these practices and the people engaged in them.

Discursiveness

We have seen that reflexivity, entailing an almost constant revision of beliefs and knowledge, currently permeates teachers' working lives. The uncertainty that this generates can be appropriated by vested interests so that teachers' control over what may be meaningful in their work is constrained and limited. As a result, teachers' space for the negotiability of meaning becomes confined. A major goal for future teacher development should be the reclaiming of this space in terms of a collegial shift towards discursiveness or engagment in the kind of discourse that Habermas identified as the 'ideal speech situation' (Habermas, 1970, 1974). Such a shift will be challenging because teachers will be engaged in critically questioning their consensual beliefs, values and practices. This kind of endeavour goes beyond current approaches to development by explicitly confronting the relativism, insularity and reproduction of practices. It demands intellectual honesty and the re-contextualisation of local understandings so that these may be justified, compared and re-worked within a dialogue of critical evaluation among peers. It also demands that teachers clearly identify those conditions in their work that are mutable by their own actions and those that are not so that transformative effort is focused rather than dissipated. Such an endeavour can be seen as the preliminary step towards what Bernstein identified as 'negotiated collective purposes' (Bernstein, 1996) and, thereby, the reassertion of individual professional identity through interaction with the wider community of language teachers. This kind of discursiveness is *necessarily* collegial, not least because of common institutional antipathy towards critique and the related need for mutual support in such circumstances.

Evolutionary

The future development of English language teachers entails their explicit recognition of their pivotal role at the heart of current educational, cultural and political change and the responsibilities that such a role involves. The versions of English being taught and learned by many millions across the world mediate those contradictions inherent in society wherein the potentials for inter-ethnic and international communication exist alongside potentials for conflict between values and community identities. Learning English entails an on-going tension between access and inclusion and between cultural hegemony and the inherent diversity of local cultural systems. Teacher development may usefully address these issues in explicit ways, focusing upon how they are enacted locally while relating them to, and comparing them with, more global processes. It may support teachers as pivotal in cultural change through their exploration of the implications for them as teachers of, for example, learners' experienced shifts in identity between speech communities, the hybridity of English and its creative realisations in spoken and written texts, the negotiability of meanings, values and norms and so on.

Professional development, perhaps more than anything, can enable teachers to freely explore ways of thinking and acting collegially that focus upon the positive opportunities to be found in the present climate of change; to exploit the challenges it presents as a means towards negotiated alternatives. Such development has to be evolutionary in the sense of continually reflecting and being permeable to beneficial influences from elsewhere – from other communities of practice, other disciplines and other cultural realizations of pedagogy – and also evolutionary in the sense of having a gradual, reciprocal influence on communities beyond the classroom.

Conclusion

In this chapter, I have reviewed some of the pressures upon English language teachers that have emerged from global processes at the turn of the twenty-first century. I considered the ways in which current teacher development has reacted to these pressures. In identifying some of the limitations of current practices, I proposed certain aspects of future teacher development that may move beyond such limitations in the direction of collegial endeavour. My purpose has been to explore ways in which teachers may claim the process of teaching and learning as appropriate to all those involved in it, rather than it being appropriated by other interests. Ambiguity and paradox appear to typify our present condition and I acknowledge their presence in the proposals I have tried to express. While I have urged that future teacher development means grappling with and participating in change, change itself has both negative and positive potentials. The practical implementation of this, and the suggestions I have offered, is not easy. The notion of 'collegial development' may be regarded as idealistic. It is one particular interpretation of the direction in which teacher development is moving and being worked through in various ways by particular teachers in different parts of the world. I suggest, however, that the identification and enactment of alternative strategies for appropriating change and making it work to the benefit of language education are urgent matters at the present moment, not least because it may become more difficult to do so in the future.

Note

*This chapter is a developed version of a review of ELT professional development in *The Kluwer handbook on English language teaching, 2*, eds C. Davison and J. Cummings (2006).

References

Allwright, D. 2000. Exploratory Practice: an appropriate methodology for language teacher development? Paper presented to the 8th IALS Symposium for Language Teacher Education, Edinburgh, UK.

Allwright, D. 2001. Three major processes of teacher development and the appropriate design criteria for developing and using them. In: *Research and practice in language teacher education: voices from the field*, eds B. Johnson and S. Irujo, CARLA Working Paper 19:115–33. Minneapolis, MN.

Allwright, D. 2006. Six promising directions in Applied Linguistics. In: *Understanding the language classroom*, eds S. Gieve and I.K. Miller. Palgrave Macmillan, Chapter 1 in this volume.

Allwright, D. and K.M. Bailey 1991. *Focus on the language classroom: an introduction to classroom research for language teachers*. Cambridge: Cambridge University Press.

Atkinson, T. and G. Claxton, eds 2000. *The intuitive practitioner*. Buckingham: Open University Press.

Barnett, R. 1997. *Higher education: a critical business*. Buckingham: SRHE/Open University Press.

Beck, U., A. Giddens and S. Lash 1994. *Reflexive modernisation: politics, tradition, and aesthetics in the modern social order*. Cambridge: Polity Press.

Bernstein, B. 1996. *Pedagogy, symbolic control and identity*. London: Taylor & Francis.

Borg, S. 2003. Teacher cognition in language teaching: a review of research on what language teachers think, know, believe and do. *Language Teaching* 36, 2:81–109.

Bottery, M. 1998. *Professionals and policy: management strategy in a competitive world*. London: Cassell.

Bourdieu, P. et al. 1999. *The weight of the world: social suffering in contemporary society*. Cambridge: Polity Press.

Breen, M.P. 1991. Understanding the language teacher. In: *Foreign/second language pedagogy research*, eds R. Phillipson, E. Kellerman, L. Selinker, M. Sharwood-Smith and M. Swain, 213–33. Clevedon: Multilingual Matters.

Breen, M.P., C.N. Candlin, L. Dam and G. Gabrielsen 1989. The evolution of a teacher training programme. In: *The second language curriculum*, ed. R.K. Johnson, 111–35. Cambridge: Cambridge University Press.

Breen, M.P., B. Hird, M. Milton, R. Oliver and A. Thwaite 2001. Making sense of language teaching: teachers' principles and classroom practices. *Applied Linguistics* 22, 4:470–501.

Burns, A. 1993. An exploration of the relationship between teacher beliefs and written language instructional practice in beginning ESL classes. Unpublished PhD thesis, Macquarie University, Sydney, Australia.

Burns, A. 1999. *Collaborative action research for English language teachers*. Cambridge: Cambridge University Press.

Calderhead, J. and P. Gates, eds 1993. *Conceptualising reflection in teacher development*. Lewes: Falmer Press.

Canagarajah, S. 1999. *Resisting linguistic imperialism in language teaching*. Oxford: Oxford University Press.

Carlgren, I. and S. Lindblad 1991. On teachers' practical reasoning and professional knowledge: considering conceptions of content in teachers' thinking. *Journal of Curriculum Studies* 7:507–16.

Carr, W. and S. Kemmis 1986. *Becoming critical: education, knowledge and action research.* Lewes: Falmer Press.

Chouliaraki, L. and N. Fairclough. 1999. *Discourse in late modernity.* Edinburgh: Edinburgh University Press.

Clark, C. and P. Peterson 1986. Teachers' thought processes. In: *Handbook of research on teaching*, ed. M.C. Whittrock, 255–96. 3rd edition, New York: Macmillan.

Davison, C. and J. Cummings 2006. *The Kluwer handbook on English language teaching.* Boston, MA: Kluwer Academic.

Day, C., J. Calderhead and P. Denicolo 1993. *Understanding professional development.* Lewes: Falmer Press.

Day, C., M. Hope and P. Denicolo 1990. *Insights into teachers' thinking and practice.* Lewes: Falmer Press.

Edge, J. and K. Richards, eds 1993. *Teachers develop teachers research: papers on classroom research and teacher development.* Oxford: Heinemann.

Elbaz, F. 1983. *Teacher thinking: a study of practical knowledge.* New York: Nichols Publishing.

Ellis, G. 1996. How culturally appropriate is the communicative approach? *English Language Teaching Journal* 50, 3:213–18.

Exploratory Practice Centre www.lehras.puc-rio.br/epcentre/epcentre.htm

Flowerdew, J., M. Brock and S. Hsia, eds 1992. *Perspectives on second language teacher development.* Hong Kong: City Polytechnic of Hong Kong.

Foucault, M. 1980. Truth and power. In: *Power/knowledge: selected interviews and other writing by Michel Foucault*, ed. and trans. C. Gordon (1972–7), 109–33. New York: Pantheon.

Freeman, D. 1991. The same things done differently: a study of the development of four foreign language teachers' conceptions of practice through an in-service teacher education programme. Unpublished PhD thesis, Harvard University.

Freeman, D. and J. Richards, eds 1996. *Teacher learning in language teaching.* Cambridge: Cambridge University Press.

Furlong, J. 1992. Reconstructing professionalism: ideological struggle in initial teacher education. In: *Voicing concerns: sociological perspectives on contemporary education reform*, eds M. Arnot and L. Barton, 163–85. Wallingford: Triangle.

Furlong, J., L. Barton, S. Miles, C. Whiting and G. Whitty 2001. *Teacher education in transition: re-forming teacher professionalism?* Buckingham: Open University Press.

Gee, J.P. 1996. *Social linguistics and literacies: ideology in discourses.* London: Taylor & Francis.

Giddens, A. 1991. *Modernity and self-identity.* Cambridge: Polity Press.

Gimenez, T.N. 1995. Learners becoming teachers: an exploratory study of beliefs held by prospective and practising EFL teachers in Brazil. Unpublished Ph D thesis, Lancaster University, UK.

Giroux, H. 1997. *Pedagogy and the politics of hope.* Boulder, CO: Westview Press.

Habermas, J. 1970. Towards a theory of communicative competence. *Inquiry* 13:89–113.

Habermas, J. 1974. *Theory and practice.* London: Heinemann.

Hargreaves, A. 1994. *Changing teachers, changing times: teachers' work and culture in the post-modern age.* London: Cassell.

Hargreaves, A. 1995. Development and desire: a postmodern perspective. In: *Professional development in action*, eds T.R. Guskey and M. Huberman. New York: Teachers' College Press.

Holliday, A. 1994. *Appropriate methodology and social context*. Cambridge: Cambridge University Press.

Johnson, K.E. 1989. The theoretical orientations of English as a second language teachers: the relationship between beliefs and practice. Unpublished PhD dissertation, Syracuse University.

Kemmis, S. 1985. Action research in the politics of reflection. In: *Reflection: turning experience into learning*, eds D. Boud, R. Keogh and D. Walker. London: Croom Helm.

Kemmis, S. and R. McTaggart, eds 1988. *The action research planner*. Geelong, Vic: Deakin University Press.

Kramsch, C. and P. Sullivan 1996. Appropriate pedagogy. *English Language Teaching Journal* 50, 3:199–212.

Kumaravadivelu, B. 1994. The postmethod condition: (e)merging strategies for second/foreign language teaching. *TESOL Quarterly* 28, 1:127–48.

Little, J.W. 1993. Teachers' professional development in a climate of educational reform. *Educational Evaluation and Policy Analysis* 15, 2:121–51.

Lortie, D.C. 1975. *School-teacher*. Chicago IL: University of Chicago Press.

Lyotard, J.-F. 1984. *The postmodern condition: a report on knowledge*. Manchester: Manchester University Press.

Olsen, J.K. 1991. *Understanding teaching*. Milton Keynes: Open University Press.

Popkewitz, T.S. and M. Brennan, eds 1998. *Foucault's challenge: discourse, knowledge and power in education*. New York: Teachers' College Press.

Richards, J.C. and C. Lockhart 1994. *Reflective teaching in second language classrooms*. Cambridge: Cambridge University Press.

Schön, D. 1983. *The reflective practitioner*. San Francisco, CA: Jossey-Bass.

Schön, D. 1987. *Educating the reflective practitioner*. San Francisco, CA: Jossey-Bass.

Shulman, L. 1987. Knowledge and teaching: foundations of a new reform. *Harvard Educational Review* 57:1–12.

Wallace, M.J. 1991. *Training foreign language teachers: a reflective approach*. Cambridge: Cambridge University Press.

Whitty, G.D. 1996. Marketisation, the state and the re-formation of the teaching profession. In: *Education, culture, economy and society*, eds A.H. Halsey, H. Lauder, P. Brown and A.S. Wells, 299–310. Oxford: Oxford University Press.

Woods, D. 1996. *Teacher cognition in language teaching*. Cambridge: Cambridge University Press.

Woodward, T. 1991. *Models and metaphors in language teacher training*. Cambridge: Cambridge University Press.

Zeichner, K.M. 1994. Research on teacher thinking and different views of reflective practice in teaching and teacher education. In: *Teachers' minds and actions: research on teachers' thinking and practice*, eds I. Carlgren, G. Handal and S. Waage, 9–27. Lewes: Falmer Press.

11
Language Teacher Educators in Search of 'Locally Helpful Understandings'*

Maria Antonieta Alba Celani

Introduction

For the title of this chapter I have borrowed from Dick Allwright's[1] (2006) view of the role of practitioners as seekers of 'locally helpful understandings', extending the idea to teacher educators, whom I also see as practitioners. In the light of the *Six Directions in Applied Linguistics* proposed by Allwright (2006, Chapter 1 in this volume), my purpose is to describe and attempt to discuss, so as to better understand, some of the challenges ('puzzles', according to Allwright, 2003: 123,129) encountered in navigating along a wide-scale in-service English teacher education programme.[2] As will be explained further on, this programme is connected with two different, though related areas; one is the area of continuing teacher education and the other is the area of applied linguistics research. This particular feature contributes to some of the 'puzzles'.

As an initial observation, the name of the programme itself – *Continuing English teacher education: a context for the reconstruction of practice* – might be the first aspect to be commented on, as it provides the theoretical assumptions informing the programme. It implies that some sort of change is needed and that it might be achieved by trying to offer tools for the job to be done in a different and *better* way. This means: looking at language and learning as discursive practices (Habermas, 1984; Vygotsky, ([1934]1986); seeing participants as agents of change and not as subjects (Fullan, 1993); believing in the practice of collaborative action based on dialogue (Duranti, 1986; Freire, 1970; Magalhães, 1990); and mostly relying on critical reflection (Freire and Shor, 1986; Schön, 1983, 1987). This necessarily leads to a view of continuing education as a *never-ending* process (Freeman, 1996; Smyth,

1987; Zeichner and Liston, 1996;). Actually, these features of the programme were established to counterbalance what seems to be the norm in many initial and in-service teacher education courses: a disproportionate attention, either to purely *theoretical* aspects or more frequently to only *technical* ones. This seems to help construct the representations which teachers of English tend to bring with them: in order to become a better teacher of English they expect to be taught the 'appropriate' use of teaching techniques or the 'best' method (Celani, 1988; Celani and Magalhães, 2002).[3] These aspects can be related to Allwright's picture of the 1950s and 1960s and also to the simplistic view of the search for the 'one best method' that would solve all problems.

The opportunities for development available in the system have not been very helpful in this respect. *Recycling* courses provided by the educational authorities or by other institutions are usually based on the assumption that all classroom situations and all teachers are essentially similar and usually leave no room for personal reflection or questioning of idiosyncratic features (Allwright, 2006). The main focus of such courses is transmission of knowledge, thus indicating that professional development consists only of knowledge of the language and technical skills updates. They are not planned to create a reflective and questioning atmosphere so as to make it possible for practitioners or future teachers to become aware of and try to understand the social nature of their work in the foreign language classroom and the social function of that kind of work in the Brazilian school system.

As mentioned before, the programme under consideration here is connected with two different, though related, areas. One is the area of continuing teacher education, having as its objective helping teachers to develop as critical professionals, to become aware of their practices by trying to understand them, and to be able to analyse them in the light of the objectives to be reached and of the knowledge to be constructed jointly in the classroom by teachers and learners The other is the area of applied linguistics research, to which the programme aims to contribute with a better understanding of how Brazilian teachers of English construct their social identity and how identity awareness affects discursive practices and social relations:

- How do public school English teachers see themselves as professionals?
- How do they see their educational work?
- How do they see the social function of the language they teach in the sociohistorical context in which they are *participants*?

While trying to look for answers to questions of a more theoretical nature connected with continuing teacher education, the programme intends to play a practical intervention role in the public school social context, thus making it possible for the participating teachers to eventually become not only agents of change in their professional context, but also 'knowledge-makers' in the field (Allwright, 2006). This aim necessarily implies a view of continuing education that must not be seen merely in terms of course results but should be understood in terms of a process that enables teachers to educate themselves as they move on in their attempts to understand their task as educators.

The educational scenario I am referring to offers fertile ground for reflection on Allwright's proposal in relation to one of his main directions – for example, who are the most productive researchers: the academics with their standard academic research practice or the classroom teachers with their close contact with classroom puzzles (direction 6)? This has been a constant preoccupation in the programme and in fact there have been useful contributions from teacher–students as researchers of their own practice (Cortez, 2003; Cunha, 2003; Mendonça, 2003; Sousa, 2003), most of them concentrating on reflection on lived experience.

Having presented the general background to the main challenges felt in the context of the programme, I now proceed to deal with some of these aspects, trying to examine and understand them in the light of Allwright's proposals.

Trying to understand the 'puzzles'

Managing social interactions in a multifarious context

In the initial phase, a great challenge was managing social interactions in a programme involving participants with many different roles and different cultures and expectations: there are those who plan, those who coordinate different aspects of the programme, those who implement plans and decisions, at both the administrative and at the academic levels and those who are being educated and there is also the public school system from which they come. There are two institutions involved – an English language teaching institution, which provides both funding for the programme and language tuition, and a university, which is in charge of the professional improvement component – each one with their own cultures, roles and expectations. There are also the teachers in the language school, the educators at the university and the public sector teachers taking the course – all playing their different roles, and bringing in different cultures and expectations.

The world of action soon showed us that there were 'white gaps' (Botkin, Elmandjra and Malitza, 1979) which had to be investigated in order to be understood. So, on looking back at the genesis of the programme and at the way it developed, it becomes apparent that at the top management level the integration between the two institutions was good and was being conducted in a highly collaborative way, with no impositions from the sponsors. Work and interactions within the teams and communication across the team leaders in each institution was fluent, open and democratic, resulting in an optimistic atmosphere. Notwithstanding this, there was not enough integration across institutions between the team responsible for language improvement and the one responsible for professional improvement. Furthermore, the actual design of the programme as a whole had originated following a prescriptive model, in the sense that there had been no 'bottom-up' establishing of priorities as a result of a needs analysis, for example. It was the result of what the planners, based on the global knowledge available at the time, thought would be good for the local situation. And this was the result of the work of planners who saw themselves as up-to-date applied linguists, who firmly believed in the importance of adopting a non-prescriptive posture as far as teacher education was concerned.

On looking back, now, it is possible to see that to some extent the same thinking underlay the way in which the different components – both language and professional – were structured. It is true that the professional component, for instance, was planned by the educators in open discussions, even with healthy conflicts sometimes, in order to decide what kind of profile the teacher education course should have, particularly in relation to what was to be avoided in the 'old maps' (Stacey, 1992), the technical training kind of 'map'. Our reflections, however, led us not to the construction of a new 'map', but to a refining of old ones, in spite of the innovative aspect emphasizing teacher education as a continuous reflective process. The view of teacher education was different from that of the 'old maps', no doubt, but the new 'map' indicating the conception of a teacher education programme did not take into account aspects of risk and uncertainty, did not anticipate aspects which would involve all the participants – for example, the partner institution, on the one hand and the teacher–students themselves, on the other. Differences in the cultural identity of the groups were not being taken into account, particularly concerning human relations and the representations and images that participants, in their different roles and with their different expectations, brought to the programme. For instance, discussing problems and trying to find ways to solve them, which for the university members of the team was quite a natural thing to do, was felt as threatening by the teachers in the language teaching institution, because in their culture problems might be equated with inefficiency.[4]

The same, although in a slightly different way, was true of the relations between teacher–students and educators. It took time for the educators to gain the teacher–students' confidence and for the latter to understand and accept the new ways of looking at teacher education, teaching of English and classroom work as proposed by the programme. In order to cope with this 'puzzle' the educators have been continuously improving the analysis of teacher–students' perceived needs. This created a feeling among the educators, perhaps not clearly perceived or expressed, that it was necessary to look at the question from a slightly different perspective. As suggested by Allwright (2006), *describing* is not enough, if the aim is *understanding*. With experienced teachers, understanding their situations prior to devising ways of how to change them might be more easily achieved if understanding is seen as an aim in its own right and not as a means to technical 'improvement in teaching efficiency' (Allwright, 2006). But, as mentioned earlier, most teachers join the programme expecting to be taught the best method for English language teaching and also to become near-native speakers of the language. What is needed, it seems, is to create situations for them to understand and look at change in a new way: this applies to the educators as well.

Meeting the needs of teacher–students

Being able to define the teacher–students' perceived needs was another important 'puzzle'. It was soon clearly felt that mere adjustments to the programme would not be enough for the programme objectives to be reached; some basic changes would be required. We turned to Hannay and Ross (1997) and Fullan (1993, 1996, 1997) for help and looked at the ways in which they discussed the question of change in educational systems. For our purposes we took the programme – and, more particularly, the teacher education course[5] – as the system to be changed and looked at our own actions as participants, in a process of self-evaluation. We also looked at the change process concerning the teacher–students, as revealed by their reflections expressed in diaries, class discussions and informal conversations. These showed feelings of uncertainty, disquiet, of disruption of views previously held. At the same time, it gradually became apparent that the team responsible for the programme was also undergoing a process of change similar to that perceived among the teacher–students: the same uncertainty as to the direction the programme should take, the same disquiet in relation to the decisions taken. This perception was fundamental in making us understand our specific situation better, and consequently, in giving us elements for re-directing the course. This stresses the relevance of Allwright's (2006) suggestion that *understanding must necessarily precede change*. Trying to achieve greater clarity and coherence in regard to our job as providers of a continuing teacher education programme became an important concern in our discussions. We started to look at our 'puzzles' with an open mind as to what might be 'solutions' for them, and always from the point of view of trying to find reasons and explanations, leading to better understanding. I can now relate this to Allwright's (2006) view that 'the proper concern of both research and teacher development work [is] to focus on understanding rather than problem-solving'.

As one of the underpinnings of the programme is the belief that cultures can undergo a process of change – for example, that there can be re-culturing of individuals or groups (Fullan, 1993, 1996) by means of a reflective process, which Allwright (2006) calls understanding, conducive to new views of teaching and new forms of professionalism, the 'puzzle' was and still is how to create conditions to foster this change/understanding process without too much suffering and threat. Before any kind of re-culturing can be achieved, however, there must be a serious endeavour to understand what is to be re-cultured, why it is necessary, how it is to be achieved and what the consequences might be. This seems to be part of the process of understanding. Needless to say, this ought to be a joint effort between educators, programme coordinators and the teacher–students themselves.

Changes are constantly being revised and when practice indicates that a particular change is not viable, sometimes simply for administrative reasons, the original pattern is restored. A case in point was the need to cancel an option which offered several routes within the programme, but which proved to be administratively unmanageable in practice. This was regrettable, because we could have had a scenario which offered a productive variety of learning opportunities to be chosen by participants according to their preferences – 'scattergun as opposed to precision', the 'throwing seeds by "broadcasting"' metaphor (Allwright, 2006, direction 4).

The widest and richest variety of productive learning opportunities is also to be found in the role of peers in creating a supportive atmosphere in the development process. In a way, this peer support fills in the lack of interaction in the school context. Multipliers working together with their peers will also have the role, as proposed by Allwright (2006), of acting as researchers, the role of 'practitioners as knowledge-makers in the field', in the sense of 'reaching locally helpful understandings, not [necessarily] new knowledge' (direction 6).

Quality in classroom action

So far, the programme has seen change of quality in classroom action as a major challenge. On reflecting on Allwright's (2006) proposal for viewing teaching–learning as 'life' rather than as 'work' (direction 5), however, we might want to look at the programme objectives in a different light, even if not necessarily taking the more radical view that the quality of classroom life is itself the most important matter. In relation to quality of life in the classroom, the programme has to be evaluated in terms of what has been achieved at the local level, in single classrooms, in the voice of the teachers themselves (Cortez, 2003; Cunha, 2003; Mendonça, 2003; Sousa, 2003), in spite of the maintenance of working conditions that go against the grain of reflective learning–teaching, and consequently ultimately affect the quality of life. Change in the quality of work deriving from personal growth can result in change in the quality of life in the classroom as well (Allwright, 2006, direction 5). But, it depends on having the time to try out new ways, to dive deeply into the culture of the students, so as to be able to understand their difficulties. This implies also being able to understand the social function of English language teaching–learning in Brazil. There are indications in the voices of a good many of the teacher–students and multipliers that the programme has played a role in positively affecting the quality of life in their classrooms, particularly in terms of teacher–student relationships, even if not the quality of work, seen as increased efficiency, as perhaps initially envisaged.

There are no indications that the working conditions of our teacher–students in terms of workload or physical facilities will improve in the near future. The programme is a rich and protected environment that welcomes the teacher and creates opportunities for professional and personal contacts; by means of reflection and a genuine endeavour to understand the general Brazilian public school context, it opens the way to improvement in the quality of life in the classroom. The programme has been providing teachers with a lively, encouraging, forward-looking site for sharing their experiences, good or bad, and their change process with other teachers of English. Outside, in the real world of their own schools, however, there have not been and there are no indications that there will be in the near future any opportunities for sharing this experience with the teachers of other subjects. In fact, there is no 'network of change' (Fullan, 1996) in our teachers' schools. Quality of life and its effect on efficiency goes far beyond the actual classroom. Perhaps the statement made above that 'change in the quality of work deriving from personal growth can result in change in the quality of life in the classroom as well' (Allwright, 2006) might be reformulated as 'quality of work and quality of life in the classroom go hand-in-hand with quality of life outside the classroom'.

A final reflection

In the programme as originally conceived, the concept of teacher education sees the teacher as learner, education as a career-long proposition, really a continuum of learning (Fullan, 1993: 289). It is based on the dialogue as understood by Freire (1970, 1980, 1985); hence, it is neither the mere imposition of ideas on others by a few holders of knowledge, nor the simple interchange of ideas to be consumed. It is the meeting place for reflection and action, in an attempt to identify and understand what needs improvement, and why. Learning to ask questions is the basis of this kind of teacher education. So, within this framework, problems are embraced by those who face them; no ready-made solutions are offered (Fullan, 1993). This necessarily implies a critical stance, which results in an anti-method pedagogy in the sense that critical teacher education provides no specific road to the way a critical educator must teach or a student must learn.

From the point of view of those responsible for the programme, a point never forgotten is that there is no 'best method' for teacher education, and that, as proposed by Allwright (2006), solutions have to be sought deriving from idiosyncratic and not from common considerations (direction 3). And in our case, the circumstances are large number of teachers with no time availability and very little official institutional support for personal development, either at the school level or at the higher hierarchical levels. So, although a vigilant critical eye is essential for making progress, albeit elusive, those responsible for its development also need the 'strong sense that [our] past was not exclusively populated with fools' (Allwright, 2006). The programme has to be evaluated in terms of the circumstances for which it was designed. Even if not generalizable, the production of 'situated under-standings' is not only directly valuable to the participants themselves, but might represent a considerable achievement in itself (Allwright, 2003: 121).

Looking at Allwright's (2006) 'six promising directions', and trying to relate them to the underpinnings of the programme discussed in this chapter, I would say that some of the directions, if not overtly present, can be said to underlie our view of a continuing teacher education programme. The idea of continuing education being a complex process, implying the acceptance of the fact that there is no 'best method' for teacher education just as there is no such thing for language teaching was a premise in the programme design. Gradually through lived experience it became clear that idiosyncratic aspects related to people and institutions should take precedence in any reflective evaluation of actions and consequently should be the source for the introduction of any changes leading to local solutions. The thinking is global, but the action should be local (Allwright, 2003: 115).

Lessons to be learned from Allwright's (2006) proposals are connected mainly with aspects relating to the idea of understanding as an objective in its own right rather than 'simply as a road to technical "improvement in teaching efficiency"'. The programme places great value on understanding situations and the people acting in them, but one main concern has been looking at expected changes in the quality of work. We have not fully realized, perhaps, that there has been an enormous amount of improvement in the quality of life of a great many people and of a great many classrooms as a result of the many productive learning opportunities generated by the different kinds of interactions among the different participants in the programme. The most important aspect has been the role of the practitioners, teacher–students and multipliers, as knowledge-makers for their own practice. The educators could be seen as triggers of the process, but in fact one must acknowledge the fact that an enormous amount of synergy has developed in this process, making both groups become one in some respects. So, Allwright's (2003: 115) 'loop' diagram:

> ┌──Think globally, act locally, think locally──┐

could inspire a new one (Figure 11.1) which attempts to represent all participants acting in concert as knowledge-makers, as practitioners who seek for understandings of their own respective actions, in their own particular local circumstances.

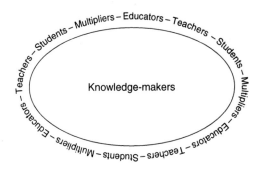

Figure 11.1 Participants in concert as knowledge-makers

Notes

*I thank the Brazilian National Research Council (CNPq) for supporting my research connected with teacher education (Proc. 306722/2003–8). I also thank Leila Barbara for discussing the first draft of this article with me.

1. Every time Allwright appears in the text without a reference date it refers to Chapter 1 in this volume (Allwright, 2006).
2. Descriptions of the programme as a whole can be found in Celani (2003), Celani et al. (2001), Celani and Collins (2003), Goldchleger (2003), Barbara and Ramos (2003) and for the distance mode in Collins et al. (2003), Collins (2003), Collins and Ferreira (2004), Collins and Braga (2004).
3. Only more recently has Brazilian research been paying attention to teacher education, rather than teacher training (see Romero, 1998; Liberali, 1999; Liberali, Magalhães and Romero, 2003; Castro, 1999; Ortiz, 2002; Lima, 2002; Miller, 2001; Miller and Bannell, 1998; Miller and Cunha, 1997; Kuschnir and Machado, 2003; Lyra, Braga and Braga, 2003; Duarte, 2003; Damianovic, Penna and Gazzotti-Vallim, 2003; Freire and Lessa, 2003, among others).
4. This finding concurs with Allwright (2003: 117)
5. Called *Reflection on action: the English teacher learning and teaching.*

References

Allwright, D. 2003. Exploratory Practice: rethinking practitioner research in language teaching. *Language Teaching Research* 7, 2:113–41.

Allwright, D. 2006. Six promising directions in Applied Linguistics. In: *Understanding the language classroom*, eds S. Gieve and I.K. Miller. London: Palgrave Macmillan, Chapter 1 in this volume.

Barbara, L. and R.C.G. Ramos, eds 2003. *Reflexão e ações no ensino-aprendizagem de línguas.* Campinas: Mercado de Letras.

Botkin, J.W., M. Elmandjra and M. Malitza 1979. *No limits to learning: bridging the human gap.* Oxford: Pergamon Press.

Castro, S.T.R. 1999. A linguagem e processo de construção do conhecimento: Subsídios para a formação do Professor de Inglês. Unpublished PhD thesis, PUC-SP, Brazil.

Celani, M.A.A. 1988. A educação continuada do professor. *Ciência e Cultura* 40, 2:58–163.

Celani, M.A.A., ed. 2003. Professores e formadores em mudança: relato de um processo de reflexão e transformação da prática docente. Campinas: Mercado de Letras.

Celani, M.A.A. and M.C.C. Magalhães 2002. Representações de Professores de Inglês sobre suas identidades profissionais: uma proposta de reconstrução. In: *Identidades: recortes multi e interdisciplinares*, eds L.P. Moita Lopes and L.C. Bastos, 319–38. Campinas: Mercado de Letras.

Celani, M.A.A. and H. Collins 2003. Formação contínua de professores em contexto presencial e a distância: respondendo aos desafios. In: *Reflexão e ações no ensino-aprendizagem de línguas*, eds L. Barbara and R.C.G. Ramos, 69–105. Campinas: Mercado de Letras.

Celani, M.A.A., S.T.R. Castro, L.P. Goldchleger, F. C. Liberali, R.C.G. Ramos and T.R. Romero 2001. The ups and downs of educating teachers to become multipliers. Paper presented at the Symposium Risk and Uncertainty: Reflective Teacher Education in Three Culturally Diverse Contexts. *Cultures of Learning. Risk and Uncertainty and Education Conference*. University of Bristol, UK.

Collins, H. 2003a. Re-estruturação e re-culturação no trabalho com o texto e a gramática. In: *Professores e formadores em mudança: relato de um processo de reflexão e transformação da prática docente*, ed. M.A.A. Celani, 133–47. Campinas: Mercado de Letras.

Collins, H. 2003b. Design, ensino e aprendizagem online: uma experiência em LE junto a professores de escolas públicas. *Revista ANPOLL* 15: 87–11.

Collins, H. 2004. Interação e permanência em cursos de línguas via Internet In: *Relatos de ensino e aprendizagem de línguas na Internet*, eds H. Collins and A. Ferreira. Campinas: Mercado de Letras.

Collins, H. and D. Braga 2004. Interação e interatividade no ensino de língua estrangeira via redes de comunicação. In: *Globalización y nuevas tecnologías: nuevos retos y 'nuevas reflexiones'*, 7, ed. M.I. Montes. Madrid: Organización de Estados Iberoamericanos para la Educación, la Ciencia y la cultura (OEI).

Collins, H. and A. Ferreira, eds 2004. *Relatos de ensino e aprendizagem de línguas na Internet.* Campinas: Mercado de Letras.

Collins, H., A. Ferreira, T. Mazzillo, S. Gervai, E. Lang, L. de Santi, S. Leites and J.C. Mello Filho 2003. Porque é difícil participar de chats? *Revista da Associação de Linguística Aplicada do Brasil – ALAB* 3, 2:41–72.

Cortez, C.D.C. 2003. Estudar . . . aprender . . . ensinar . . . mudar . . . transformar-se: um processo contínuo. In: *Reflexão e ações no ensino-aprendizagem de línguas*, eds L. Barbara and R.C.G. Ramos, 221–34. Campinas: Mercado de Letras.

Cunha, A.M.A. 2003. Dividindo para multiplicar. In: *Reflexão e ações no ensino-aprendizagem de línguas*, eds L. Barbara and R.C.G. Ramos, 235–55. Campinas: Mercado de Letras.

Duarte, V.C. 2003. Que querer é esse que eu quero? Despertando o querer usando atividades teatrais. In: *Reflexão e ações no ensino-aprendizagem de línguas*, eds L. Barbara and R.C.G. Ramos, 259–85. Campinas: Mercado de Letras.

Damianovic, M.C., L.Penna and M.A. Gazzotti-Vallim 2003. O instrumento descrição de aula visto sob três olhares. In: *Reflexão e ações no ensino-aprendizagem de línguas*, eds L. Barbara and R.C.G. Ramos, 109–30. Campinas: Mercado de Letras.

Duranti, A. 1986. The audience as co-author: an introduction. *Text 6*, 3.

Duranti, A. 1992. Collaboration: constructing shared understandings in a second language classroom. In: *Collaborative language learning and teaching*, ed. D. Nunan. New York: Cambridge University Press.

Freeman, D. 1996. Renaming experience/reconstructing practice: developing new understanding of teaching. In: *Teacher learning in language teaching*, eds D. Freeman and J. Richards, 221–41. New York: Cambridge University Press.

Freire, P. 1970. *Pedagogia do oprimido*. Rio de Janeiro: Paz e Terra.

Freire, P. 1980. *Conscientização. Teoria e prática da libertação: uma introdução ao pensamento de Paulo Freire*. São Paulo: Moraes.

Freire, P. 1985. *The politics of education: culture, power, and liberation*, trans. Donaldo Macedo. South Hadley, MA: Bergin & Harvey.

Freire, M.M. and A. Lessa 2003. Professores de Inglês da rede pública: suas representações, seus repertórios e nossas representações. In: *Reflexão e ações no ensino-aprendizagem de línguas*, eds L. Barbara and R.C.G. Ramos, 167–94. Campinas: Mercado de Letras.

Freire, P. and I. Shor 1986. *Medo e ousadia: o cotidiano do professor*. Rio de Janeiro: Paz e Terra.

Fullan, M.G. 1993. *Change forces: probing the depths of educational reform*. Lewes: Falmer Press.

Fullan, M.G. 1996. Turning systemic thinking on its head. *Phi Delta Kappa 77*, No. 6: 420–3.

Fullan, M.G., ed. 1997. Broadening the concept of teacher leadership. In: *Professional development in learning-centered schools*, ed. S. Caldwell, 34–48. Oxford, OH: National Staff Development Council.

Goldchleger, L.P. 2003. Projeto COGESP: narrando a história por parte da Cultura Inglesa: Nove anos em sete páginas. In: *Reflexão e ações no ensino-aprendizagem de línguas*, eds L. Barbara and R.C.G. Ramos, 61–7. Campinas: Mercado de Letras.

Habermas, J. 1984. *The theory of communicative action*. Cambridge: Polity Press.

Hannay L.M. and J.A. Ross 1997. Initiating secondary school reform: the dynamic relationship between reculturing, restructuring and retiming. *Educational Administration Quarterly* 33:576–603.

Kuschnir, A.N. and B.S. Machado 2003. Puzzling and puzzling about puzzle development. *Language Teaching Research 7*, 2:163–80.

Liberali, F.C. 1999. O diário como ferramenta para a reflexão crítica. Unpublished PhD thesis, PUC-SP, Brazil.

Liberali, F.C., M.C.C. Magalhães and T.R.S. Romero 2003. Autobiografia, diário e sessão reflexiva: atividades na formação crítico-reflexiva de professores. In: *Reflexão e ações no ensino-aprendizagem de línguas*, eds L. Barbara and R.C.G. Ramos, 131–65. Campinas: Mercado de Letras.

Lima, N. de 2002. Desconstruindo e reconstruindo conhecimentos pedagógicos: uma experiência de formação/transformação em serviço. MA dissertation, PUC-SP, Brazil.

Lyra, I., S. Fish Braga and W.G. Braga 2003. What puzzles teachers in Rio de Janeiro, and what keeps them going? *Language Teaching Research 7*, 2:143–62.

Magalhães, M.C.C. 1990. A study of teacher/researcher collaboration: reading instruction for Chapter One students. Unpublished PhD thesis, Virginia Polytechnic Institute & State University.

Mendonça, M.L. 2003. The king, the mice and the cheese: uma reflexão crítica. In: *Reflexão e ações no ensino-aprendizagem de línguas*, eds L. Barbara and R.C.G. Ramos, 207–20. Campinas: Mercado de Letras.

Miller, I.K. 2001. Researching teacher-consultancy via Exploratory Practice: a reflexive and socio-interactional approach. Unpublished PhD thesis, Lancaster University, UK.

Miller, I.K. 2003. Researching teacher-consultancy via Exploratory Practice. *Language Teaching Research* 7, 2:201–20.

Miller, I.K. and M.I.A. Cunha 1997. Exploring our classrooms – and our teacher development sessions. In: *Perspectivas: O ensino da língua estrangeira*, ed. E. Taddei, 54–72. Prefeitura da Cidade do Rio de Janeiro, Brazil.

Miller, I.K. and R.I. Bannell 1998. Teacher education, understanding and Exploratory Practice. *IATEFL Teacher Trainer SIG Newsletter 22*: 20–8. Kent, UK.

Ortiz, H.M.E. 2002. Educadores em formação: uma experiência colaborativa de professores em (trans)formação inicial. MA dissertation, PUC-SP, Brazil.

Romero, T.R.S. 1998. A interação coordenador e professor: um processo colaborativo? PhD thesis, PUC-SP, Brazil.

Schön, D. 1983. *The reflective practitioner* New York: Basic Books.

Schön, D. 1987. *Educating the reflective practitioner*. San Francisco: Jossey-Bass.

Smyth, J. 1987. *Educating teachers: changing the nature of pedagogical knowledge*. Lewes: Falmer Press.

Sousa, M.B.N. 2003. A tormenta do buscar: refletir para transformar. In: *Reflexão e ações no ensino-aprendizagem de línguas*, eds L. Barbara and R.C.G. Ramos, 195–205. Campinas: Mercado de Letras.

Stacey, R.D. 1992. *Managing the unknowable: strategic boundaries between order and chaos in organizations*. San Francisco: Jossey-Bass.

Vygotsky, L.S. [1934]1986. *Thought and language*. Cambridge, MA: MIT Press.

Zeichner, K.M. and D.P. Liston 1996. *Reflective teaching*. Mahwah, NJ: Lawrence Erlbaum Associates.

12
Teaching and Learning in 'The Age of Reform': The Problem of the Verb

Donald Freeman

From simplicity to complexity: the core premise

In his *Six Promising Directions in Applied Linguistics*, Dick Allwright (2006, Chapter 1 in this volume) makes the case that we have moved from seeing language teaching and learning as a singular, unified undertaking to one that is multi-faceted, messy and even chaotic (the latter are my words, not his.) Allwright describes this shift as a movement from simplicity to complexity, noting that:

> Another way of looking at the shift from prescription to description and then to understanding is to think of it more generally as a move from a simplistic way of looking at the world ... towards a recognition of the essential and irreducible complexity of the phenomenon of classroom language learning and teaching. (Allwright, 2006)

Since the 1990s, there has been a great deal of work in both research and theorizing in second language education that supports this statement. For example, the research on teacher decision-making (for example, Woods, 1996) portrays teaching as a complex process of socio-cognitive negotiation, while recent theorizing in complexity theory (Larsen-Freeman, 1997) and in sociocultural views of second language (2L) acquisition (Watson-Gegeo, 2004) bear out this movement towards complexity. So it is ironic that the public discourse in the media and in political spheres is moving in the opposite direction – towards a view of teaching in relationship to learning that is more simplified than complex and more focused on the necessity of common standards than on the value of idiosyncratic practices.

In this chapter, I want to argue that this counter-movement in the social and political discourse is based on a fundamental misunderstanding about the nature of teaching and its complexity, and on a comparable misconception about how teaching relates to learning. I begin by framing the educational context, which I will call 'the age of reform', in which this counter-view has taken root. I then outline three misunderstandings about the relationship between teaching and learning, and conclude with suggestions about how we need to rethink contexts of professional learning along the lines of Allwright's (2006) premise. The discussion is conceptual; it is not an evidence-based argument, which would be another, different undertaking. But in the spirit of Allwrightian analysis, I want to suggest that we need to rethink how we understand and support teachers' professional learning, particularly given the social and political demands in this 'age of reform'.

Professional learning in 'the age of reform'

That education is under extreme stress in most contexts around the world is evident in the headlines of the popular press, comments in the electronic media and in the claims and counter-claims of the many political and public policy arguments. In communities in the global north,[1] there are arguments about the role of education in creating and sustaining democratic access as societies become more multilingual and multicultural. Arguments about the importance of social access and inclusion emphasize the role of language learning and teaching, as in the following observation from the *European profile for language teacher education*:

> Diversity is one of Europe's main assets. Language teaching, learning, and teacher education help safeguard Europe's plurilingual and pluricultural heritage. Language learning encourages cooperation and exchange and a diversity of languages enriches Europe and high-lights cultural and linguistic variety. (Kelly et al., 2004:10)

In communities in the global south, financial and human resources remain critical issues to supporting and expanding the reach of education to under-served groups. It is not surprising, therefore, that increasing demands are being made on all aspects of education – from classroom teaching to school administration and teacher education. In virtually every aspect, there are calls for change and reform. While curriculum, assessment and resource allocations each receive their share of attention in these discussions, a great deal of critique and comment is directed towards teachers, and what they do in classrooms. For example, Brazil's Ministry of Education and Culture (MEC) notes in its 1996 reform document:

Teachers are the main agents for a policy on quality in education, which is why the teaching profession must be publicly given its due. Three lines of action are to be taken simultaneously in order to boost the teaching profession: career, working conditions, and qualifications. (MEC, 1996:61)

Within this focus on the teacher, the notion of 'teacher quality' as in the Brazilian document, is often central to reform efforts. Initiatives try to improve how people learn to be teachers – what they learn through preparation and pre-service training before they enter the teaching force – as well as what they learn through in-service training on the job – through various strategies including coaching, mentoring and other means of in-service development. Taken together, these interventions can be grouped under the general rubric of 'teachers' *professional* learning': *Teacher learning that is supported through organized interventions before and during the teacher's professional career* (for example, Kennedy, 1991). This definition contrasts with 'teacher learning' in the broader, generic sense, which includes not only 'professional learning' above as a sub-set, but also the non-formal, individual and social processes of learning in which people participate as they are becoming teachers and doing the work of classroom teaching.

Within this definitional framework, pre-service 'teacher training' as well as in-service 'teacher development' (which is also referred to as 'professional development' in the USA and Canada) are in essence ways of delivering input and providing support for teachers' professional learning (see Freeman, 2001). From the level of individual schools to that of national educational systems, educational reforms – such as initiatives in curricular change or to introduce new technologies, among other examples – hinge on teachers' professional learning. The stakes are high; the South African government (National Department of Education, NDOE, 1996) noted in a *White paper on teacher supply, utilisation, and development* drafted as part of the creation of the post-apartheid education system that:

The Ministry has attached great significance to the role of teacher education in the transformation process. The Ministry regards teacher education as one of the central pillars of national human resource strategy and growth of professional expertise and self-confidence is the key to teacher development. Teacher education has the awesome task of playing a central role in our commitment to redress and national reconstruction and development within a context of global change. (NDOE, 1996:2)

In spite of such high hopes, there is a real question, however, whether such professional learning can be effectively centrally organized and facilitated at a systemic level (for example, Darling-Hammond and Sykes, 1999). It may well be that the 'irreducible complexity of... classroom language learning and teaching', to use Allwright's (2006) phrase, does not succumb readily to centrally organized interventions and standardized approaches to professional development. In part the problem with such systemic attempts may be that they underplay the role of individuals and what they do – their individual agency – in such professional learning. Thus an alternative to the systemic view, which focuses on the centrality of the individual teacher in creating educational change (for example, Bailey, Curtis and Nunan, 2001), may make more sense. In this view, individual agency underlies professional development alternatives such as exploratory practice (Allwright, 2003), teacher research (Freeman, 1998) and action research (Nunan and Lamb, 1995). These interventions (and others like them) advance the notion that teachers' professional learning on a micro or individual level can contribute to what Allwright refers to as 'the quality of life'. Allwright paraphrases South African teacher educator Michael Joseph, saying that:

> Education...must first and foremost be good for teachers' lives if it is ever to be good for learners' learning...It must make a contribution to the quality of life in the language classroom before it can hope to make a contribution to the quality of teaching and learning there. (Allwright, 2003: 120)

In focusing on the 'quality of life', Allwright and others (for example, Cochran-Smith and Lytle, 1993) want to re-centre the idea of individual agency. They have argued that individual agency, when it is taken to a technicist extreme, can be diverted away from its core values of knowledge and understanding (Freeman, 1998) into a sort of glorified problem-solving. Thus when action research or teacher research become overly focused on addressing classroom 'problems' rather than, in Allwright's wonderful phrase 'the essential idiosyncracy of humanity', their purposes can be diverted from understanding to an orientation which puts the onus on the teacher to improve what Allwright calls 'the quality of the work'. For teachers, this can lead to an extended sense of hyper-responsibility for everything in the classroom, which can overwhelm a deeper engagement to think and understand more fully how their lives and their work, and those of learners, are interconnected.[2]

The problem stems in part from a perception that the focus on the 'quality of life' fostered by individual approaches to professional learning such as Exploratory Practice, teacher research or action research is overly general. In the climate of reform, such breadth risks blurring the basic social premise – that classrooms exist for the learning of both students and teachers. Whether we fully agree or not, in the public mind, teaching is evaluated on the 'quality of work' rather than on the 'quality of life' in the classroom. Logically when Exploratory Practice, teacher research, or inquiry focus on better understanding learning, such examinations are anchored in classrooms, so that the connection between quality in the classroom and quality of life generally is understood. But in the public discourse of reform, unfortunately, classroom learning is more often viewed as 'work' than it is viewed as 'life'. Further, efforts to improve the 'quality of work' seem focused, goal-oriented and achievable, while improving the 'quality of life' can seem elusive and evanescent.

Understanding learning on two levels: or 'the problem of the verb'

This pull between focusing on 'the quality of work' and focusing on 'the quality of life' runs head on into the intense pressures in public and political discourse to relate changes in teaching to improvements in student learning. This conceptualization, which relates teacher professional learning to student learning, creates a parallel between what teachers know and do and what students come to know and be able to do through teachers' efforts. This parallel is a key tenet in improvement efforts in what I am calling 'the age of reform'. The problem is that while understanding learning at the professional level for the teacher and understanding learning for students in the classroom are conceptually parallel challenges, neither is straightforward or easily done.

Understanding teachers' professional learning is somewhat uncharted territory (Freeman, 1996). We actually know very little about how the level of professional learning, (what teachers learn in professional development) connects to what they do and to what students learn in their classrooms (the level of student learning) (for example, Freeman and Johnson, 2004; Hawley and L. Valli, 1999). The challenge of the two levels is then to show the ways in which teachers' professional learning contributes – directly, indirectly, or perhaps not at all – in improving classroom practice. In other words, in what ways does teaching matter to learning? This question, which is central to the high-stakes arguments in this 'age of reform', demand different ways of conceiving the relationships among teacher knowledge, professional learning and classroom teaching.

If we know relatively little about these two levels of teacher and student learning and how they may connect, why is it that public discussions and critique, in both language education and in general education, seem to focus so intensely in this issue? Part of the reason lies in an underlying assumption based in common-sense: that what teachers know and do is somehow connected to what students know and do. If this assumption is the case, then what teachers know and do should be able somehow to 'drive' improvements in what students know and do. In other words, to use a shorthand, teacher learning should be able to 'drive' student learning.

At the heart of this assumption is what I would call the problem of the verb: *What teachers know and do———what students know and do.* There are many ways to 'verb' this statement and depending on which verb we choose, we posit a different relationship between teacher learning and student learning. For example, we could say:

(1) What teachers know and do *causes/shapes/directs* what students know and do. Or...
(2) What teachers know and do *contributes to/influences/supports* what students know and do. Or...
(3) What teachers know and do *creates learning opportunities for* what students know and do...

and there are many other options. These options for the verb form a sort of continuum from strong causality – as in (1) 'causes/shapes/directs' – through some sort of interaction (2) 'contributes to/influences/supports', to influence and subordination as in (3) 'creates learning opportunities for' (Freeman and Johnson, 2004).

If the basic syllogism of change and reform is: to improve what students know and do (and what we want them to be able to know and do), we must address what teachers know and do, then each of these verbs defines a different approach to changing or improving what happens in classrooms at the individual and the systemic levels. Thus the verb links teacher learning to student learning – and, more broadly, educational change and reform to professional development.

The verb, and the assumptions it carries with it, are critical to better understanding this key relationship between teachers (and their professional learning) and students (and their classroom experiences). As critical as this analysis of the verb is, however, it is circumscribed by problematic assumptions, cul-de-sacs in reasoning that tend to stymie thinking, often directing us towards blame and inaction rather than towards positive movement, new practices and new avenues of activity. I want to explore three of these problematics in how teacher learning and professional development are conventionally approached and linked to student experience and learning. I refer to these approaches as 'problematics' because I believe they can box us into reasoning and programmes that are ineffective. And a major part of the problem is the verb.

The first problematic: of individualism

The first problematic lies in the assumption that what individuals think and do *as individuals* is central to the quality of life in the classroom. In other words, classrooms are made up of individuals; it is a setting in which the individual teacher directs the learning of individual students. Instances of this individualist perspective are so widespread that they are common currency in our experience. For example, we generally experience classroom teaching as students with an individual teacher, so our 'apprenticeship of observation' suggests to us that teaching is an autonomous, individual activity involving one adult with a group of (generally younger) student (Lortie, 1975). Teachers' work responsibilities are usually organized on a per-class basis, with one teacher having responsibility for a group of learners for a period of time in what Lortie called 'the egg crate profession'. Similarly for students, tasks and grades are generally organized and assessed on an individual basis. This is, in essence, the 'factory module' of education (Tyack and Cuban, 1995).

The corollary follows that at its core teachers' professional learning and development is also about individuals, what each teacher knows and can do, and what s/he needs to learn and/or be able to do. This reasoning is based in the fundamental belief that the individual teacher is central to good teaching; it is a belief on which policies of educational reform are being built.

In many instances, the assumption that teachers matter most as individuals is a viable one. Certainly teachers as individuals often undertake professional learning, which in turn influences what they do in their classrooms. This affirmative logic of improvement – that a teacher can improve and change her practice such that students have a different, more productive experience – is evident in many cases. The problem comes, I would argue, when the logic is applied across the board. If you think, for example, of a lesson which, in spite of all the teacher's best efforts and intentions, still goes badly and does not reach the aims or those of the learners, we often ask ourselves what happened... what went wrong? In effect, we seek to assign individual responsibility for what we did or did not do, or perhaps to a learner or group of learners, what they did or did not do.

Viewing teacher and student learning as strictly and exclusively an individual matter, it follows that *if* the class does not go well, *if* several students do not learn what was taught, *then* there must be an individual issue at work – someone must not be doing something s/he should be doing. From the individualist perspective, when students flourish and do well, teachers are usually granted some of the credit. But when things do not go well, the argument is made that to improve what students know and do, the teacher needs to be 'fixed'. This line of reasoning is evident, for example, in the various proposed pay-for-performance schemes that are under consideration in several US communities in which a portion of the individual teacher's compensation would be linked to student results on standardized assessments (Darling-Hammond, 1998).

The individualist perspective is a problematic for several reasons, however. If logically it were true that improving individual teachers alone would improve student learning, then many educational reforms that have attempted to do so would have succeeded. That many such reforms have not succeeded fully and permanently, would suggest that there is more to the quality of life in classrooms that simply what a single teacher can do, as various commentators have pointed out (for example, Darling-Hammond and Sykes, 1999). To address the short-comings in the problematic of the strict individualist perspective, we need to adopt an alternative view, one that speaks to the shared, social, and collective aspects of classroom teaching and learning.

Focusing on the classroom as a social practice, as contrasted to a network of individual interactions, presents such an alternative view. The idea of social practices (for example, Chaiklin and Lave, 1996) examines how individuals participate in organized, recognizable activities towards common ends or purposes. A birthday party, or shopping in a market, or the waiting room at a clinic, are each instances of social practices. This view shifts the focus from the individual *per se* to the activity as a fabric of social interaction. In the context of the language classroom, social practices capture Stevick's now classic admonition that teaching needs to focus on 'what goes on inside and between people' in the classroom (1976: 4). On the level of professional learning, working with the ideas of exploratory practice, Allwright and his colleagues have pursued a similar direction away from the exclusive focus on the individual when they argue that improvement in classrooms depends on 'collegiality' at many levels – among students and teacher, among teachers themselves, among teachers, administrators and the wider community (Allwright, 2003: 131–5). In essence, this collegiality refocuses us on the group and away from the individual.

When professional learning and student learning are seen as social practices, the complexity of the classroom is recast. The focus moves away from what individuals do as teacher or students towards how participation in classroom as a system of activity works to realize certain ends or purposes, both explicit and tacit (Lantolf, 2000; Wells, 1999). In this view, the teacher and the students *together* participate in the activity system of the particular classroom. The shared social purpose or common object defines that activity, at least on an explicit level, so in an English class you learn English, in a maths class, maths, and so on. This shared, explicit goal circumscribes how individuals participate, as well as the personal goals or outcomes they are seeking to achieve in the setting. From the standpoint of a social practice, classroom activity is reframed from what the teacher *or* the students are doing as individuals to what the teacher *and* the students do collectively. In this 'both/ and' viewpoint, what the teacher does is contingent on what the students are doing, and vice versa.

This shift in analysis may be more clearly understood if it is placed in the context of a specific example. The following comes from memory; it is a story rather than a case study. I want to use it as a case in point, as a sort of rudimentary illustration of the problematics, which I elaborate in the chapter. The story comes from outside the realm of language teaching, but perhaps that 'otherness' is useful in clarifying the issues at hand.

A case in point: the algebra class

Some time ago, I was talking with one of my daughters about the algebra class she was taking in high school. She said it was boring which, given adolescence, is hardly an uncommon response. When I asked why, she said that the teacher always told students 'how to do things, but she didn't explain why'. My daughter continued, 'We're working with graphing lines and the teacher just says, "Now you press zero on your calculator, and then you enter $Y = 25 \ldots$ ", and we never end up understanding *why* we're supposed to do it this way'.

'Part of the problem', she added, 'is that it's a big class and a lot of kids in the back of the room would rather talk than listen to her. So the teacher probably feels that she has to keep us doing things so that we don't just talk or space out.'

If one were to adopt the extreme individualist perspective, one might say the problem lies with the teacher, who isn't explaining graphing concepts effectively, and with certain individual students at the back of the room, who are disruptive and would rather chat with their friends than focus on algebra and graphing lines. To address these shortcomings, the individualists would argue that the teacher needs more training in how to manage and discipline the class and how to explain maths concepts. And were we to talk with the teacher, she might agree with this analysis, or she might add other concerns such as the level of student interest and motivation, how well they had been prepared for algebra and so on. My point is not that these perspectives are wrong or right, but rather that by focusing on individuals they may be missing something crucial about both student learning in algebra and professional learning in how to teach it.

From the viewpoint of social practice, we might begin by recognizing as we do above that the teacher and the students have different, possibly overlapping, reasons for being in the algebra class. While the explicit, publicly recognizable goal is to learn/teach algebra, that goal is refracted by the participants in different ways, which reflect their roles within the activity system of the classroom. For example, the teacher may rely on *telling how* to graph on the calculator rather than *explaining why* it works because she wants to keep the students occupied. Or she may believe that through having students do the actions on the calculator, they will establish a basis for understanding the maths involved. She may want to explain things, but feel that the students need to master the mechanics first.

Similarly, the students will have differing and overlapping reasons for what they do. Some may want to learn how to graph lines; some may want to learn why graphing works in this way; some may want to catch up with their friends; and so on. Participants' purposes in the classroom activity, why they do what they do, are complex, multiple, overlapping and mutually contingent. The individualist perspective is problematic in that simplifies or unifies purposes, thus diminishing what Allwright (2006: 13) calls 'the essential and irreducible complexity of classroom language learning and teaching'. For this reason, I would argue that viewing teaching and learning as a matter of individuals is conceptually problematic.

The alternative social practice view holds that, by definition, there are always tensions or contradictions in the purposes or object of an activity system (Engeström, Miettinen and Punamäki, 1999). In that the various purposes imply *either/or choices* in which one purpose trumps others, they tend to pull participants in the activity in various directions thus creating momentum or dynamism in the system. Some of these contradictions are intrapersonal (within individuals), such as the student who wants to learn to graph lines *and* wants to chat with friends, while others are interpersonal (among people), as in the contradiction between the teacher's purpose and that of the chatting students. These contradictions in purpose extend beyond the class in that they reflect the various communities on which the classroom draws and of which it is a part. 'Communities' is here understood to mean the extended groups to which participants belong, see themselves as belonging, or wish to be part of. For example, from the teacher's point of view if she keeps the students occupied, she is managing the class well; she thus connects herself to the community of 'good teaching practice' in which 'well-run classes' have students engaged. A visitor who might stop by would see a 'well-managed' classroom in which students are doing something. On another level, the tension in purpose between explaining graphing and mastering its mechanics on the calculator echoes major debates within the maths teaching community about how students need to understand the content but also need to know the mechanics so that they can apply that content in the world.

From the student standpoint, there are also multiple communities to which the students belong, or want to belong; these communities bear on purposes in the classroom. Chatting with friends cements certain social groups as sub-communities within the school. Learning maths and being successful academically links students to the communities of potential careers and the expectations of parents and so on. And communities and their purposes are not strictly stratified by role; for instance, teachers have the capacity to engage students in potential communities which they might think of joining.

Among other things, these various communities cast long shadows of multiple and contradictory expectations over what is going on in this classroom, expectations that contribute in shaping what is happening. Purpose, and how to act on it in the classroom, is not as simple and clear-cut as the individualist perspective of 'fix-the-teacher-to-improve-the-students' logic would suggest.

The second problematic: of immediacy

These notions of contradiction among participants' purposes and the pull exerted by various communities on what goes on in the social practice of the classroom places teaching and learning in a larger virtual space than the lesson itself. The multiplicity of purpose and the shadows of communities also suggest a second problematic – that of immediacy and of focusing only on the present. Teaching is often focused on the here-and-now, on the individual teacher concerned with what is happening in front of her. If the students are not prepared, the teacher may adjust the lesson. If the technology does not work or some material is missing, she may adjust the task. If some students are absent, the groupings and social relations adjust. And so on. This immediacy is characteristic of teaching; it is what is captured in the theoretical notion of teachers' interactive decision-making (for example, Johnson, 1999). However, this interactive immediacy of teaching does not necessarily mean that the present alone, the here-and-now, is all that matters or even what matters most in the social practice of the classroom.

Lessons unfold over the course of an hour or more, curricula unfold over the course of a school year. Like an activity, teaching and learning take place in time; they are historical processes. Everything involved – the students, the teacher, the curriculum and materials, the classroom space – comes from somewhere; everything has a past. And in a real sense the past is prologue.

The case in point continued: parents' night about the algebra class

At a parents' meeting earlier that year, I recall the maths teacher talking about the algebra curriculum and in particular the value of the hands-on work with graphing calculators.

'These machines are everywhere now', she said, 'You can buy them in the supermarket. Students need to know how to use them.'

The teacher used a power point display to show us how she was working with the calculators, how complex issues in changing X and Y values could be made clear and accessible.

'But isn't this just a short cut? Will the kids learn the basic mechanics?', one parent asked.

'They'll learn both', the teacher replied, 'They'll learn the mechanics, but I want them to go beyond that to understand how they can use this tool to think mathematically. Students now need to know that. They can even use these calculators on many of the advanced academic exams.'

The teacher talked about her hopes and intentions for using the graphing calculators. She was clearly positioning these tools as offering access to a different level of mathematical thinking than what we had had in school. As we left the meeting, one parent commented, 'I can remember having to do all that stuff on a slide rule. It took forever, but even that was better than using paper and pencil.'

When we think about the classroom only in the present we risk becoming trapped in the here-and-now and ignoring the past and how things got to be the way they are. If we accept that activity exists in time, then it is by nature historical (Wertsch, 1998). Any social practice comes from somewhere, and where it comes from shapes what it is, as well as what it can become.

We tend to think of the roles in the classroom, (who does what), and the norms (the social rules that govern what is appropriate or inappropriate), as being elements that carry this historical influence most clearly in the social organization of classroom activity. For example, the division of labour – who does what, the social roles and hierarchies – seems to be fairly traditional in this algebra class. The teacher is telling students what to do – 'which buttons to press on their calculators' – and the students, for the most part, are doing it. Similarly, the social norms, both explicit and tacit, seem to be fairly conventional to the classroom. The teacher is directing the lesson and the students are following her instructions. There are explicit social rules of school, for example, that students are not supposed to talk while the teacher is talking; and there are tacit norms of student socializing, that you can chat with your classmates as long as you are not too disruptive.

How the division of labour and social norms got to be the way they are is a function of their history. Since the early 1900s, the social organization of schooling in industrialized societies has distinguished between elementary and secondary teaching (Tyack and Cuban, 1995). Broadly speaking, teaching at the elementary level focused on basic skills and socializing students, while teaching at the secondary level focused on content and preparing students for careers. Elementary schools are usually organized by age/grade level; high schools are organized by academic department. In the former, teachers are usually identified by grade level and the students they teach. In the latter, the norm is to identify teachers by their content expertise (as a maths or an English or a history teacher). In high school, this organization by subject matter has led historically to an emphasis on knowledge transmission, on teaching as telling, on content as talk (for example, Sizer, 1992). So the social norms and division of labour in high school teaching often boil down to what we see in the algebra class.

Although the division of labour and the social norms carry history, it is a mistake to think they do so alone. In fact, the instruments used in the activity system – the physical and/or symbolic tools – often show the history most clearly. In a lecture for example, the instruments might include the pen and paper as physical tools, while the language of the lecture is a symbolic tool. In the algebra class, the instruments include symbolic tools such as the teacher's instructions, the algebraic symbols and the talk that supports the lesson. The physical tools are the chalk writing on the blackboard and, of course, the graphing calculator.

Many physical tools such as graphing calculators, word processors, language labs, the internet and so on, make possible new types and levels of thinking. From the presentist perspective, these new tools should work to enhance teaching and extend the here-and-now of the lesson. The problem is that the conventional rules and division of labour which circumscribe who does what and how they do it in the classroom can often constrain the potential of new tools. Engeström, Miettinen and Punamäki (1999) point out that these contradictions among aspects of the activity system – between the instrument on the one hand and the rules and the division of labour on the other – make the activity inherently unstable and thus highly dynamic. For example, although the algebra teacher knows how she wants to use the graphing calculator as a tool to teach her students, she seems to encounter, parti- cipate in and even unwittingly contribute to classroom norms and a conventional division of labour that do not accommodate it. Thus there is a contradiction between the potential of the calculator on the one hand, and the traditional norms and the conventional classroom divi- sion of labour in which the teacher tells and the students do, on the other. So often what can seem to be resistance to change or even 'poor teaching' may be unresolved tensions between the new and the conventional aspects in the activity system

Swedish educational psychologist, Roger Säljö (1997) who has worked extensively with sociocultural theory, describes eloquently this tension of time in the tool:

> If we think of what we now consider as a relatively simple device such as a mini-calculator, we find that sophisticated knowledge about mathematical operations (how to divide and multiply, for

instance), about the notational system (the use of the zero and decimals) and about how to perform certain frequent operations (such as calculating percentages, finding inverse numbers or square roots) have all been incorporated into the machine. Thus, when pupils, even in the lower grades in school, press the buttons of their calculators, they are literally operating with conceptual tools that have developed over thousands of years... and that have eventually been implemented in the calculator.

Echoing the algebra teacher's explanation in the parents meeting, Säljö continues:

[T]he learning of elementary mathematics is rapidly transformed by means of such technology. The drill and practice of elementary multiplication and division that used to take a very long time is challenged by such technology that literally hides the operations within the pressing of keys on the calculator.

He then draws an interesting comparison:

In antiquity when, in one of Plato's dialogues, Socrates complained about the lazy youngsters who did not learn to memorize the great texts... but rather cheated by reading them. [Similarly] there [are] conflicts within educational circles [as to whether] children are really learning mathematics when [they are] using such tools.

Säljö concludes that:

What we see in socio-cultural terms is a new division of labour between the human mind, the body, and an artifact [or tool], but all elements are still necessary in order to perform mathematical reasoning. (Säljö, 1997)

Säljö's analysis speaks to the presentist perspective in which teachers are seen entirely in the here-and-now of their individual classrooms. New physical tools such as using word processors to teach writing or using the internet to research information are literally redefining, the division of labour – who does what – in the activity. But these new tools and their potential re-division of labour must take place within often conventional classroom norms and roles. So unless the whole activity system of the classroom is taken into account, the changes may fall apart. The new tools are likely to be subsumed by traditional rules and divisions of labour, as in the algebra class. Professional development that does not take these dynamics into account is unlikely to be successful in realizing improvement. And in that failure, there is the risk that teachers are blamed for what does not happen.

The third problematic: of causality

The third problematic focuses on the relation between teaching and student learning, which brings us back to the verb. This problematic of causality holds that it is the behaviour of the individual teacher that 'causes' individual students to learn. As I have argued with the first two problematics, of individuality and of immediacy, this view greatly simplifies a complex situation. Teachers are influential in classroom learning, but that does not mean that they cause it to happen.

The notion that teaching causes learning is permeating public policy and debate in many countries. In the USA, for example, federal education policy has attempted to link teacher compensation to student performance on standardized tests through so-called 'merit pay' for teachers or 'pay for performance'. Such policies that are anchored in an extreme view of causality have had unintended consequences. In some 'pay for performance' environments, teachers are shying away from assignments in classrooms and schools where the students are difficult to teach. If pay depends in part on how students perform on standardized measures, and if these students have multiple and complex needs, it is likely that they will not perform as well as their counterparts who do not have such needs (for example, Darling-Hammond, 1998). The problem with the causal view of teaching and learning is that it can lead to a single standard by which success is judged. As Professor Walter Haney has observed in testifying in a lawsuit brought by the Mexican–American Legal Defense Fund on behalf of poor and language minority students against pay-for-performance practices in Texas: 'When principals and teachers and students are all judged by the same test score, the weakest will inevitably suffer: the students' (see also Haney, 1993). His words crystallise this problematic of causality, that it creates an either/or proposition: either the problem lies with the teacher *or* it lies with the students. The solution becomes either to 'fix the teacher' or to 'fix the students'.

In contrast to this Manichaean view of causality which shuts down complexity, the social practice perspective which we have explored seems to open up possibilities. When the classroom is seen as a social practice, *both* the teacher *and* the students are participants in its activity system. So it is not logical to try and locate a problem with learning in either the teacher *or* in the students. If together the participants make up a single, complex system, any analysis has to account for this contingency and collectivity, and this calls into question the notion of *causality*. How can teaching 'cause' learning when teacher and learners are part of, and mutually influence and shape, what one another does? It is this broader view that Allwright captures when he writes about teaching as 'creating learning opportunities'. He observes that, 'the best task design will not seek to determine what shall be learned, but only to guarantee the provision of a wide range of learning opportunities among which all of the participants will be able to find something of use' (2005: 14). To contrast this notion of learning opportunities with the causal view of teaching in relation to learning, another example can be useful.

Case in point: choosing vs. assigning groups

In the mid-1980s, when word processors were being introduced into US elementary school classrooms, Sarah Michaels (1985) looked at how students were learning to use the new technology to edit their writing. Writing workshop and peer editing (see Calkins, 1986) were popular pedagogies at the time and so the interesting question was how might word processors affect this approach to teaching? From a social practice standpoint, there was a new physical tool, the word processor, to be integrated into an existing activity system, a middle-school writing class.

Michaels chose to focus on two classrooms in particular. Neither of the teachers considered themselves computer literate nor had they received any special professional development in how to use the word processor in teaching writing. Each was given a brief training on basic word processing and then left to integrate the technology as they chose into their teaching.

There were some differences in the social organization of the two classrooms, however. In the first class, the teacher had her students work in assigned groups to give feedback on each other's writing drafts. The groups were reassigned every few weeks in the belief that students would profit from working with different peer groups over time. In contrast, the teacher in the second class allowed students to work with whomever they chose to review and critique their writing. She believed that the small groups organized based on friendship and other social reasons were most useful if peers were to critique each other's writing honestly. So groups tended not to shift very much over time, and best friends often worked together for most of the year (or at least as long as their friendships lasted).

On the surface, these two classrooms presented similar activity systems and particularly, in the social rules and divisions of labour. In both classrooms, the division of labor was small-group work and the rules structured peer editing of writing and students learning to work with each other. There were subtle but importance differences, however. In the classroom where groups were assigned, students ended up working with every one of their classmates at some point during the year, whereas in the classroom where students chose their partners, this random mixing did not occur. So the two classrooms had different histories when the word processors were introduced.

So what were the consequences? Michaels examined several aspects of these two classrooms, but one indicator of computer literacy in particular stood out. At the start of the school year, the researchers gave the students in both classrooms a test on basic word processing skills including how to cut and paste text, delete text, spell check and so on. Then at the end of the school year, students in both classes were tested again. They found that in the classroom in which students worked in assigned groups, most of the students had mastered the basic word processing skills. In the classrooms in which students chose their groups, some students became quite proficient in word processing while others could do little more than they had been able to do at the start of the year.

It seems that the small differences in the social rules and in how labour was divided made an enormous difference in terms of learning outcomes. In the class in which students chose their groups, students whose friends were skilled with computers for whatever reason learned the skills from these peers. But students whose friends were not skilled did not make much progress. The researchers did observe instances in which some students would ask more skilled peers for help, but the basic small-group units did not change over the course of the year and so the skills were not widely or equally distributed. In contrast, in the classroom with assigned groups, most of the students learned the basics of word processing. Because the groups were reassigned regularly, over time the more skilled students inevitably worked with their less skilled peers.

The histories of the two classrooms made an enormous difference in how the present change, introducing word processors, developed. The study was carried out over a school year, so at the beginning all the students were new to each other, to the teacher and to the rules of their respective classrooms. As the school year started, the two classrooms established different norms that, among other things, socialized students into different forms of group work. The teachers had subtly different ways of doing things and these differences provided an environment in which the new tool worked in very different ways.

The differences in how the students learned to use the word processors might also show up in different students' knowledge of writing. In other words, if the knowledge of word processing was not travelling throughout the class in one case because of the different divisions of labour, the knowledge of writing might not have been travelling as well. Thus the differential use of the word processor as new tool might make visible a basic issue in learning and access to knowledge that would have remained hidden.

Michaels also reported that in the classroom in which students chose their groups, some students became highly skilled at word processing, while others learned very little. In the classroom in which groups were assigned, the skills seemed to cluster towards the middle; most of students became competent, but there were no clear extremes in skill at the end of the year. The latter finding is important to note, lest we conclude that one classroom was good while the other was bad. In fact, this research illustrates how new tools come into historically rich classroom environments. It seems to be the unique mix of norms – how work is divided, social groupings, and so on – that shapes the learning opportunities in each setting. To fully understand how these learning opportunities are shaped and re-shaped, we need to consider the whole activity system, past and present.

Returning to 'the problem of the verb'

These three notions – of individuality, of immediacy and of causality – are problematic precisely because they suggest a mirage of simplistic approaches when faced with a puzzle in the classroom: assign it to the teacher *or* the student (individuality); examine it only in the here-and-now (immediacy); try to address by 'fixing the teacher' or 'fixing the students' (causality). Each of these approaches takes us in the wrong direction, away from the complexity and interdependence of the teaching–learning relationship.

Which brings us back to Allwright's (2006) notion of complexity, and what I have called 'the problem of the verb': How we complete the statement, *What teachers know and do*————*what students know and do*, shapes how we approach and support teachers' professional learning.

I have argued that this relationship is commonly understood as highly individual, focused in the here-and-now to the exclusion of the past, both recent and more distant and based in a notion of causality. I have used the framework of social practices to counter these three problematics of individuality, immediacy and causality. Fully to support development of the 'quality of life' in the classroom, I contend that we need to think differently about teachers' professional learning and the professional development designs and interventions which support it.

In returning to the problem of the verb, I will summarize my argument as follows:

- **To the degree that teachers' professional learning is connected to the classroom, it will have greater influence**

  Focusing on classrooms entails focusing on complexity and on the web of connections among individuals rather than the individuals themselves. While classrooms involve individuals, they function as collective activity systems. To influence what happens in them, one needs to be engaged on a first-hand basis in that collective complexity. When professional development is separated in time and space from the classroom and what learners are doing, it risks minimizing or even missing out on that 'essential idiosyncrasy of humanity' as manifested in that particular classroom.

- **Teachers' professional learning needs to take classroom history in account**

  Classrooms as an activity systems have pasts, so the question of how things in this classroom and school got to be the way they are is important to understanding where they may go next. Clearly teaching is anchored in the here-and-now, in what participants are doing together in the present. But the social norms – who does what and the ways in which roles develop and are assigned – bring past reasoning and logic into the present activity. When teachers pose questions or articulate puzzles, as they do when they undertake teacher research or Exploratory Practice, they probe the present of the classroom to examine, reflect on and perhaps change what they have done and understood in the past. In essence, this type of professional learning traces aspects of teaching back, while projecting them forward towards a hopefully new or different outcome.

  Contrast this approach to professional development that concentrates on training teachers in new ways of acting – perhaps using new technologies, as in the example of Sarah Michaels' research, or

new curricula or pedagogies. Such professional development interventions risk achieving less impact because they overlook the past to
focus on introducing new ways to do things in the future.

- **Professional learning depends on tools**
  I have argued that teachers use tools – both physical and symbolic –
  to create learning opportunities. A class that is doing an information-
  gap activity may use documents with different information (physical
  tools) and language (a symbolic tool) to complete the task. Similarly,
  professional learning makes use of tools, such as ideas, procedures
  and even physical materials. These tools or instruments often trigger
  changes in classrooms as activity systems, as in the case in point of
  the word processors in Sarah Michaels' research.
  But tools are not only physical. Often symbolic tools, concepts
  and ideas that are collectively developed through such professional development interventions as reflective teaching groups,
  inquiry seminars or teacher research groups, can offer potent
  instruments in professional learning. For example, when Allwright
  (2003) began to argue in favor of the idea of 'puzzles' as triggers for
  Exploratory Practice, in contrast to the more accepted idea of
  'problems' as the focus of action research, he introduced an
  important conceptual tool, one which re-centred classroom investigations on what was puzzling instead of what needed to be fixed.
  These conceptual tools do not solve things in the classroom; they
  can introduce alternative ways for participants to conceive of and
  act in the classroom.
- My final contention, in view of what I have said about tools as potentially (re)shaping conceptions of classroom activity, is that **professional
  development can influence professional learning, it cannot
  create ready-made solutions.** Classrooms as activity systems are
  shaped by 'what goes on inside and between' their participants, to use
  Stevick's (1980: 4) phrase. For the teacher, professional development
  can introduce new tools, for both doing the work of teaching and,
  perhaps more critically, for thinking about it. But like the graphing
  calculator or the word processor, physical tools alone do not change
  what happens. The new tools do create new possibilities, which in
  turn create contradictions, often between past ways of doing things
  and future possibilities. The graphing calculator created a tension in
  the activity system of the algebra class, just as the word processors
  led to contradictions in activity systems of the two writing classes.
  As teachers worked to make the tools part of their teaching, the
  classroom activity (re)adjusted. So in a sense, these tensions and

contradictions moved teaching and learning forward (for example, Engeström, Miettinen and Punamäki, 1999).

Focusing on the quality of life

Although teaching does not cause learning, the relationship between the two processes is clearly crucial. Re-thinking this relationship, as Allwright has done throughout his work, can help to lead us out of the problematics of individuality, immediacy and causality that have trapped how we conceive of, and what we do in, professional development to support teachers' professional learning. As Allwright concludes (2006, emphasis in the original):

> [We need] a way of getting teaching and learning done so that the teachers and learners simultaneously develop their own understanding of what they are doing as learners and teachers. And they can perhaps best do this by focusing on trying to understand the factors that affect the quality of *life* in the language classroom. (2006: 15–16)

The current demands of social needs and national policies in 'the age of reform' make this approach all the more imperative. In many settings, teachers are increasingly held accountable for what students know and do not know. The challenge to improve student learning will not diminish. What is needed is a different way to approach the problem of the verb: this central relationship between what teachers know and do and what students know and do.

Notes

1. The terms 'global north' and 'global south' refer to differing socioeconomic realities that exist in, for example, the countries of Western Europe, the USA, the UK, Canada, Japan, South Korea in the northern hemisphere, as compared to those primarily in the southern hemisphere. The geographic distinction is not hard and fast, as the 'global north' also includes Australia and New Zealand. This 'north–south' distinction is seen as descriptive and less value-laden than the terms 'developed' and 'developing' world.
2. This reframing of purpose is particularly evident, I think, in the ways in which action research, which was at its core a movement of social critique and transformation, became in some settings in language education overly focused on addressing classroom issues. Thus the frame shifted from the social organization of work to the role of the teacher in improving classroom practices (see Freeman and Richards, 1993).

References

Allwright, R. 2003. A brief guide to exploratory practice: rethinking practitioner research in language teaching. *Language Teaching Research 7*, 2:113–42.

Allwright, D. 2006. Six promising directions in Applied Linguistics. In: *Understanding the language classroom*, eds S. Gieve and I.K. Miller. London: Palgrave Macmillan, Chapter 1 in this volume.

Bailey, K.M., A. Curtis and D. Nunan 2001. *Pursuing professional development: the self as source*. Boston, MA: Heinle & Heinle.

Calkins, L.M. 1986. *The art of teaching writing*. Portsmouth, NH: Heinemann.

Chaiklin, S. and J. Lave, eds 1996. *Understanding practice: perspectives on activity and context*. New York: Cambridge University Press.

Cochran-Smith, M. and S. Lytle 1993. *Inside/outside: teacher research and knowledge*. New York: Teachers College Press.

Darling-Hammond, L. 1998. Teachers and teaching: testing policy hypotheses from a National Commission Report. *Educational Researcher 27*, 1:5–15.

Darling-Hammond, L. and G. Sykes, eds 1999. *Teaching as the learning profession: handbook of policy and practice*. San Francisco: Jossey-Bass.

Engeström, Y., R. Miettinen and R.-L. Punamäki, eds 1999. *Perspectives on activity theory*. New York: Cambridge University Press.

Freeman, D. 1996. The 'unstudied problem': research on teacher learning in language teaching. In: *Teacher learning in language teaching*, eds D. Freeman and J.C. Richards, 351–77. New York: Cambridge University Press.

Freeman, D. 1998. *Doing teacher research: from inquiry to understanding*. Boston, MA: Heinle & Heinle.

Freeman, D. 2001. Second language teacher education. In: *The Cambridge guide to teaching English to speakers of other languages*, eds R. Carter and D. Nunan, 72–9. Cambridge: Cambridge University Press.

Freeman, D. and K.E. Johnson 2004. Towards linking teacher knowledge and student learning. In: *Second language teacher education: international perspectives*, ed. D. Tedick. Mahwah, NJ: Lawrence Erlbaum.

Freeman, D. and J.C. Richards 1993. Conceptions of teaching and the education of second language teachers. *TESOL Quarterly 27*, 2:193–216.

Haney, W. 1993. Minorities and testing. In: *Beyond silenced voices: class, race and gender in United States schools*, eds L. Weis and M. Fine, 45–73. Albany, NY: State University of New York Press.

Hawley, W. and L. Valli 1999. The essentials of effective professional development: a new consensus. In: *Teaching as the learning profession: handbook of policy and practice*, eds L. Darling-Hammond and G. Sykes, 127–50. San Francisco: Jossey-Bass.

Johnson, K.E. 1999. *Understanding language teaching: reasoning in action*. Boston, MA: Heinle & Heinle.

Kelly, M., M. Grenfell, R. Allan, C. Kriza and W. McEvoy 2004. *European profile for language teacher education: a frame of reference*. Graz: European Centre of Modern Languages.

Kennedy, M. 1991. *An agenda for research on teacher learning*. East Lansing, MI: National Center for Research on Teacher Learning.

Lantolf, J., ed. 2000. *Socio-cultural theory and second language learning*. New York: Oxford University Press.

Larsen-Freeman, D. 1997. Chaos/complexity science and second language acquisition. *Applied Linguistics 18*, 2:141–65.

Lortie, D. 1975. *Schoolteacher: a sociological study.* Chicago, IL: University of Chicago Press.

Michaels, S. 1985. Classroom processes and the learning of text-editing commands. *Quarterly Newsletter of the Laboratory of Human Cognition* 5:30–34.

Ministry of Education and Culture (MEC), Brazil 1996. *Development of education in Brazil.* Brasilia: NDOE.

National Department of Education (NDOE), Republic of South Africa 1996. An agenda of possibilities: national policy on teacher supply, utilisation, and development. Pretoria: Author.

Nunan, D. and C. Lamb, eds 1995. *The self-directed teacher.* New York: Cambridge University Press.

Säljö, R. 1997. Learning and socio-cultural change: inaugural lecture for the van Zuylen Visiting Professorship. Faculty of Social Sciences, University of Utrecht.

Sizer, T. 1992. Horace's school: redesigning the American high school. Boston, MA: Houghton-Mifflin.

Stevick, E. 1980. *Teaching languages: a way and ways.* Rowley, MA: Newbury House.

Tyack, D. and L. Cuban 1995. *Tinkering toward utopia: a century of public school reform.* Cambridge, MA: Harvard University Press

Watson-Gegeo, K.A. 2004. Mind, language, and epistemology: toward a language socialization paradigm for SLA. *Modern Language Journal* 88, 3:331–50.

Wells, G. 1999. *Dialogic inquiry: towards a sociocultural practice and theory of education.* New York: Cambridge University Press.

Wertsch, J. 1998. *Mind as action.* New York: Oxford University Press.

Woods, D. 1996. *Teacher cognition in language teaching.* New York: Cambridge University Press.

Author Index

Subject Index

Printed in the United States
139837LV00001B/82/P